COMPETITIVE DEBATE

THE OFFICIAL GUIDE

COMPETITIVE DEBATE

THE OFFICIAL GUIDE

BY

RICHARD E. EDWARDS, PH.D.

ALPHA

A member of Penguin Group (USA) Inc.

ALPHA BOOKS

Published by the Penguin Group

Penguin Group (USA) Inc., 375 Hudson Street, New York, New York 10014, USA

Penguin Group (Canada), 90 Eglinton Avenue East, Suite 700, Toronto, Ontario M4P 2Y3, Canada (a division of Pearson Penguin Canada Inc.)

Penguin Books Ltd., 80 Strand, London WC2R 0RL, England

Penguin Ireland, 25 St. Stephen's Green, Dublin 2, Ireland (a division of Penguin Books Ltd.)

Penguin Group (Australia), 250 Camberwell Road, Camberwell, Victoria 3124, Australia (a division of Pearson Australia Group Pty. Ltd.)

Penguin Books India Pvt. Ltd., 11 Community Centre, Panchsheel Park, New Delhi—110 017, India

Penguin Group (NZ), 67 Apollo Drive, Rosedale, North Shore, Auckland 1311, New Zealand (a division of Pearson New Zealand Ltd.)

Penguin Books (South Africa) (Pty.) Ltd., 24 Sturdee Avenue, Rosebank, Johannesburg 2196, South Africa

Penguin Books Ltd., Registered Offices: 80 Strand, London WC2R 0RL, England

International Standard Book Number: 978-1-59257-693-7
Library of Congress Catalog Card Number: 2007941341

10 09 08   8 7 6 5 4 3 2 1

Interpretation of the printing code: The rightmost number of the first series of numbers is the year of the book's printing; the rightmost number of the second series of numbers is the number of the book's printing. For example, a printing code of 08-1 shows that the first printing occurred in 2008.

Printed in the United States of America

CONTENTS

Appendixes

Acknowledgments

M y love for competitive debate began as the result of an outstanding high school debate coach—Frank Kruse at Newton Senior High School in Newton, Iowa. Frank Kruse was one of those teachers who dramatically changed the lives of his students for the better—I can with certainty say that happened in my case. Robert Kemp was my teacher, colleague, and friend during the eight years I spent as a debater and graduate student at the University of Iowa. I dedicate this book to Frank Kruse and Bob Kemp, the debate coaches who introduced me to the life of the mind.

I am grateful to the participants in the national final debates in 2006 and 2007 for agreeing to the publication of their speeches in this volume. The 2006 public forum debate finalists were Valerie Hobbs/Michelle Schmit from Bishop Heelan High School in Sioux City, Iowa (coached by Elizabeth Dalton), and David Nadle/Jennifer Goldstein from Marjory Stoneman Douglas High School in Parkland, Florida (coached by Diane McCormick). The 2007 Lincoln-Douglas debate finalists were Taarini Vohra of The Hockaday School in Dallas, Texas (coached by Stacy Thomas), and Bilal Malik of James Logan High School in Union City, California (coached by Tommie Lindsay, Jr.). The 2007 policy debate finalists were Andrew Baker/Sarah Weiner of Shawnee Mission West High School in Shawnee Mission, Kansas (coached by Ken King), and Stephanie Spies/Matt Fisher of Glenbrook North High School in Northbrook, Illinois (coached by Christina Tallungan).

I am indebted to Tim Averill, the debate coach at the Waring School in Beverly, Massachusetts, who was willing to share his extensive teaching resources for the coaching of public forum debate. Scott Wunn, Executive Director of the National Forensic League, and Kent Summers, Associate Director of the National Federation of State High School Associations, also provided essential resource materials.

Finally, I appreciate the assistance and encouragement of my wife Connie, the love of my life.

TRADEMARKS

CHAPTER 1

THE VALUE OF DEBATE

If you have chosen to read this book, you no doubt enjoy a good argument! But *competitive debate* means more than arguing with a friend about whether video games cause violence or some other subject of interest. In an organized system now almost a century old, thousands of American high schools and middle schools offer opportunities to participate in debate tournaments. Homeschool debate leagues also now sponsor debate tournaments. In these tournaments, students present and defend pre-prepared arguments in competition with the opposing arguments from another school or league. The topics for these competitions are selected by national organizations, meaning that students throughout the United States are debating the same topics. Each debate "round" is judged by experienced critics who have the responsibility to declare a "winner" and a "loser." Debate tournaments produce regional, state, and national champions in each style of debate.

This first chapter discusses the benefits of competitive debate. These benefits have been shared by hundreds of thousands of students who have participated in debate, not simply the smaller group of state and national champions.

DEBATE MAKES LEARNING FUN!

Debate competition turns learning into an exciting game. Unlike some other academic games, winners are not those who have memorized the greatest number of "facts." Debate competition introduces its participants to a much broader world of ideas. Successful debaters are able to articulate "why" something is true, uncovering sometimes hidden value assumptions.

The search for the "why" comes naturally to the human spirit. Normal three- or four-year-old children go through a phase of asking "why?" to every statement made by their parents. The parents soon discover that every answer or explanation will still be met with "why?" Ultimately, the adults end the game with "I don't know" or "because I said so." Some children grow tired of inquiry and simply accept the statements of others as inscrutable truth. Yet for most of us, the search for the "why" never ends. If the question is gun control, it isn't enough to know that a prominent senator supports it; we want to know more.

CRITICAL THINKING

Critical thinking does not mean to be critical of others or to think negatively. Instead, it refers to an ability to arrive at decisions through a systematic and logical process. Dr. Raymond S. Nickerson, professor of psychology at Tufts University, has listed numerous characteristics of the "critical thinker," including the following:

- Uses evidence skillfully and impartially

- Organizes thoughts and articulates them concisely and coherently

- Distinguishes between logically valid and invalid inferences

- Can learn independently and has an abiding interest in doing so

- Can strip a verbal argument of irrelevancies and phrase it in its essential terms

- Habitually questions one's own views and attempts to understand both the assumptions that are critical to those views and the implications of the views (Schafersman)

Competitive debate promotes all six of these elements as it pits argument against argument; through a process of trial and error, debaters learn the difference between strong and weak arguments. Ironically, many beginning debaters win every round of debate—from their perspectives, their arguments were vastly superior to their opponents. No matter that the judge awarded the win to their opponents. With more experience, however, debaters develop the ability to recognize when they have lost. Learning to recognize the strength of an opposing argument plays a major role in the cultivation of critical thinking skills.

LOVE FOR LEARNING

Too much of the educational process in contemporary American education involves teachers telling students *what* to think. Thus education becomes a dull process of memorizing mountains of facts. Competitive debate takes a different approach: it teaches students *how* to think. The thought process begins by gathering evidence with an open mind.

Most forms of competitive debate involve the switching of sides. Suppose that the national debate question is "Resolved: The United States federal government should regulate handguns." Switching sides means that a debater will be called upon to advocate gun control in one round and to oppose it in the very next round. In the later rounds of a tournament, debaters toss a coin to determine whether they will support or oppose the debate resolution.

Switching sides produces numerous benefits. Prominent among these benefits is the ability to understand the arguments of an opponent. All of us have a tendency to underestimate our opposition until we have truly considered the strength of the evidence supporting their position. Competitive debate provides students a safe space for the testing of ideas.

RESEARCH SKILLS

Debate teaches cutting-edge research skills. Because the quality of an argument often depends on the strength of the supporting evidence, debaters quickly learn to find the best evidence. This means going beyond run-of-the-mill Internet sources to government hearings, law reviews, professional journal articles, and book-length treatments of subjects. Debaters learn how to evaluate study methodology and source credibility.

Debaters also learn how to process massive amounts of data into usable argument *briefs*. Argument briefs bring together the strongest logical reasons and evidence supporting various positions. The ability to gather and organize evidence into logical units is a skill that is treasured by business decision-makers, government policy-makers, legal practitioners, scientists, and educators.

EMPOWERMENT

Debate training offers empowerment—empowerment for women, empowerment for disadvantaged minorities, and empowerment for young people in general. Because of their backgrounds, some individuals feel powerless, as if their opinion does not matter. Yet powerful adults typically react with surprise (and sometimes even with awe) when in the presence of logical and articulate young people.

Robert Reich, former secretary of labor and now professor of social and economic policy at Brandeis University, has described competitive debate as the "great leveler": "Debate leagues can help reduce the educational-opportunity gap that separates rich and poor communities and thus they can help our children's chances and our nation's future" (Winkler et al.).

Eddie Wexler is a social studies teacher and debate coach in Oakland, California. He has described how debate helps students "find their voices": "Urban debate is transformative in an individual sense. It directly changes the lives of kids in a way that big, sweeping school reforms do not. ... My kids' analytical skills have taken off. And some of the most shy, timid kids have been emboldened in the most positive way. Debate has helped my kids find their voices. ... And now, in a society that has pretty much ignored them, they will have a greatly improved ability to make themselves heard" (Winkler et al.).

Many of the instruments of power in our democratic society are more readily available to those with economic or political resources. But the driving power of logical persuasion is available equally to all who are interested in learning its secrets.

THINK RAPIDLY ON YOUR FEET

All forms of competitive debate involve cross-examination as a debater fires questions at an opponent. Debaters develop skills in framing questions and in answering them. This skill in managing cross-examination pays dividends both in the short term and in the long term. In the short term, it improves students' test-taking abilities. Essay examinations typically test the ability to think quickly and to organize persuasive answers. For me, the ultimate essay exam came when I completed the course work for my doctorate and I appeared before my doctoral committee for an oral defense of my dissertation. I approached this task with confidence because of my years of experience in competitive debate.

Over the long term, cross-examination prepares students for success in the "real world" beyond school. Sales presentations are often followed by questions from prospective buyers. Expert witnesses in the courtroom are questioned by an opposing attorney who is determined to discredit the testimony. Debaters learn to overcome attempts at intimidation and to frame persuasive responses.

COMMUNICATION SKILLS

Competitive debate offers a laboratory for the development of numerous communication competencies. Public speaking heads the list of communication skills developed through debate.

Confidence in public speaking comes only through experience. In the typical semester-long course in public speaking, students deliver five or six speeches at the most. In a single six-round debate tournament, a debater delivers twelve speeches (two per round). In an entire year, a typical debater will deliver seventy speeches—more than ten times the number of speeches in a public speaking course.

Small group and interpersonal communication skills are also byproducts of debate participation. This happens because debaters work with other members of a team, working together to prepare argument briefs and organize practice sessions. Interviewing skills, consisting of the asking and answering of questions, are cultivated as debaters participate in dozens of cross-examination periods.

COMMUNITY RELATIONS

Debate programs offer an opportunity for high schools to put the power of their educational programs on public display. Demonstration debates on issues of community or national interest can make allies out of community groups. Kiwanis International, Rotary International, Lions Club, Junior Chamber of Commerce, the Young Lawyers division of the American Bar Organization, and numerous other community service clubs have been known to host demonstration debates featuring local debaters.

As a high school debater, I participated in numerous demonstration debates before community groups. My debate coach convinced a local television station to broadcast a series of debates between various high schools in central Iowa. My debate partner and I participated in demonstration debates before high school assemblies. On one occasion, we traveled 200 miles by passenger train to do a demonstration debate before a high school assembly in Omaha, Nebraska.

These demonstration debates offer educational and public relations benefits. Public debates cultivate persuasive speaking skills in ways that nicely complement the skills involved in tournament debates. Tournament debates are typically judged by professional *critics of argument*, meaning former debaters or current debate coaches from neutral schools. Such judges tend to focus more on the quality of logical arguments and supporting evidence rather than on public speaking skills. By participating in public debates, students hone the persuasion skills necessary to appeal to general audiences.

The public relations benefits of demonstration debates are substantial. Influential members of the community are able to see firsthand the impressive knowledge and skill displayed by bright high school students.

LEADERSHIP TRAINING

Dr. Alfred Snider, the Edwin W. Lawrence Professor of Forensics at the University of Vermont, has offered the following explanation of how competitive debate promotes leadership: "Debaters are more often seen as leaders. Studies in America show that those who communicate often and well, and give a balance of positive and negative comments, are seen as leaders. Leadership is given, not taken. Debaters are more likely to be given leadership. Debaters tend to become citizens in the real sense of the word—informed, active, participating, a force to be harnessed for the betterment of all."

CAREER PREPARATION

Dr. Joseph Zompetti, professor of communication at Illinois State University, describes the career benefits of debate in the recent book *Discovering the World Through Debate*: "Debaters learn how to think on their feet and to express themselves clearly in front of an audience. These skills can serve them, of course, throughout their academic careers, but they are also fundamentally important in a variety of professions, such as teaching, law, business management, or citizen activism. In sum, there are broad educational benefits to participating in debate."

Many successful attorneys began their training as high school debaters. San Francisco area attorney Raoul Kennedy said the following about his own debate experience: "I truly believe I would have been as prepared for law school had I simply debated and not attended college at all. I have found that the practice of law—and I assume this is true of a large number of other jobs—consists basically of trying to solve problems in an organized manner. ... Debate placed a premium on the factors that I believe are essential to effective problem solving" (Kay, p. 8).

John Sexton, president of New York University, has written the following about the value of competitive debate: "Those four years in debate were the educational foundation of everything I did. And I don't mean that in some simple form. ... I'm saying the finest education I got from any of the institutions that I attended, the foundation of my mind that I got during those four years of competitive debate: that is, 90% of the intellectual capacity that I operate with today; Fordham [University] for college, Fordham for the Ph.D., Harvard for law school—all of that is the other 10%" (Winkler et al.).

President John F. Kennedy once said, "I think debating in high school and college is most valuable training whether for politics, the law, business, or for service on community committees such as the PTA and the League of Women Voters" (Kay, p. 3). President Lyndon Baines Johnson was a high school debate coach before he became a member of Congress and later president of the United States.

KNOWLEDGE OF CURRENT EVENTS

Topics for competitive debate are typically the hottest political issues of the day. Former U.S. Secretary of Defense Donald Rumsfeld, in his 2004 testimony before the National Commission on Terrorist Attacks upon the United States (commonly called the 9/11 Commission), said the following: "I used to think one of the most powerful individuals in America was the person who could select the annual high school debate topic. Think of the power to set the agenda, and determine what millions of high school students will study, read about, think about, talk about with friends, discuss with their teachers, and debate with their parents and siblings over dinner" (Minch, p. 5).

Recent national debate topics have included public health assistance to sub-Saharan Africa, U.S. immigration policy, juvenile justice, gun control, global warming, and protection of ocean ecosystems.

BUILDING STRONGER AND SAFER COMMUNITIES

First Lady Laura Bush describes how competitive debate can become an alternative to violence: "Unfortunately, some teens turn to anger or violence as a means of expression. Debate is a healthier option, safer for children and for their communities. Students in the CAD [Computer Assisted Debate, part of the Atlanta Urban Debate League] program learn what it's like to be on a team, a lesson much better learned in the classroom than in a gang. They learn to see both sides of an issue, which helps them diffuse potentially dangerous situations. Debaters learn how to identify a good argument and reject a bad one, so they're better equipped to deal with the hazards of negative peer pressure" (NAUDL).

Michael Scott, president of the Chicago Board of Education, writes that "debate is a wonderful way to learn. It encourages critical thinking, analyzing issues at their core, and then articulating your view in a sound, reasonable, rational fashion. If more people could argue their points, there would be less shooting on our city streets" (NAUDL).

FRIENDSHIPS

Beginning debaters develop close friendships with the debaters on their own team. Experienced debaters also develop close friendships with their competitors. After a few years of competitive debate experience, a debater will have established a network of friends who are destined for success in their chosen career paths.

From my own high school experiences, I have a network of friends including numerous attorneys, two members of Congress, a judge recently appointed by the International Criminal Court to investigate genocide charges in Darfur, three college professors, two high school teachers, and several business executives. I also have numerous friends who met their life partners through debate competition.

TRAVEL

Participation in debate tournaments usually involves travel to neighboring cities and often to other states. This travel is an education in itself as it offers shared experiences with other students and adult sponsors.

COLLEGE SCHOLARSHIPS

There are also practical advantages to participation in high school debate. Numerous organizations sponsoring debate tournaments offer scholarships to outstanding participants. The National Forensic League, in partnership with several sponsors including the Lincoln Financial Group, provides over $150,000 each year in scholarships to top competitors at the national tournament. Among state associations offering scholarships for debaters, the University Interscholastic League (UIL) in Texas leads the way. Students who qualify for elimination rounds at the UIL state tournament are eligible for college scholarships provided through the Texas Interscholastic League Foundation (TILF), which amounted to $1.18 million in 2007–2008.

Hundreds of colleges and universities provide debate scholarships. Baylor University (where I am a professor of communication studies) currently offers eight full tuition scholarships to outstanding high school debaters who are interested in participating in intercollegiate debate competition.

WHAT IS THE COST?

This first chapter has been about the benefits of competitive debate. Yet with all benefits, there are also costs. What are the costs of involvement in competitive debate?

Debate requires a commitment of time and energy. Successful debaters spend hours of preparation for each hour of actual competition. This preparation involves research, organization, and rehearsal.

Debate also requires a willingness to risk embarrassment. There will be times when a superior opponent demonstrates the inadequacies of your arguments. Losing is never pleasant, but it is educational. The best debaters learn as much from the rounds they lose as the ones they win.

Debate requires a commitment of resources. Tournament participation involves the payment of entry fees and travel expenses. Some progressive-thinking school districts pay for all these expenses because they recognize the educational benefits of competitive debate. In most cases, however, tournament expenses are funded by parental contributions and/or fundraising campaigns.

FURTHER READING

Kay, Jack. *The Value of Forensics*. Indianapolis, IN: National Federation of High Schools, 1994.

Minch, Kevin. *The Value of Speech, Debate, and Theatre Activities: Making the Case for Forensics*. Indianapolis, IN: National Federation of High Schools, 2006.

NAUDL: National Association of Urban Debate Leagues. "What People Are Saying About Urban Debate." www.urbandebate. org/endorsements (accessed July 24, 2007).

Schafersman, Steven D. "An Introduction to Critical Thinking." January 1991. www.freeinquiry.com/critical-thinking.html (accessed July 24, 2007).

Snider, Alfred. "Debate as a Method for Improving Critical Thinking and Creativity." May 15, 2001. http://debate.uvm. edu/travel/china/chinaspeng.html (accessed July 24, 2007).

Winkler, Carol, Melissa Wade, and Larry Moss. "National Debate Project: Excellence Through Debate." 2007. www.nationaldebateproject.org/ (accessed July 24, 2007).

Zompetti, Joseph P., and William J. Driscoll. *Discovering the World Through Debate: A Practical Guide to Educational Debate for Debaters, Coaches, and Judges*. Budapest, Hungary: Central European University Press, 2002.

CHAPTER 2

MAKING SENSE OF ARGUMENT

For many people, an argument means little more than a "yes it is" versus "no it isn't" exchange. Consider the "Argument Sketch" from *Monty Python's Flying Circus:*

A man walks into an office.

Man: Good morning, I'd like to have an argument, please.

Receptionist: Certainly, sir. Have you been here before?

Man: No, this is my first time ....

Man: Is this the right room for an argument?

Other Man: (pause) I've told you once.

Man: No, you haven't!

Other Man: Yes, I have.

M: When?

O: Just now.

M: No, you didn't!

O: Yes, I did!

M: You didn't!

O: I did!

M: You didn't!

O: I'm telling you, I did!

M: You didn't!

O: Oh I'm sorry, is this a five-minute argument, or the full half-hour?

M: Ah! (taking out his wallet and paying) Just the five minutes.

O: Just the five minutes. Thank you.

O: Anyway, I did.

M: You most certainly did not!

O: Now let's get one thing perfectly clear: I most definitely told you!

M: Oh no, you didn't!

Unless our intention is humor, argument must consist of more than assertion. Argument should be *reason-giving*—it should offer data to support a conclusion. Debaters learn to prove their claims, rather than merely to assert them.

LIMITATIONS OF FORMAL LOGIC

There was a time when debaters were encouraged to use formal logical structures to support their arguments. The classic example of formal logic is the syllogism. The example Aristotle provides of the syllogism in *The Organon* (350 B.C.) is as follows:

All men are mortal (A = B)

Socrates is a man. (C = A)

Therefore, Socrates is mortal. (C = B)

The syllogism uses the mathematical law of transitivity, creating an illusion that the claim ("Socrates is mortal") has been proven absolutely. There are, however, weaknesses in the syllogism. Aristotle himself was well aware of these weaknesses. He referred to the first statement in the syllogism as the *major premise* and the second statement as the *minor premise*. A *premise* is an assumption, so the conclusion is true *only if* the two premises are true. The problem is that the "major premise" is such a huge assumption that it makes the conclusion trivial. Suppose I phrase the logic chain this way: "Look, folks, if you will grant me the assumption that *every man* who has ever lived is mortal, then, using my mathematical skill, I will prove to you that *one man* is mortal!" If you grant me that all men are mortal, isn't it child's play to draw the conclusion that one man is mortal? The careful mathematical movement becomes, therefore, little more than a distraction. It certainly doesn't merit a claim that I have proved something to you absolutely!

Must I always begin from a premise (or an assumption)? Consider the problem of proving that international terrorism is wrong. To prove anything, I must first have "where to stand"—I have to begin somewhere. I might try to anchor my "terrorism is wrong" argument to a beginning statement that "killing is wrong." Yet careful questioning might uncover problems with my premise. An opposing debater might ask whether it was wrong for our Revolutionary War forefathers to fight for independence in 1776—was killing wrong in that instance? I might have to refine my beginning statement to say that "killing innocent people is wrong." Some critics, pointing to examples such as the dropping of the atomic bomb on Hiroshima and Nagasaki, might still find fault with my premise. The point of this discussion is that argument must begin from assumption; the challenge comes in finding an assumption that a listener (or debate judge) is willing to *believe* is true.

A Definition of *Proof*

Because formal logic is incapable of absolute proof, the necessity of forcing verbal argument into mathematical models loses its luster. Douglas Ehninger and Wayne Brockriede, in their classic 1965 book *Decision by Debate,* were the first to suggest that debaters abandon the formal logical model in favor of a more modest and useful approach. Their definition of *proof* is as follows: "Proof is the process of securing belief in one statement by relating it to another statement already believed." This definition abandons any claim that argument can provide absolute proof. We should simply admit, said Ehninger and Brockriede, that proof starts from belief and attempts to move a listener to a higher level of belief.

THE TOULMIN MODEL

Ehninger and Brockriede introduced debaters to the informal logical model of Stephen Toulmin, a British philosopher of science. Now almost every modern debate text uses the Toulmin Model as the method of teaching argument. Toulmin first explained this model in his 1958 book *The Uses of Argument.*

Toulmin suggested that every argument (if it deserves to be called an argument) must consist of three elements: data, warrant, and claim.

The claim answers the question "What are you trying to get me to believe?"—it is the ending belief. Consider the following unit of proof: "Uninsured Americans are going without needed medical care because they are unable to afford it. Because access to health care is a basic human right, the United States should establish a system of national health insurance." The claim in this argument is that "the United States should establish a system of national health insurance."

Data (also sometimes called *evidence*) answers the question "What have we got to go on?"—it is the beginning belief. In the foregoing example of a unit of proof, the data is the statement that "uninsured Americans are going without needed medical care because they are unable to afford it." In the context of a debate round, a debater would be expected to offer statistics or an authoritative quotation to establish the trustworthiness of this data.

Warrant answers the question "How does the data lead to the claim?"—it is the connector between the beginning belief and the ending belief. In the unit of proof about health care, the warrant is the statement that "access to health care is a basic human right." A debater would be expected to offer some support for this warrant. Such support might come from the United Nations Universal

Declaration of Human Rights, from the preamble to the U.S. Declaration of Independence, or by quoting a statement from a health care expert.

The most common argumentative inadequacy is the *unwarranted claim*—a debater merely makes a claim without attempting any type of support. Suppose a debater attacks the national health insurance proposal by declaring that "the cost of a national health insurance system would cause the U.S. deficit to skyrocket." This is a claim, but it is not an argument because there is neither data nor warrant.

Sometimes a debater will offer data and claim but omit the warrant. Suppose the debater reads evidence that the U.S. deficit now stands at $8.9 trillion and then makes the claim that "the cost of a national health insurance system would cause the U.S. deficit to skyrocket." Now the statement has data and claim, but the warrant is missing—there is nothing connecting the currently sizable U.S. deficit to a claim that national health insurance will make this deficit substantially worse. Accordingly, the statement does not meet the definition of an argument.

Occasionally a debater will present data without offering either a warrant or a claim—the debater simply presents an "interesting fact." Suppose in our national health insurance debate, a student reads a piece of evidence showing that Hillary Clinton, when she was first lady, proposed national health insurance in 1994. This data may well be accurate, but it doesn't lead anywhere. There is no argument unless the data is connected to a claim through a warrant.

Is-Ought Gap

Many beginning debaters make the mistake of assuming that effective argument consists entirely of stacking up "the facts." The problem is that facts by themselves don't lead anywhere. Suppose I am trying to prove that the United States federal government should restrict possession of handguns. I could approach this task by citing dozens of "facts" concerning the number of handgun owners, the number of accidental deaths of children, the number of murders committed with handguns, the text of the Second Amendment to the U.S. Constitution, statements about a citizen's right to self-defense, and so on. Would amassing these facts ever answer the question of whether handgun ownership should be restricted? Would we say that if one side has ten facts and the other side has only eight then the side with the greater number of facts should win? Responsible decision-makers would never make judgments in this way. Facts mean nothing without a system for weighing or evaluating them. This requires the injection of one or more value premises. We must have a way to decide whether the risk of accidental death or gun-related murders is outweighed by the Constitutional right of self defense.

All debaters, whether debating questions of value or policy, must concern themselves with value assumptions. This is true because of the inevitable gulf between "is statements" and "ought conclusions." Philosopher David Hume was the first to fully explain the problem of the "is-ought gap" in his 1739 work *A Treatise of Human Nature*. Most questions of public policy involve "ought questions"—we are asked to decide what ought be done. Should handguns be restricted? Should the government restrict the burning of fossil fuels? Is capital punishment morally justified? "Facts" can never, by themselves, answer these questions.

The problem is that a great logical gulf exists between "is statements" (facts) and "ought conclusions." It is logically impossible to cross this gulf without the injection of value premises.

PATTERNS OF ARGUMENT

Debaters create the sense that something has been logically demonstrated by following systematic reasoning processes or patterns. In each case, these logical patterns answer the three key questions asked by the Toulmin Model: (1) Claim: What are you trying to get me to believe? (2) Data: What have you got to go on? (3) Warrant: How does the data lead to the claim? Each pattern, however, answers the questions in somewhat different ways.

Deductive Reasoning

The first pattern for argument is *deduction*—meaning a type of reasoning that derives claims from premises. This is the method of the syllogism. Using deduction, a debater might argue as follows: "Citizens should have a right to defend themselves and their families from attackers. Handguns are necessary as a means of self-defense. Therefore, citizens should have the right to possess handguns." To establish the probability that the claim is true, the debater would have to offer support for the two premises. Authoritative quotations or explanations could be offered to support the premise that citizens should have a basic right to self-defense. The premise that "handguns are necessary as a means of self-defense" would be more difficult to prove. The debater would need to offer an authoritative quotation or explanation as to why rifles or passive security systems (locks, motion detectors, and so on) could not take the place of handguns as means of self-defense.

There are two primary tests of deduction: (1) Are the premises sound? and (2) Do the premises lead to the conclusion? In the case of the self-defense example, the first premise is that "citizens should have the right of self-defense." An opposing debater might object that it is the responsibility of government rather than the individual to ensure safety in the community. When individuals take public safety into their own hands, the result is vigilantism. Sometimes debaters construct a defective deductive reasoning chain such that the premises, even if true, simply do not lead to the conclusion. Consider the following example: "Nuclear weapons threaten world peace. The United States possesses nuclear weapons. The United States should unilaterally disarm and dismantle its nuclear weapons." This claim (that the United States should disarm) does not logically follow from the premises. Even if the premises are true, there is no logical justification for unilateral disarmament. Russia and numerous other nations also possess nuclear weapons. Although it may be true that nuclear weapons threaten world peace, an even more threatening situation could be created if only nations such as Russia, North Korea, and Iran possessed these weapons.

INDUCTIVE REASONING

A second widely used logical pattern is *induction*—meaning a type of reasoning in which previous experience or observation is used to support a claim. Using induction, a debater might argue as follows: "The government of Iran is a threat to world peace and security. Consider their behavior over the past decades: They used hostage-taking as official government policy in the 1980s when they took 63 Americans captive and held most of them for two years. They have been a state-sponsor of terrorist groups, providing funding for Hezbollah and Hamas. Iranian President Mahmoud Ahmadinejad has said that the nation of Israel is a 'fake regime' that 'should be wiped off the map.' Now Iran is openly attempting to obtain nuclear weapon capability. These actions have been typical of Iranian behavior over the past decades." In this example of induction, the claim is that Iran is a threat to world peace and security. The data shows numerous instances of behavior threatening to world peace. The warrant says that the examples are typical (they are the norm rather than the exception).

There are four primary tests for inductive reasoning:

- Are the examples accurately described?
- Was the number of examples sufficient?
- Are there counter-examples?
- Are the examples or the counter-examples more representative?

A debater responding to the claim that "Iran is a threat to world peace and security" might argue that the examples are inaccurately described. Consider, for example, the claim that Iranian President Mahmoud Ahmadinejad threatened to "wipe Israel off the map." Our opposing debater might object that this statement misrepresents the whole context of what Ahmadinejad actually said. The opposing debater might also question whether support for Hezbollah and Hamas constitutes support for international terrorism. Iran's pursuit of nuclear power could be justified by its desire to acquire nuclear reactor technology. The hostage-taking incident in the 1980s came immediately following the overthrow of a brutal dictator and predated the establishment of the modern democratic government in Iran.

Sometimes the number of examples offered provides too small a sample from which to draw a conclusion. A debater could, for example, read a piece of evidence describing a heinous murder committed by an illegal immigrant before drawing a conclusion that illegal immigration is a major source of crime in America. The sample size is simply too small to support the conclusion. In properly conducted empirical studies, mathematical formulas are used to determine whether a finding is "statistically significant." The smaller the sample size, the less likely the researchers will arrive at a statistically significant result. In the context of argument, the same principle holds, though on a smaller scale. A single example rarely provides a convincing basis for inductive proof. In the foregoing Iran example, the arguer obviously felt the need to offer numerous instances of threatening behavior before drawing the conclusion that Iran is a threat to world peace and security.

Offering counter-examples is one of the means of opposing inductive argument claims. A debater could answer the claim that "Iran is a threat to world peace and security" by citing instances in which Iran has acted peacefully. The United Nations International Atomic Energy Agency reports that Iran is cooperating with its nuclear inspections and does not seem to be diverting nuclear materials. Iran is one of only a few countries in the Middle East where the government is democratically elected. Furthermore, Iran has agreed to meet with Bush administration officials over the issue of limiting the killing of civilians in Iraq.

A final test of inductive reasoning asks whether the examples are representative. Debate topics are chosen because they are controversial. This means that examples will be available to support both sides of the resolution. The key question is which examples are more representative or typical.

ABDUCTIVE REASONING

A third logical pattern is *abduction*—the framing of a hypothesis that best fits a set of facts. Aristotle's term for this form of reasoning was *apagoge*. Physicians use abduction when they ask a patient to describe his or her symptoms and then make a diagnosis as to the likely disease the patient is experiencing. Debaters also, on occasion, attempt to diagnose symptoms. How, for example, would a debater prove that globalization produces economic stagnation in developing countries? This is a hypothesis advanced to support a group of facts: globalization is proceeding at a rapid pace; developed countries are getting richer as globalization proceeds; and developing countries are getting poorer as globalization proceeds. The debater arguing this case claims that stopping the spread of globalization will be the solution to improving economic growth in developing countries.

The three primary tests of abduction are as follows:

- Are the facts (or symptoms) accurately described?
- Are other facts ignored that would contradict the hypothesis?
- Are other hypotheses available to explain the same set of facts?

Facts are sometimes slippery things. For example, the statement that "globalization is proceeding at a rapid pace" may be true in some places but not in others. An opposing debater might be able to prove that globalization is rapidly advancing in precisely those countries where economic growth is highest. Accordingly, developing countries might need more globalization rather than less. A key way to defeat argument by abduction is to show that the facts are incorrect or improperly interpreted.

A second problem with abduction is that an arguer may conveniently leave out certain facts. A physician is likely to misdiagnose a patient if a few symptoms are considered but others are ignored. Similarly, a debater might improperly choose a hypothesis because too few facts are considered. In our globalization example, an opposing debater might succeed in identifying some developing countries that have embraced globalization and have experienced outstanding economic growth as a result.

A final method of defeating abduction is the support of alternative hypotheses. A debater responding to the attack on globalization might be able to support several other explanations:

- Economic stagnation in developing countries results from a failure to embrace globalization.

- Economic stagnation in developing countries results from rampant government corruption in these countries.

- Economic stagnation in developing countries results from the dependency-effects of too much foreign assistance.

Cause-Effect Reasoning

Another method of reasoning uses *cause-effect analysis*—the claim that one phenomenon is caused by another. A debater might make the following argument: "Poverty is the most immediate cause for the spread of HIV/AIDS in sub-Saharan Africa. Malnutrition weakens the body's immune system, making it more susceptible to HIV/AIDS. Poverty also forces breadwinners to travel long distances from home in an effort to find work; such itinerant lifestyles make it more likely that men will be unfaithful. Poverty also means that people in sub-Saharan Africa can't afford the antiretroviral medications needed to control HIV/AIDS. Therefore, if we truly wish to stop the spread of HIV/AIDS, we must address the problem of poverty in sub-Saharan Africa."

There are five questions that should be asked about causal claims:

- Is the cause a necessary condition for the effect?

- Is the cause a sufficient condition for the effect?

- Did the cause precede the effect?

- Is there a logical explanation as to how the cause generated the effect?

- What other causes might explain the effect?

When asking whether a cause is a necessary condition for an effect, we are really asking whether the effect would exist without the alleged cause. Suppose I am a prosecutor presenting a case in court claiming that the negligence of a drunk driver caused an accident victim to die. In this case the death of the victim would not have happened but for the negligence of the drunk driver. Accordingly, this negligence was a necessary cause for the victim's death. In the case of our HIV/AIDS example, we would be asking whether it is possible to have HIV/AIDS without being in poverty. Clearly, there are people who contract HIV/AIDS who are not living in poverty. Thus, living in poverty is not a necessary condition for contracting HIV/AIDS.

When asking whether a cause is a sufficient condition for an effect, we are really asking whether the cause is *by itself* enough to produce the effect. Consider our example of the drunk driver whose negligence killed an innocent victim. If I were the prosecuting attorney, I would be trying to argue that the driver's negligence was a sufficient condition for the victim's death. In other words, there were no other significant causes in play (such as the victim wandering aimlessly in the middle of the road when hit or a foggy morning that would have obscured the vision of even the most careful driver). The prosecuting attorney has the strongest causal case if it can be shown that the driver's negligence was both a necessary and sufficient cause of the victim's death. Consider, however, the claim that poverty causes HIV/AIDS in sub-Saharan Africa. Would it be true that living in poverty is a sufficient cause for contracting HIV/AIDS? Clearly not! Poverty might arguably be one of the factors increasing susceptibility to HIV/AIDS, but many people live in poverty while never contracting HIV/AIDS.

Why is it important for the debater to know that poverty is neither a necessary nor sufficient condition for contracting HIV/AIDS? This means that a program designed to reduce poverty in sub-Saharan Africa is unlikely to have a large impact on solving HIV/AIDS.

Another question to ask about causal claims is whether the alleged cause preceded the effect. Suppose a debater points out that the latest report of the U.S. Justice Department shows that major crime has declined over the past year. The debater claims that the passage through Congress last year of a tougher sentencing bill caused the decline in major crime. An opposing debater could simply point out that major crime has declined steadily over the past decade; it would make little sense to give the credit for this decline to a measure that has only recently been implemented. A causal claim has little validity if it can be shown that the effect was already underway before the alleged cause.

Causal claims must also offer some persuasive explanation as to how the cause generated the effect. It is never enough to show that a cause preceded the effect. One could say, for example, that "a bell in a church tower rang and two minutes later it began to rain; the bell must have caused the rain." Such an argument is silly, of course, but many equally silly causal claims are made in the course of debates. A debater must be able to provide a reasonable explanation as to why the cause brought the effect into being.

ARGUMENT FROM SIGN

Another method of reasoning uses *sign*—the claim that one phenomenon is associated with another. We might say, for example, that a local restaurant must be a good place to eat because the parking lot there is always full. By making such a statement, we are accepting a full parking lot as a sign of business success. The full parking lot does not, of course, cause a restaurant to be successful; the restaurant could be sharing its parking lot with a used car lot next door.

Sign reasoning is very similar to a method of exploration that is now widely accepted in the social sciences—the computation of correlation coefficients. Suppose a communication scholar wants to explore how the amount of direct eye contact contributes to communication success. Any such study would have to account for numerous other intervening variables such as culture, gender, and socioeconomic status. At the end of the study, the researchers might find a high correlation between business success and the amount of eye contact for males in a Middle Eastern culture. This does not necessarily prove that by increasing your eye contact you can become more successful; it has simply found that one is a sign of the other.

Sign reasoning also appears within the debate context. Suppose a debater wishes to argue that violent video games are bad for America's teenagers. The major studies conducted in this area are based on correlation; they ask how often the watching of violent video games is associated with violent teenage behavior.

There are three primary questions that should be asked about sign reasoning:

- How strong is the association between the variables?

- Are there other unexamined variables that might better explain the relationship?

- Is the arguer attempting to base a causal claim on sign reasoning?

Properly conducted studies in the social sciences do much more than simply declare a relationship between two or more variables—they also calculate the degree of correlation. Correlation coefficients are always between plus one and minus one. A correlation coefficient of +1.0 means that a one-to-one relationship exists between the two variables. Suppose we are asking how likely it is that a person growing up in a household with a smoker will choose to smoke in adulthood. A +1.0 correlation would mean that all persons growing up in such a household become smokers in adulthood. A −1.0 correlation would mean that no persons growing up in such a household become smokers in adulthood. A correlation coefficient of 0 would mean that there is no correlation between the variables—or at least that the study could not detect a relationship. In general, a correlation coefficient in the range of .7 or more is considered a high correlation, while a correlation coefficient in the range of .3 or less is considered a low correlation.

A second question to ask about sign reasoning is whether there are unexamined variables that might better explain the relationship. Suppose, for example, a debater is making the claim that lowering the high school dropout rate will strengthen the American economy by hundreds of billions of dollars. The argument is based on a study that shows that high school graduates earn nearly twice as much as high school dropouts. An opposing debater can point out that this study is merely showing a correlation between income and high school graduation. The ignored intervening variable may well be the amount of drive and initiative people possess. People who have a great deal of initiative might be successful at whatever they do, and this success might have little to do with their level of education. Conversely, people who drop out of high school lack initiative. They will be unsuccessful regardless of their level of education. Any solution that forces all the dropouts to remain in school might have very little impact on overall earning power in the American economy.

A final question to ask about sign reasoning is whether it is being inappropriately used to make causal claims. The major reason social scientists have avoided causal claims in favor of correlational analysis is that they are trying to frame studies that are more modest and scientifically careful. Yet debaters often take the results of correlational studies and present them as if a causal connection has been demonstrated. The studies showing a correlation between violent video games and real violence offer just such an example. A debater might use these studies as the basis for claiming that banning violent video games would reduce teenage violence. Such a claim assumes a causal connection between the two variables. It might well be that the same teenagers who have violent tendencies in real life are also drawn to video games that are violent. Accordingly, there is a strong correlation between real violence and video violence. This does not, however, prove that banning video games would change the violent tendencies of teenagers.

ARGUMENT BY DIVISION

Yet another method of reasoning uses *division*—the process of elimination to arrive at a conclusion. A computer program uses division as its method of reasoning; at every point in a computer's binary logic, the decision is always between zero and one.

Many of our everyday uses of argument also employ division. Consider the following example: "The safe in the office was robbed sometime last evening. Only Smith, Jones, and Thompson knew the combination to the safe. Smith is on vacation in Australia; Jones was with several friends the whole evening. It must have been Thompson who robbed the safe." This logic sample illustrates numerous flaws with division, which are explored later.

Following is an example of the way a debater might use division: "Iran doesn't deny that it is developing the ability to produce highly enriched uranium. Iran's motive for doing so must be either to use enriched uranium in nuclear reactors or to store material for constructing nuclear weapons. The first possibility makes no sense. After all, Iran is sitting atop one of the world's richest supplies of oil; they have less need for nuclear power than any other nation on earth. It is clear that Iran is enriching uranium in preparation for the building of nuclear weapons." Notice that the debater uses the process of establishing alternatives and then sorting/discarding the alternatives.

There are three primary questions that should be asked about argument by division:

- Have we identified all the alternatives?

- Are the alternatives mutually exclusive?

- Are there good reasons for rejecting other alternatives?

A common problem with argument by division is a failure to start with all the alternatives. Consider the previous example of the safe that has been robbed. Why do we assume that the person robbing the safe must have been one of the three with the combination? Consider the other alternatives: a professional safe cracker robbed it, the combination was left where another person discovered it, someone failed to lock the safe, or an employee of the company manufacturing the safe robbed it.

A second problem with argument by division is that sometimes debaters present phony alternatives—options that are not mutually exclusive. A debater might, for example, say, "You have a choice between upholding the Second Amendment to the Constitution *or* requiring the registration of handguns. We have shown you many reasons why you should choose to uphold the Second Amendment." An opposing debater should ask why one has to choose between these two alternatives. It is certainly possible to do what the Second Amendment says (have a well-regulated militia) while also requiring the registration of handguns.

A final problem with argument by division is that sometimes mistakes are made in the rejection of alternatives. Consider our earlier argument about the reasons Iran wants to produce highly enriched uranium. The debater argued that it is unreasonable to believe that Iran wants to support nuclear power because it has an abundance of oil. Yet environmentalists have been predicting for the past quarter century that the world oil supply will run dry. Why is it unreasonable that Iran should choose to use some of its oil wealth to prepare for the world beyond fossil fuels?

ARGUMENT FROM ANALOGY

Another method of reasoning uses *analogy*—a figurative comparison. Some theologians have argued for the existence of God based on the analogy of the watchmaker—the belief that the complexity of the universe speaks of a creator. Astronomers explain their theories of the universe by comparing it to spots on the surface of an expanding balloon. Philosopher John Rawls explained his notion of justice by using the analogy of standing behind a veil (he called it a "veil of ignorance"). Supreme Court Justice William Brennan used the analogy of the "slippery slope" to warn that a seemingly innocuous step down the slope of restricting civil liberties could result in a slide all the way to the bottom.

Analogies also find a place in political debates. A February 16, 2007, article in *USA Today* by Darlene Superville detailed the ways that members of the U.S. Congress have used analogies in debating U.S. policy with respect to Iraq. Republican Representative Ric Keller of Florida offered the following analogy:

> Imagine your next-door neighbor refuses to mow his lawn and the weeds are all the way up to his waist. You decide you are going to mow his lawn for him every single week. The neighbor never says thank you, he hates you, and sometimes he takes out a gun and shoots at you. Under these circumstances, do you keep mowing his lawn forever? Do you send even more of your family members over to mow his lawn? Or do you say to that neighbor, you better step it up and mow your own lawn, or there are going to be serious consequences for you? Mr. Speaker, sending more young American troops now into the middle of Iraqi civil war violence is not the answer.

Texas Republican Congressman Ron Paul used a "visit to the doctor" analogy to make his case against the war:

> A wrong diagnosis was made at the beginning of the war, and the wrong treatment was prescribed. Refusing to reassess our mistakes and insisting on just more and more of a failed remedy is destined to kill the patient. In this case, the casualties will be our liberties and prosperity, here at home, and peace abroad.

Debaters make a serious mistake when they underestimate the persuasive power of analogies. One can, of course, point out the obvious: the Iraq War is not much like mowing a lawn, the universe is much larger than a watch, and civil liberties do not really rest on a muddy slope. The real power of an analogy, however, comes not from its literal force, but from the way it illuminates the imagination.

The two most successful strategies for responding to an analogy are as follows: (1) Extend the analogy (on its figurative side) until it breaks down and (2) Offer a counter analogy. Consider Representative Ric Keller's analogy asking how long we should mow our neighbor's lawn. In response, you might ask whether it changes the equation if you have borrowed and broken your neighbor's lawnmower? We took responsibility for maintaining order in Iraq when we destroyed its own capability to do so. How long must we mow Iraq's lawn? Until we can get its lawnmower repaired.

As many of Representative Keller's colleagues seemed to realize, often the best answer to an analogy is a counter analogy. Georgia Representative Jim Marshall, a Democrat, used just such a method:

> The anti-surge resolution is akin to sitting on the sidelines and booing in the middle of our own team's play because we don't like the coach's call. I cannot join midplay naysaying that might discourage even one of those engaged in this current military effort in Baghdad.

John Shaddegg, a Republican from Arizona, used the analogy of stepping on a landmine:

The best analogy I heard was one that said, "This is like stepping on a land mine, where you put your foot on it, but you know that if you lift your foot off it will blow up." We have put our foot on a land mine in Iraq. But if we lift our foot off before the Iraqi government can defend itself, it will blow us up, and it will blow them up.

Representative Joe Wilson, a Republican from South Carolina, used a fire fighting analogy to argue for staying the course in Iraq:

Just as we know our fire chiefs would call up additional fire-fighters to contain a spreading fire, we must give our troops in Baghdad the chance to suppress violence and stabilize the region, which protects American families. In conclusion, God bless our troops and we will never forget September the 11th.

Todd Akin, a Republican from Missouri, used an historical analogy, comparing what we are doing in Iraq to defending the Alamo:

Picture Davy Crockett at the Alamo. He has his back to the wall. Santa Ana has got thousands of troops. So he gets his BlackBerry out. He checks with Congress. Congress says, "Hey, Davy, we really support you, but we're not going to send you any troops." That doesn't make a whole lot of sense to me.

ARGUMENT FROM NARRATIVE

A final method of reasoning uses *narrative*—proving a point by telling a story. Consider the example of Frederick Douglass as he provided persuasive proof of the horrors of slavery. In the following section of his *Narrative of the Life of Frederick Douglass, an American Slave,* he is describing his master, Captain Anthony (Douglass said he never knew his master's first name):

He was a cruel man, hardened by a long life of slave-holding. He would at times seem to take great pleasure in whipping a slave. I have often been awakened at the dawn of day by the most heart-rending shrieks of an own aunt of mine, whom he used to tie up to a joist, and whip upon her naked back till she was literally covered with blood. No words, no tears, no prayers, from his gory victim, seemed to move his iron heart from its bloody purpose. The louder she screamed, the harder he whipped; and where the blood ran fastest, there he whipped longest. He would whip her to make her scream, and whip her to make her hush; and not until overcome by fatigue, would he cease to swing the blood-clotted cowskin.

The narrative approach works by asking the listener to identify with the plight of the person described in the story. But narrative also has some key disadvantages. First, telling stories takes a lot of time—something that is a scarce commodity in most debates. Second, stories offer only a single example of a problem. Few stories carry the emotional power of the Douglass narrative; most narratives can be answered rather simply by pointing out examples in support of the opposing case. Third, narratives appeal more at the emotional than a logical level. When debate judges are forced to choose between logical support and emotional appeal, most side with the logical support.

Further Reading

Douglass, Frederick. 1845. *Narrative of the Life of Frederick Douglass, an American Slave.* http://sunsite3.berkeley.edu/Literature/Douglass/Autobiography/ (accessed July 28, 2007).

Monty Python Scripts. 2007. "The Argument Sketch." www.intriguing.com/mp/_scripts/argument.asp (accessed July 26, 2007).

Superville, Darlene. "Analogies Made During Iraq War Debate." *USA Today,* February 16, 2007. www.usatoday.com/news/washington/2007-02-16-iraq-analogies_x.htm (accessed July 28, 2007).

CHAPTER 3

GETTING THE MOST OUT OF RESEARCH

Debaters are expected to support their positions with authoritative evidence. It is, therefore, no surprise that the best debaters are usually the most competent researchers. Mastery of research techniques is also one of the major educational benefits of participating in competitive debate. This chapter is, therefore, dedicated to helping beginning debaters become acquainted with the intricacies of research.

The best researchers are those who can uncover the most credible authoritative evidence to support their positions. This means it is important for debaters to explore the full range of sources, including books, newspapers, periodicals, government documents, law reviews, and the reports of advocacy groups and research think tanks.

Research tools have been revolutionized over the past decade as reliance on paper-based library resources has given way to online research tools. Only a few years ago, the best advice for beginning researchers was to begin by familiarizing themselves with the "traditional" library resources (using the old-fashioned card catalogs and bound volumes of the *Reader's Guide to Periodical Literature*). But libraries are increasingly doing away with paper indexes in favor of computerized, Web-based search tools. Accordingly, this chapter begins by exploring the terms and methods involved in online research. Ironically, online research tools are now the best way to gain access to traditional resources such as books and periodicals.

TERMINOLOGY USED IN ONLINE RESEARCH

An understanding of online research requires the learning of a new vocabulary. Terms such as *Internet provider*, *browser*, and *search engine* have entered our language only in the past two decades.

Internet provider refers to the commercial service used to establish a connection to the Internet. Examples of a service provider are America Online, Sprint, AT&T, MSN, and Road Runner.

Internet browser refers to the software used to manipulate information on the Internet. The four major browsers in use are Netscape, Mozilla Firefox, Safari (the Apple product), and Internet Explorer (the Microsoft product). Each type of browser gives you access to the same group of search engines, which is the main thing you will care about.

Netscape and Firefox have one important feature that Safari and Internet Explorer lack: they can report to you the date that a web page was created or last modified (select Page Info from the top View or Tools menu to access this function). Ignore the date information listed to the right of Modified—that date is almost always the date you are conducting the search. The date information you seek is usually reported in the box labeled Meta. By scrolling through the information in this box, you can usually discover both the date of original creation of the web page and the date it was last modified. A web page may be dated from the last revision date if no other date is shown on the page; Internet Explorer and Safari offer no way to know this date.

Why would you need to know the date of creation or last revision? As you will discover later in this chapter, the National Forensic League (NFL) evidence citation standard requires evidence to have a date listed. If the web page does not list a date of creation or last revision, the evidence would be unusable in debate unless it can be discovered in some other way. It is never acceptable in competitive debate to list a piece of evidence as "n.d."—meaning "no date"—as some notation systems suggest for class projects and term papers.

Internet Explorer, Firefox, and Safari have one very useful feature that Netscape lacks: the user can "copy" an image from the Internet (to move over to a PowerPoint presentation, for example) by simply right-clicking the desired image and selecting Copy. It is easier to build a PowerPoint presentation using this feature. You can have PowerPoint running at the same time as Internet Explorer (or Firefox or Safari), copy an image using the method previously described, click the bottom Start menu bar to make PowerPoint the active window, and then simply issue the Paste command (either by pressing Ctrl+V or by selecting Paste from the top menu choice for Edit). You can accomplish the same thing from Netscape, but it is more cumbersome. You have to right-click the image and select the choice for Save This Image (there is no choice for Copy in Netscape). Save the image to a place on your hard drive or on a floppy; then from the top Insert menu, you can select Insert Picture (the choice for Insert Picture from File). The only problem is that this requires a couple of extra steps and you have to make sure you know where on your hard drive you saved the image.

URL or Universal Resource Locator refers to the Internet address for websites. An example would be www3.baylor.edu/~Richard_Edwards/.

Internet search engine refers to the software used to search for information on the Internet. You will use the same group of search engines regardless of which browser (Explorer, Firefox, Netscape, or Safari) you might be using. Examples of search engines are Google, AllTheWeb, HotBot, Teoma, InfoSeek, Yahoo!, Excite, LookSmart, and AltaVista.

Metasearch engines are Internet search engines that submit your search to other search engines. The best of the metasearch engines are SearchOnLine, Dogpile, Mama, and Webcrawler. The metasearch engines advertise that they are superior to any one search engine because they report results from four or five major Internet search engines. Although this is useful for some purposes, it is not the best means to conduct debate research. The metasearch engine sends a simple search request to other search engines, meaning you are foregoing the opportunity to use the advanced search function that almost all major search engines make available to you. This means you often lose the capability to do exact phrase searching, limitation by date, limitation by domain, and limitation by file type. It is also often true that you receive fewer hits from each of the major search engines than if you were to issue the search from directly within that search engine.

The *domain* of a web page tells you something about the origin of that page. Each web page on the Internet has a closing three-letter code such as *.com*, *.edu*, *.gov*, or *.net*—this is its domain. In most instances, the .edu domain means the web page is housed in or provided by a college or university. The .gov domain means the web page is maintained by a federal, state, or local government. The .com and .net domains usually mean a commercial enterprise hosts that page. Most of the major search engines (in the advanced search options) allow you to limit a search to particular domains.

PDF stands for portable document file and indicates that a document is being made available in a format that will look just like an original document in print (complete with page numbers). PDF files are designed to be viewed and printed in Adobe Acrobat Reader (available free for download from the Internet). The advantage for the debater is that information gathered from a PDF file can be cited at a particular page number (the same page number it would have if you had access to the original printed document). Almost all congressional hearings (starting with the 105th and 106th Congresses) are available in PDF format. This not only means that you can download a hearing that's identical to the printed one, but it also means you have almost immediate access to a hearing after it has been held.

PDF files also carry the advantage that they are usually made available from well-established sources on the Internet. Again, however, the software necessary to "read" PDF documents is available free on the Internet. You will know that a document for download is available in PDF format if the Internet URL ends in .pdf. Most of the major search engines allow you to search for only those web pages that make a PDF download available.

HTML stands for HyperText Markup Language and is the code used for creating web pages. You don't really need to be an HTML programmer to be able to write a web page because numerous programs such as Netscape Composer and Microsoft FrontPage can create the code for you from simple-to-operate menu choices. If you want to view the HTML code used to construct a web page, you can do so by selecting the top menu choice for View (in either Netscape or Internet Explorer) and then selecting the choice for Page Source. You will see displayed the native HTML code that creates the web page.

MAXIMIZING THE USE OF THE SEARCH ENGINE

Why use a search engine? This is the only way to find material on the Internet unless you already know the URL you are looking for. The problem is that you must know the URL precisely; close will not be good enough. In the early days of the Internet, folks used to use printed resources such as *Internet Yellow Pages*. But now there are simply too many pages for these types of publications to be very useful. Google and AllTheWeb, for example, index more than two billion Internet pages.

CHARACTERISTICS OF A GOOD SEARCH ENGINE

Comprehensiveness is the most important quality in a search engine. Powerful search engines index as much of the Internet as possible through two means. First, they invite web page creators to send a request to have their pages indexed. This is in the interest of web designers because they almost always want their pages to be easily found. Second, they employ automatic searching programs that continually find new (and unindexed) pages on the Web and index them.

The best search engines also do full text indexing. This means you could literally pick a phrase out of the middle of a web page and enter the phrase in Google or AltaVista in quotation marks, and the search engine will find the page for you within about a second. This capability is especially important for the debater. You might have written down a portion of a quotation used against you that you would dearly like to find (either because you want to check its context or you want to locate the quotation to use in your own briefs). If the quotation is from an Internet source, you can quickly find it using a comprehensive search engine. There are, however, some limitations to the capability to find text within a web page. Google, for example, indexes only the first 101 kilobytes of a web page (under normal circumstances, this is the first eight to ten pages of text).

Speed of operation is also important in choosing a search engine. In the early days of search engines, you could sometimes issue a search and wait a long time (ten or twenty seconds) for the search to be completed. Those days are gone. All the major search engines are really almost instantaneous now. If you are experiencing problems with speed, it is probably due to your own modem's speed or to the limitations of your own computer processor's capability to handle the web page graphics.

Proximity searches are a big concern for the debater. If you enter terms such as <categorical imperative> into your search engine, you will receive dramatically varying results depending on the search engine you are using. Google does the best job of performing automatic proximity searching, meaning that it orders your search results by examining how close your search terms are in proximity to one another. Older or less capable search engines merely report the pages that contain some or all of these words.

Exact phrase searching is an essential feature, for the debater, of a good search engine. By placing your phrase in quotation marks, you can instruct the search engine to return only those pages containing the whole phrase as a phrase. When searching for "public health assistance," you want to find the whole phrase of the resolution, not just pages that contain the individual words *public* and *health* and *assistance*. Almost all major search engines allow for exact phrase searching, but there are some unfortunate exceptions. Be aware, though, that unless you place your phrase in quotation marks, you are not getting an exact phrase search.

Image search is not important for debate research but is great when you are looking for visual images to build PowerPoint presentations for class projects.

PROCEDURES FOR EFFECTIVE SEARCHING

What about capitalization? For the major Internet search engines, capitalization no longer matters. Searching for "VEIL OF IGNORANCE" will produce the same results as "Veil of Ignorance" or "veil of ignorance."

What about quotation marks? Use quotation marks whenever you want the search engine to look for words together as a phrase (assuming you are using a search engine that enables exact phrase searching). If you search for Public Health Assistance (without the quotation marks), the search engine will look for web pages containing the word *public* and *health* and *assistance*, but it will not require that the words be next to each other. By putting quotation marks around "Public Health Assistance", you are requesting only those pages containing the whole phrase. There is no need to put quotation marks around a single word.

How can you limit a search to a particular domain? The best Internet search engines have an advanced search or power search capability. One of the options in the advanced search engine is the capability to limit by domain. Limiting your search to the .gov domain will, for example, provide an efficient means of finding government publications on the desired search.

How can you search for a particular URL (if you know part but not all of the URL)? Many of the advanced search engines provide the capability to enter a search term and then indicate whether you want to make this search apply to title only, full-text, or URL. You would, of course, select the URL option.

How does the search engine rank the web pages it reports? This is a somewhat controversial issue. Some search engines receive payment from Internet advertisers for the privilege of having their pages reported early in the search list. Most search engines, though, report the web pages in order of the greater number of occurrences of the term. Google's patented PageRank system factors in not only the proximity of the terms, but also the number of times other users have accessed the web pages.

How can "taking apart the URL" help you locate the author's qualifications? Consider the following example. You enter "John Rawls" and "social safety net" in a Google search. You get a web page returned to you titled "Notes on 'A Theory of Justice.'" The web page contains some information you find useful, but you have no information about the author other than just the name Chilton. You notice from the URL that the web page comes from an .edu domain associated with something called d.umn, but you don't know what school this is, and you don't know whether the author is a professor or an undergraduate student. The URL is www.d.umn.edu/~schilton/3652/Readings/3652. Rawls.ATheoryOfJustice.html. Take apart the URL to discover more about the author. Click with your mouse up in the URL line and eliminate all of the end of the URL back to schilton; then press Enter. See whether you can find more information about the author. If the URL comes from an educational institution with which you are unfamiliar, eliminate all the end of the URL back to the part that ends in .edu; then press Enter. By clicking the button on the author's web page for "Vita", you can discover information about his background. You find that the author of the web page is Stephen Chilton, associate professor of political science at the University of Minnesota, Duluth, and earned his Ph.D. from MIT—a good source. But some additional work is needed to determine his qualifications. It is essential that you find the person or group responsible for authoring the web page. It is NEVER a sufficient qualification that you found it on the Internet.

Google (www.google.com) is the best search engine overall for policy debate research. Other folks have discovered it as well: According to "Nielsen Netratings" of June 2007, Google is responsible for 56.3 percent of all search engine referrals worldwide. The next closest search engine is Yahoo! at 21.5 percent, followed by MSN Search (www.live.com) at 8.4 percent. What makes Google ("Go" "Ogle") so useful for debate research? Two factors: (1) It provides the most comprehensive search, and (2) It performs automatic proximity searching among the terms listed in the search box. Suppose, for example, you enter in the search box the following words: malaria sub-Saharan Africa. Google returns only those web pages containing the listed search terms, and (most importantly) it lists first those web pages that contain the search terms in the closest proximity to one another.

Google does have some quirks, however. Google searches are limited to 10 words—if you enter more than 10 words, Google ignores all but the first 10 words it finds. Also, Google indexes only the first 101 kilobytes of any web page (typically about 10–15 pages, depending on the graphic content of the page). If the quotation happens to be toward the end of a long document, Google will not find it.

The "hidden Internet" includes, by most accounts, more than twice as much material as the searchable Internet. Searches on Google (or other search engines) fail to find these documents because they exist in file formats that are invisible to indexing software. Only recently have search engines developed the capability to reach inside of portable document files (PDFs) to index their contents, but many other formats remain inaccessible. The contents of the huge ERIC database provides a prominent example of web-based materials that are not indexed in most search engines. The only means for gaining access to these materials is through the use of the search system contained on the home page where the materials are housed.

The URL for a website can be used to go directly to the desired page on the Internet. To use this function, however, you must know the whole URL and enter it precisely—periods, commas, underlines, and slashes—in the address line. Sometimes, however, a debater knows one portion of a long URL but not the whole address. Fortunately, Google provides the means to find any web page that contain that certain portion of a URL. The Google search process involves entering the term "inurl" followed by a colon and then the known portion of the URL.

Google also provides the capability to limit a search to terms found in the title of a web page. This is done by listing "allintitle" followed by a colon and the search term. An example of such a search would be <allintitle: "public health assistance">.

Selecting Google's Advanced Search page offers numerous other ways to fine-tune an Internet search. A debater might, for example, want to limit an Internet search to federal government websites; this can be done by telling Google's advanced search (in the Domain edit box) to select only documents ending in <.gov>.

Another function on the Advanced Search page allows you to select only certain types of files. This might be used, for example, to limit the search to PDF files. The main advantage of PDF files is that the user is shown a document with pagination exactly the same as the printed version of the document (especially useful for viewing congressional committee hearings).

SOURCES OF DEBATE EVIDENCE

Mastery of debate research requires source variety. Debate judges, much like the English teachers who grade your essays, are impressed by researchers who dig below the surface of a topic. Digging below the surface means looking into books, government documents, law reviews, and reports from major think tanks. Newspaper and magazine accounts are often very useful—and they are certainly the easiest to read—but the cutting-edge researcher treats these sources as merely a beginning place. The following paragraphs describe how to gain access to a wider world of ideas and arguments.

BOOKS

Books are too often neglected as a resource for modern debate research. This is unfortunate because some of the best debate evidence on debate topics appears in books.

Gaining access to books sometimes involves either travel or expense. Finding a particular book often means visiting the closest college library or purchasing the book through Amazon.com (or one of its online competitors). Before deciding to buy a book, however, check into whether your high school or public library is a member of the Online Computer Library Center (OCLC). If so, it might be able to obtain the book through interlibrary loan.

An exciting new Internet tool puts the world of books at your fingertips. Worldcat—the computerized card catalog that lists all the books available in American libraries—is now freely available on the Internet at www.worldcat.org. Worldcat is the premier research tool for locating books. After you have located a book on Worldcat, you have all the information necessary for ordering the book through interlibrary loan. In fact, Worldcat is owned and operated by the Online Computer Library Center.

Explore the power of Worldcat by clicking its Advanced search link. Try entering a search term such as "sub-Saharan Africa" and limiting the dates to nothing older than 2004. This search produces more than 2,000 books. Notice that Worldcat allows you to save this list to your computer in any order you choose (by author name, date, or relevance to your topic). By clicking one of the books, you will discover other powerful tools. If, for example, you click the book titled *A Continent for the Taking: The Tragedy and Hope of Africa*, you will see numerous additional links. By clicking the link labeled Biographical Information, you will discover that the author, Howard French, is a senior writer for *The New York Times* who has won numerous journalistic awards for his coverage of African issues. By clicking the Sample Text link, you will be shown the first two pages of the book where the author is explaining his purpose in writing the book. By clicking Cite This Item, you will be given the complete citation for the book in the five standard citation formats (Modern Language Association, Turabian, American Psychological Association, Chicago Manual of Style, and Harvard Law Review Association). You can copy and paste this book citation (using your chosen format) into your word processor to save you the trouble of constructing a citation for material quoted from the book.

GOVERNMENT DOCUMENTS

Congressional committee hearings provide a good source of information on debate topics. Most of the research work done by members of Congress is conducted in committee hearings; each congressional committee holds its own hearings on legislation that falls within its jurisdiction. Each hearing typically includes testimony from key federal government officials and leading scholars in the topic area. Hearings offer testimony from both proponents and opponents of legislative proposals. Hearings are available on the Internet in two formats: HTML and PDF. Although PDF files take longer to download, they have the advantage of pagination that precisely follows the format of the printed version of the government document. Debaters are, therefore, able to cite the page number for each quotation.

Congressional hearings can be retrieved in full text from the following website: www.gpoaccess.gov/chearings/index.html— the Government Printing Office (GPO) website for hearings. The GPO website allows you to search in any session of Congress after the 105th.

The Government Printing Office also maintains a website that searches the published reports of the U.S. Agency for International Development, the Centers for Disease Control and Prevention, and all other executive departments and agencies. This search engine is available at the following website: www.gpoaccess.gov/cgp/advanced.html.

A website called Thomas (named after Thomas Jefferson) is the place to go for access to the *Congressional Record* (a transcript of the floor debate in both houses of Congress) and for information on the status of pending legislation. Thomas, available at http://thomas.loc.gov, is maintained by the U.S. Library of Congress.

Often a debater needs to know whether a particular piece of legislation has passed Congress and become law. Thomas offers accurate, up-to-date information about legislation, including whether hearings have been held, whether legislation has passed the House or Senate, and whether it has become a public law.

Another useful group of government documents is available from the Congressional Research Service (CRS), a division of the Library of Congress. The CRS has prepared thousands of reports dealing with almost every topic imaginable. CRS reports are especially useful in providing a simple summary of current legislation (usually 6–10 pages) for any of the topics that come before Congress. Surprisingly, CRS reports also deal with numerous value questions such as separation of church and state, animal rights, and freedom of the press. Debaters should be aware of a search engine designed specifically to search CRS reports: http://2act.org/p/576.html.

The Government Accountability Office (GAO), formerly the General Accounting Office, serves Congress as part of the Office of the Comptroller General. The GAO conducts hundreds of investigations each year on topics ranging from the risk of a bird flu outbreak to the success of current efforts to limit illegal immigration. Direct access to GAO reports is available from the following website: www.gao.gov/index.html.

LAW REVIEWS

Gaining access to law reviews is a challenge for the debater. For cases dealing with technical subject matters, the evidence available in law reviews is of critical importance. Schools fortunate enough to have a Lexis/Nexis subscription have an advantage, but creative students should be able to gain access through other means. Check with your school library to find out whether you have access to a commercial database that might include some law reviews (examples of such databases include ProQuest, Academic Search Premier, Ingenta, WilsonSelectPlus, and ArticleFirst).

If you do not have access to an appropriate commercial database, try going directly to the website for the particular law review. Almost all law schools maintain an Internet site for their law review, and they often provide free access to some articles. If you still are unable to find the desired law review, try entering the title of the law review article (in quotation marks) in a Google search. Sometimes you will find a full text copy of the article posted on the author's website or at the website of an advocacy group. You also might be able to find the full text of a law review article available through the website of the University Law Review Project: www.lawreview.org. You might also try the Yahoo! Law Directory. This site provides links to hundreds of law reviews, many of which make their archives available online at http://dir.yahoo.com/Government/Law/Journals/.

RESEARCH THINK TANKS

The website associated with a typical think tank generally provides free access to thousands of pages of research on topics of interest to debaters. Although it is true that think tanks and advocacy groups push particular political agendas, the research reports are prepared by experts in their fields. Debaters interested in supporting a larger role for government in solving social problems will find support from groups such as the Urban Institute, the Brookings Institution, and the Carter Center. Evidence opposing greater government involvement is available from groups such as the Cato Institute, the American Enterprise Institute, the Hudson Institute, and the Heritage Foundation. Debaters interested in environmental advocacy can find supporting materials from groups such as Greenpeace and the World Wildlife Fund. For every public policy problem, there are think tanks or advocacy groups preparing reports on that specific problem.

The following paragraphs describe the major research think tanks "in their own words"—meaning the descriptions are those contained in the "about us" links on the groups' own websites.

American Enterprise Institute (www.aei.org/library.htm): "The American Enterprise Institute for Public Policy Research is dedicated to preserving and strengthening the foundations of freedom—limited government, private enterprise, vital cultural and political institutions, and a strong foreign policy and national defense—through scholarly research, open debate, and publications. Founded in 1943 and located in Washington, D.C., AEI is one of America's largest and most respected think tanks."

American Foreign Policy Council (www.afpc.org): "For two decades, the American Foreign Policy Council (AFPC) has played an essential role in the U.S. foreign policy debate. Founded in 1982, AFPC is a non-profit organization dedicated to bringing information to those who make or influence the foreign policy of the United States and to assisting world leaders, particularly in the former USSR, with building democracies and market economies. AFPC is widely recognized as a source of timely, insightful analysis on issues of foreign policy, and works closely with members of Congress, the Executive Branch, and the policymaking community."

Brookings Institution (www.brook.edu): "In its research, The Brookings Institution functions as an independent analyst and critic, committed to publishing its findings for the information of the public. In its conferences and activities, it serves as a bridge between scholarship and public policy, bringing new knowledge to the attention of decisionmakers and affording scholars a better insight into public policy issues. The Institution traces its beginnings to 1916 with the founding of the Institute for Government Research, the first private organization devoted to public policy issues at the national level."

Carnegie Endowment for International Peace (www. carnegieendowment.org): "The Carnegie Endowment for International Peace is a private, nonprofit organization dedicated to advancing cooperation between nations and promoting active international engagement by the United States. Founded in 1910, its work is nonpartisan and dedicated to achieving practical results."

Carter Center (www.cartercenter.org): "The Carter Center, in partnership with Emory University, is guided by a fundamental commitment to human rights and the alleviation of human suffering; it seeks to prevent and resolve conflicts, enhance freedom and democracy, and improve health."

CATO Institute (www.cato.org): "The Cato Institute seeks to broaden the parameters of public policy debate to allow consideration of the traditional American principles of limited government, individual liberty, free markets, and peace. Toward that goal, the Institute strives to achieve greater involvement of the intelligent, concerned lay public in questions of policy and the proper role of government."

Center for Strategic and International Studies (www.csis.org): "The Center for Strategic and International Studies (CSIS) seeks to advance global security and prosperity in an era of economic and political transformation by providing strategic insights and practical policy solutions to decisionmakers. CSIS serves as a strategic planning partner for the government by conducting research and analysis and developing policy initiatives that look into the future and anticipate change."

Heritage Foundation (www.heritage.org): "Founded in 1973, The Heritage Foundation is a research and educational institute—a think tank—whose mission is to formulate and promote conservative public policies based on the principles of free enterprise, limited government, individual freedom, traditional American values, and a strong national defense."

Hoover Institution (www.hoover.org): "The Hoover Institution on War, Revolution and Peace, Stanford University, is a public policy research center devoted to advanced study of politics, economics, and political economy—both domestic and foreign—as well as international affairs. With its world-renowned group of scholars and ongoing programs of policy-oriented research, the Hoover Institution puts its accumulated knowledge to work as a prominent contributor to the world marketplace of ideas defining a free society."

Hudson Institute (www.hudson.org): "In Hudson Institute's policy recommendations, articles, books, conferences, and contributions to the electronic media, we share optimism about the future and a willingness to question conventional wisdom. We demonstrate commitment to free markets and individual responsibility, confidence in the power of technology to assist progress, respect for the importance of culture and religion in human affairs, and determination to preserve America's national security."

Manhattan Institute (www.manhattan-institute.org): "For over 25 years, the Manhattan Institute has been an important force in shaping American political culture. We have supported and publicized research on our era's most challenging public policy issues: taxes, welfare, crime, the legal system, urban life, race, education, and many other topics. We have won new respect for market-oriented policies and helped make reform a reality."

Progressive Policy Institute (www.ppionline.org): "PPI's mission is to define and promote a new progressive politics for America in the 21st century. Through its research, policies, and commentary, the Institute is fashioning a new governing philosophy and an agenda for public innovation geared to the Information Age."

RAND Corporation (www.rand.org): "RAND (a contraction of the term research and development) is the first organization to be called a 'think tank.' We earned this distinction soon after we were created in 1946 by our original client, the U.S. Air Force (then the Army Air Forces). Some of our early work involved aircraft, rockets, and satellites. In the 1960s we even helped develop the technology you're using to view this website. Today, RAND's work is exceptionally diverse. We now assist all branches of the U.S. military community, and we apply our expertise to social and international issues as well."

Twentieth Century Fund (www.tcf.org): "Our efforts cut across many areas of policy, but focus particularly on four basic challenges facing the United States: persistent economic inequality combined with the shift to American households of financial risks previously borne by employers and government; the aging of the population; preventing and responding to terrorism while preserving civil liberties; and restoring America's international credibility as an effective and cooperative leader in responding to global security and economic dangers."

United States Institute of Peace (www.usip.org): "The United States Institute of Peace is an independent, nonpartisan, national institution established and funded by Congress. Its goals are to help prevent and resolve violent conflicts, promote post-conflict stability and development, and increase peacebuilding capacity, tools, and intellectual capital worldwide."

Urban Institute (www.urban.org): "To promote sound social policy and public debate on national priorities, the Urban Institute gathers and analyzes data, conducts policy research, evaluates programs and services, and educates Americans on critical issues and trends."

NEWSPAPERS

Excellent access to recent newspaper articles is available through Google News. To access Google News, go to the main Google web page (www.google.com) and click the top tab for News. Google searches newspaper databases for the most recent three months.

Numerous other websites offer free access to newspaper articles. FindArticles.com provides free access on the Web to thousands of publications, including many newspapers (http://articles.findarticles.com/p/home?tb=art). From the Library of Congress Online Reading Room website, you can find links to hundreds of online newspapers and journals (www.loc.gov/rr/news/lists.html). The Write News website provides links to all major newspapers maintaining online services (http://writenews.com/newslinks/).

PERIODICALS

Periodicals include widely circulated magazines (such as *Time* and *Newsweek*) and journals (such as *Foreign Affairs* and *Washington Quarterly*). Your library might subscribe to an electronic database and indexing system such as InfoTrac, Ingenta, ArticleFirst, Expanded Academic ASAP, or Lexis/Nexis Scholastic Universe. Most such systems provide a computer-based searching system as well as full-text access to periodical articles. Some print publications also provide limited access to their materials online. The following paragraphs provide just a sampling of the periodicals available online.

The Nation (www.thenation.com): A liberal publication, *The Nation* provides free access to approximately 40–60 percent of its articles since 1999. Subscribers can access all material since 1999. The digital archives provide access to all articles since 1895 for a fee.

National Review (www.nationalreview.com): This conservative magazine provides free access to many of its articles and web features. Subscribers can download a digital copy of the magazine.

New Republic (www.tnr.com): Subscribers can access the magazine's archives. Known for its liberal perspective, *The New Republic* provides free access to web-only content.

Newsweek (www.msnbc.msn.com/id/3032542/): This popular newsmagazine has partnered with the online news service MSNBC to provide an extensive amount of news. Users can search articles that have appeared in *Newsweek* since 1993. Searching is free, but access to archived articles requires a fee.

Time (www.time.com/time): Search issues of the popular news magazine from 1985. This site provides some free access, but archived articles require a fee for viewing.

U.S. News and World Report (www.usnews.com/usnews/ home. htm): Users can access current articles from *U.S. News and World Report* or pay a fee to view archived articles.

CITATION SYSTEM FOR ONLINE EVIDENCE COLLECTION

The National Forensic League rule for the citation of evidence is based on a modification of the Modern Language Association (MLA) standard. For Internet sources, this means the following:

- Author (the author might be a person's name or the name of a group)
- Author's qualifications
- Title of the web page
- Date the web page was created
- The retrieval statement

So, what do you do if you are unable to find the author's name? Try taking apart the URL. Suppose you find some interesting quotable information at www.perrspectives.com/articles/ art_optout01.htm. You are having trouble, however, determining the authorship of the web page. Try stripping the text from the end of the URL (always stopping at a forward slash) until you work your way back to the home page of the person or group posting the web page you want to cite. If you go to www.perrspectives.com, for example, you will find that the web page is posted by Jon Perr, a member of the Democratic Leadership Council. If, despite your best efforts, the author remains unknown, the evidence should be treated as unusable in the debate context.

The author's qualification refers to the position held by the author (that is, professor of political science at Yale University, senior analyst at the Cato Institute). The title of the web page is the name of an online periodical or other title that appears at the top of the web page. The date the web page was created is usually available somewhere on the page; in the event that no creation date is available, the last revision date is acceptable. What happens if you are unable to find either the creation date of the web page or its last revision date? If no date is available, the web page is unusable in the debate context. There may still be hope, however, in finding the last revision date. Try using Mozilla Firefox as your Internet browser. You can load the web page and then select Page Info from the top Tools menu. Firefox will report to you (in most instances) the date of last modification of the web page. The retrieval statement indicates the online source, the date of retrieval, and the URL. For documents retrieved through Google (or another Internet search engine), the online source is simply "Internet."

Following is an example of an Internet citation:

Eric Larson and Reva Adler (Director, Group Health Cooperative Center for Health Studies and Professor of Medicine at the University of British Columbia), *Seattle Times*, June 19, 2005. Online. Internet. Jan. 25, 2007. http://seattletimes.nwsource.com/html/opinion/2002339788_sungenocide19.html.

Following is an example of a Lexis/Nexis citation:

Nsongurua Udombana (Professor of Legal Studies, at the Central European University in Budapest), *San Diego International Law Journal*, Fall 2005. Online. Lexis/Nexis Academic Universe. Feb. 8, 2007.

Notice that each citation includes two dates: the date of the evidence and the retrieval date. The first of these dates is the one that should be cited orally in the debate round. Why is the retrieval date necessary? Material available on the Internet changes day-by-day. For someone trying to verify the accuracy of an Internet citation, it would be essential to know the date of the retrieval. Notice also that the Internet citation lists the URL but that the Lexis/Nexis citation does not.

For subscription databases (such as Lexis/Nexis, ProQuest, Ingenta, and so on), the listing of the URL is unnecessary—the URLs are usually incredibly long and contain information making it accessible only from the same subscriber location as your point of access. Researchers seeking to check the accuracy of their ProQuest document would need to access the database through their own subscription site.

FINDING DEFINITIONS OF TERMS ON THE INTERNET

Debaters often need evidence defining terms such as "juvenile justice" or "public health." Two Internet search engines provide significant assistance in gathering definitions. Access to more than 1,000 dictionaries is available through www.onelook.com.

Google (www.google.com) also provides two little-known definition tools. The first approach is to enter the term "define" in the main search box, followed by a colon, and then the term or phrase for which you want the definition. Try, for example, the following Google search—define: public health. You will find approximately 10 web-based definitions of the term. Notice the difference made by the colon after the word *define*. If the colon is absent, Google looks for any web pages containing the word *define* and the phrase *public health*. With the colon present, Google detects that you want to examine only those websites that intend to define the specific term *public health*. A second definitional tool built in to Google involves the capability to click any underlined term in a search phrase. Try, for example, entering the phrase "substantially increase." You will notice that when Google returns the pages for this search, it now also underlines (at the upper-right corner of your screen) each of the words contained in your search. By clicking one of the underlined words, you will see a definition of the term.

COLLECTING EVIDENCE

In the age of the information explosion, it is simply not feasible for debaters to print a hard copy of everything they think they might need to read. The two major impediments are expense and time. It is expensive (in laser printer cartridges) for a debate squad to print all the materials active researchers need. It is also time consuming to print big chunks of material; computer labs typically have many computers but only a single printer. The printer becomes the bottleneck. The overuse of printing is also environmentally irresponsible. Debaters waste huge volumes of paper, often printing a 200-page law review article to extract two or three cards. This means hundreds of pages per day of printed or photocopied materials are simply discarded.

Word-processed briefs are easier to read (no illegible handwritten tags, no red or blue ink that refuses to photocopy), and they contain much more evidence per page. This ends up saving a squad large amounts of money in photocopy costs. In fact, members of a large squad can simply distribute new positions via disc and have each squad member print her briefs on her own printer. This dramatically reduces squad photocopy costs. If briefs are to be word-processed, it simply makes sense to collect the evidence on disc. Otherwise, the debater has to retype the evidence that exists in hard copy.

The old way for debaters to construct arguments (a federalism disadvantage, for example) was to create piles of evidence that was sorted into different parts of the argument. Inevitably, as the argument was being constructed, the debater frequently thought, "I know I have that piece of evidence that says ... but WHERE IS IT?" When evidence is collected, sorted, and filed on disc, that doesn't happen. If the evidence isn't found in the right category, the debater simply uses the word processor's find function to search for the word or phrase. The card is located in seconds. When evidence is prepared on disc, the debater can simply use the sorting function of the word processor to put the evidence in order.

STANDARDS FOR THE CUTTING OF EVIDENCE

When you are reading a book, magazine, or newspaper on your research topic, how do you know what to include within a single piece of evidence? Debaters use the term *cutting* to refer to this process of pulling evidence quotations out of an article or a book. I suggest two rules and two suggestions for the cutting of evidence. First, the rules:

Cutting Rule 1: Always directly quote from the beginning of one sentence to the end of the closing sentence. There are several implications of this rule:

a. Never paraphrase the evidence; take the evidence word-for-word.

b. Never leave out words or sentences in the middle of a quotation. If you were doing research for a term paper, you could leave out words—using an ellipsis (...) to indicate the place where the words were omitted. Yet competitive debate standards forbid an internal ellipsis. National Forensic League (NFL) evidence rules state that the evidence must be taken continuously from the beginning of one sentence to the end of another. The only time you can have an ellipsis is if it already exists in the source you are quoting.

c. NFL evidence rules do not allow you to start a quotation in the middle of a sentence or to stop before the end of a sentence.

d. NFL evidence rules do not allow you to add words to a quotation; if you need to explain a reference, insert the explanation in brackets. Suppose, for example, the quotation uses the acronym UDF and you know from reading the rest of the article that the reference is to United Dairy Farmers. Simply insert in brackets [United Dairy Farmers] after the UDF. Never use a bracket insertion to change or add to the meaning of a quotation.

Cutting Rule 2: Every piece of evidence must have a source. This source must include an author (which could be an organization), a qualification for the author (professor of engineering at MIT, staff writer, and so on), a publication source, a date, and a page number. If the evidence is from an online source, it is acceptable to omit the page number but online access information must be listed in its place (accessed at www.annrand.org on July 31, 2007).

Cutting Suggestion 1: You should have a purpose in mind for each piece of evidence. Don't just collect evidence at random. What argument would the evidence support? If you don't have an answer to that question, there is little point in collecting the quotation.

Cutting Suggestion 2: Make the quotation long enough so that it gives reasons for a conclusion, but not so long that it would take several minutes to read in a debate round. Sometimes debaters take a single sentence out of an article, presenting only the author's conclusion: "Adopting the Kyoto Protocol would be ruinously expensive for the American economy." A good piece of evidence would provide reasons in support of a conclusion. Don't make the mistake of cutting the evidence down to the point that you are eliminating those reasons while only stating a conclusion. Five to six sentences is a good default standard for card length, although there are often good reasons for shorter or longer quotations.

So, what happens when competitive debaters violate evidence rules (making up evidence, distorting evidence, using evidence with improper citations, and so on)? Most tournament rules impose stiff penalties for evidence violations. Success in debate relies so heavily on having supporting evidence that the activity becomes somewhat meaningless when evidence rules are ignored. Penalties range from losing the debate round in which the infraction occurred all the way up to disqualification from the entire tournament. Because faulty evidence collection endangers all the teams competing for a given school (because they commonly share evidence), some coaches will summarily dismiss a debater from the squad when serious evidence violations are discovered.

STEPS FOR CUTTING EVIDENCE ONLINE

Open both your word processor (for example, Microsoft Word, WordPerfect) and your Internet browser (for example, Internet Explorer, Firefox). Arrange the windows for each program so they are side-by-side on your computer screen. Locate the information you want to quote from your Internet source. Now click over to your word processor and type in the source citation (using the proper NFL evidence citation format). All the information necessary for constructing the source citation should be visible on your web page screen. Highlight the text you want to quote from the web page and use the Copy command (Ctrl+C on a PC or Apple+C on an Apple computer). Now click back over to your word processor and use the Paste command (Ctrl+V on a PC or Apple+V on an Apple computer). Eliminate unwanted returns in one of two ways: (a) click at the beginning of each line and press Backspace, or (b) use the word processor's search and replace function to eliminate all paragraph breaks. Your objective is to have each evidence card in a single paragraph with the evidence citation in the same paragraph. Keeping each card within a single paragraph will allow you to use your word processor's Sort function to help you index your material. When you use your word processor Sort command, you are telling it to arrange all the paragraphs of the document into alphabetical order. If you leave internal paragraph breaks within a single card, the card is pulled apart when the Sort command is issued.

Continue pasting cards into the word processor until you have taken all the desired cards from the web page. Then copy and paste as many evidence citation tops as needed to match each of the cards.

Sorting Evidence on the Computer

Design a filing scheme that will allow the addition of categories. Suppose, for example, you are researching the topic of global warming. You might use a filing system where all the cards in this group begin with GW (for global warming).

GW101 to GW199—Harms of global warming
GW101 Sea rise harms
GW102 Agricultural harms
GW103 Hurricanes and severe storms
GW104 Loss of endangered species from warming
GW105 Diseases spread from tropical regions
Etc.

GW201 to GW299—Global Warming Inherency
GW201 Bush administration refuses to act
GW202 Other countries are waiting for us to act
GW203 Business won't act without government incentives
Etc.

GW301 to GW399—Global Warming Solvency
GW301 It is not too late to act
GW302 Kyoto Protocol can still work
GW303 Other countries will follow the U.S. lead
Etc.

GW501 to GW599—Answers to Global Warming Harms
GW501 Warming is slow
GW502 People can adjust to warming
GW503 Warming actually helps plants grow
GW504 Storms are not becoming more severe
Etc.

GW601 to GW699—Answers to Inherency
GW601 Businesses are acting on their own
GW602 Other countries are acting without the U.S.
Etc.

GW701 to GW799—Answers to Solvency
GW701 Kyoto Protocol will not slow global warming
GW702 U.S. leadership is irrelevant
GW703 Human causes are tiny compared to natural causes
Etc.

GW801 to GW899—Disadvantages to Global Warming
Solutions
GW801 Kyoto Protocol will kill the U.S. economy
GW802 Wind power kills birds
GW803 Shift away from oil will increase Middle East war
Etc.

All the research you have done on global warming is saved to a
single word processing file in which every paragraph is a card
preceded by the appropriate filing number. Examine carefully the
following sample card:

GW103 Alok Jha and Tania Branigan, (Staff Writers), *The
Guardian*, July 30, 2007, p. 10. Online. Lexis/Nexis Academic
Universe. July 31, 2007. Climate scientists have blamed global
warming for a dramatic rise in the number of storms in the
Atlantic over the past century. Their study showed the average
number of storms that develop every year has doubled since 1905.
They suggest the trend is due to the rise in sea surface temperatures in the Atlantic, a phenomenon with a well-established link to
climate change. Tropical storms are powered by the energy in the
oceans they pass over, with warmer sea surfaces leading to more
intense storms. In the past century, the surface temperature of the
Atlantic has risen by 0.7C. The increase in storm frequency was

most recently visible in 2005, with more than double the average number of storms, including Hurricane Katrina, the most costly natural disaster in U.S. history. It claimed almost 2,000 lives.

The evidence card contains a complete source, listing all the required elements of an NFL citation. The evidence card contains a complete quotation with nothing left out in the middle. In the original newspaper article, this quotation had four paragraph breaks; these paragraph breaks were removed so the card will not be pulled apart when sorted. Notice also that the text of the evidence card is within the same paragraph as the evidence source—this is also important to prevent the card's source from becoming separated from the text during the sorting process.

The evidence card has its filing number first so the word processor's sort function will place together all similar evidence. In Microsoft Word, the Sort command can be found under the Table menu; simply select all the paragraphs in your document (do this by using the Edit menu and selecting the Select All option) and then issue the Sort command. You will discover that all your paragraphs have been rearranged into alphabetical order using your filing category numbers.

After they're filed and sorted, your on-disc evidence file functions just like the "piles of cards" on the table. You use the index to see where the cards are that support the part of the argument you are putting together and then use the search function on the word processor to find the cards, by searching for GW301, for example. Read the cards filed there, and select the card or cards you want to insert in the brief. Then cut and paste them.

ETHICAL STANDARDS FOR ONLINE EVIDENCE COLLECTION

The accessibility of information on the Internet has revolutionized the process of evidence collection in policy debate. The Internet places billions of pages of information at our fingertips. With this bountiful blessing also comes the necessity for some careful ethical choices. The same Google search can return web pages from world-class scholars, hate groups, and elementary school students. Just as in the print media, one must make a distinction between *The New York Times* and the *National Enquirer.* Because most debate research is squad-based, meaning it is shared by many students, it is essential that there be agreement on minimum standards for the types of web pages that can be used for debate research. Following are some recommended standards:

No use of web pages that come from discussion groups or chat rooms.

No use of news blogs where you are quoting from the comments on a news story posted by a reader of the news story. Most blogs invite readers of news stories to post their own reactions; there is no reason to believe that the people who post their comments have expertise on the subject at hand. Often the people who post to a blog are identified only by the anonymous web name they used to register at the blog website.

No use of web pages where the author's qualifications are unknown.

No use of web pages where the author is a student in grade school, high school, or college.

No use of web pages from hate groups or unidentified organizations.

No use of web pages that are undated or for which a "last revision date" is unavailable.

Prefer web pages sponsored by one of the following groups:

A government institution

A major educational institution or a professor at such an institution

A recognized think tank or advocacy group (RAND, Brookings Institution, Heritage Foundation, CATO Institute, Hudson Institute, Center for Strategic and International Studies, Hoover Institution, Amnesty International, and so on)

A reputable journalistic organization (CNN, *The New York Times*, *Washington Post*, *Christian Science Monitor*, Fox News, and so forth)

Evidence rules in debate require that quotations from authority be preserved exactly as they appeared in the original, meaning words are not to be added and internal ellipses are not allowed. This means the debater is not allowed to take words out of the middle of a quotation.

FURTHER READING

Emory University Libraries. "Internet Critical Evaluation." August 23, 2005. http://web.library.emory.edu/services/ressvcs/ howguides/internet.html (accessed July 31, 2007).

Kingwood College Library. "MLA Style: Paper and Online." 2006. http://kclibrary.nhmccd.edu/mlastyle.htm (accessed July 31, 2007).

University of Michigan. "Political Science Resources: Think Tanks." August 17, 2005. www.lib.umich.edu/govdocs/psthink.html (accessed July 31, 2007).

CHAPTER 4

CHOOSING THE DEBATE FORMAT THAT IS RIGHT FOR YOU

Three major types of competitive debate are practiced in American high schools: policy debate, Lincoln-Douglas debate, and public forum debate. This chapter provides a brief overview of each type of debate. No one style of debate is better than another, but each has characteristic advantages and disadvantages.

POLICY DEBATE

Policy debate is the oldest form of competitive debate in American high schools, dating from the early 1900s. For the first eighty years of the twentieth century, it was the only form of debate competition. Policy debate is called *team debate* in some parts of the country, even though public forum debate also involves a two-person team. In other parts of the country, policy debate is called CX *debate* (short for cross-examination), even though all three forms of competitive debate have cross-examination.

Policy debate gets its name from the types of resolutions (topics) that are debated. Debate resolutions can be questions of fact, value, or policy. A resolution of fact would be something like "Resolved: O.J. Simpson murdered his wife Nicole." Court cases usually deal with questions of fact. A value resolution might say, "Resolved: Civil disobedience is justified in a democracy." Policy resolutions suggest action; an example is "Resolved: The United States should change its foreign policy toward the People's Republic of China." The use of policy resolutions means that debaters are encouraged to become thoroughly familiar with current events and matters of public policy.

The resolutions in policy debate are selected through a process administered by the National Federation of State High School Associations (NFHS) where every high school sponsoring policy debate has an opportunity to influence the topic selection. After the resolution is selected, however, schools throughout the nation debate the same topic for an entire year.

Policy debate is team debate, meaning each school must have at least one two-person team to compete. Some schools enter numerous two-person teams into competition.

Each round of policy debate requires eighty minutes to complete, consisting of eight speeches and four cross-examination periods (during which the debaters ask questions of the members of the other team).

Lincoln-Douglas Debate

Lincoln-Douglas debate competition began in American high schools in the late 1970s. The competition gets its name from the famous series of debates between Abraham Lincoln and Stephen Douglas when they were campaigning for an Illinois Senate seat in 1858.

Lincoln-Douglas competition uses resolutions of value, such as "Resolved: The individual ought to value the sanctity of life above the quality of life." The use of value resolutions means debaters are encouraged to familiarize themselves with major philosophical systems—concepts such as John Stuart Mill's marketplace of ideas, Immanuel Kant's categorical imperative, and John Rawls's theory of justice.

The resolutions used in Lincoln-Douglas debate are selected by committees appointed by the National Forensic League (NFL) or by individual state associations sponsoring the tournaments. The NFL Lincoln-Douglas topics change every two months during the debate season.

Lincoln-Douglas debate is one-on-one debate as distinguished from the team debate formats of policy debate and public forum debate. Lincoln-Douglas competitors do not have a partner, but compete individually against competitors from other schools.

Each round of Lincoln-Douglas competition requires about thirty-five minutes to complete—less than half the time for a round of policy debate. A Lincoln-Douglas round consists of five speeches and two cross-examination periods.

PUBLIC FORUM DEBATE

Public forum debate is the most recent addition to competitive debate formats; the first national competition in the event was in 2002. Public forum debate has also been called *Controversy debate* and *Ted Turner debate* (so named because CNN founder Ted Turner was one of the early sponsors of the event).

The topics for public forum debate are selected by a committee of the NFL, and they change monthly. The NFL committee selecting public forum topics places great emphasis on finding topics "ripped from the headlines"—meaning they try to find the "hot" national topic for that month. Some public forum topics have been resolutions of fact: "Resolved: The United States is losing the War on Terror." Some topics have been resolutions of value: "Resolved: The costs of legalized casino gambling in the United States outweigh the benefits." Most public forum topics are, however, resolutions of policy: "Resolved: The United States should issue guest worker visas to illegal aliens."

Public forum debate is team debate, meaning that a two-person team competes for each school. Each round of public forum debate requires about thirty-five minutes to complete—about the same as Lincoln-Douglas debate, but much less than a round of policy debate. A round of public forum debate consists of eight speeches (some of them as short as one minute) and three "crossfire" periods.

SIMILARITIES BETWEEN DEBATE FORMATS

In all three forms of competitive debate, students must be prepared to switch sides. This means debaters must be prepared to support the resolution as well as to oppose it. Suppose, for example, the topic is "Resolved: The private ownership of handguns should be banned in the United States." A debater must prepare a case for banning handguns as well as a case opposing such a ban. You will not know for sure which side you will be called upon to support until shortly before the round of debate begins.

The structures of all three types of debate tournaments are similar regardless of the format. The most common format for a two-day tournament is five or six preliminary rounds of competition, in which each round involves a competitor from one school meeting a competitor from another school. In each such round, a neutral judge declares a winner and a loser while also assigning speaker points. At the end of the preliminary rounds, competitors are seeded into an elimination bracket. If the first elimination round is octafinals, only the top 16 teams continue debating; the remaining teams are eliminated. Seeding means that the top preliminary round competitor meets the 16th, the 2nd meets the 15th, and so on in toward the middle of the bracket. In elimination rounds, there are typically three judges for each debate; the winner of each round advances and the loser is eliminated. This process continues until only two competitors remain, competing against each other in the final round.

In all three forms of debate, competitors give speeches and participate in cross-examination (questioning) of their opponents.

CONSIDERATIONS FOR CHOOSING A DEBATE FORMAT

Which type or types of debate does your school sponsor? To enter tournaments, you must have the support of your debate coach and your school. Not all schools compete in all three forms of debate.

How much time do you have to commit to debate competition? Policy debate is the most time-intensive form of competition because it requires the greatest commitment to research and pretournament practice.

Do you have an interest in philosophy? Lincoln-Douglas debate, because of its focus on value resolutions, rewards those who have a good grasp of philosophical concepts. By committing to Lincoln-Douglas debate, you are likely to learn a great deal about the great philosophers from Aristotle to John Locke.

Do you have an interest in media debates? In that case, public forum debate is probably your best choice. This format has actually been modeled after media debate formats such as on *Crossfire* and the *McLaughlin Group.*

Are you interested in trying to earn a college debate scholarship? If so you should determine the type of debate offered by the college of your choice. Colleges participating in parliamentary debate will be more impressed by your success in Lincoln-Douglas or public forum debate. Colleges participating in the Cross Examination Debate Association (CEDA), American Debate Association (ADA), or National Debate Tournament (NDT) styles will be more impressed by your success in policy debate.

Do you see debate competition as a way to improve your skills as a public speaker? Although all debate competition will improve your confidence in public speaking, public forum and Lincoln-Douglas debate are clearly superior to policy debate in this area. Policy debaters generally talk more rapidly than is advisable for effective public speaking.

Are you starting to debate in the middle of the school year? If so, you would find more competitive success in public forum or Lincoln-Douglas debate than in policy debate. This is true because policy debaters utilize the same topic all year long. If you are starting in the middle of the year, other students will have a con-siderable head start in researching the topic. Public forum topics change every month. If you are starting in December, for example, you would be starting to debate a new topic at the same time as your competitors.

Do you see debate competition as preparation for a future in the law? Policy debate, because of its intensive focus on research and preparation of argument briefs, offers superior training for the future law student.

Is there another person at your school who is interested in becoming your debate partner? If not, you should consider Lincoln-Douglas debate; in this debate format, you compete as an individual. If you have a partner who shares your goals and work ethic, you should consider policy debate or public forum competition.

Are you willing to attend a summer debate institute? Many colleges and universities sponsor summer debate workshops. These workshops provide excellent training, but they also require a commitment of time and money. The most successful competitors in policy and Lincoln-Douglas debate typically attend a summer institute. The same is not yet true for public forum debate. If you do not plan to attend a summer institute, you might have more competitive success in public forum debate.

FURTHER READING

Edwards, Richard. *An Introduction to Debate.* Indianapolis, IN: National Federation of High Schools, 2002.

Ulrich, Walter. *Selecting and Attending a Forensic Institute.* Indianapolis, IN: National Federation of High Schools, 1991.

CHAPTER 5

AN INTRODUCTION TO POLICY DEBATE

Policy debate involves debating in teams, meaning that two students from one school debate two students from another school. Each member of the team delivers two speeches, the first of which is called a *constructive speech*. The constructive speech is so-named because the contestant is "constructing" his or her case; new arguments are allowed in constructive speeches. The second speech given by each debater is called a *rebuttal speech;* in this speech no new arguments are allowed. In a situation analogous to an attorney's closing argument in a court case, the rebuttal attempts to answer the arguments of the other side and to reestablish the debater's own case arguments.

THE FORMAT FOR POLICY DEBATE

A single *round* of policy debate includes eight speeches and four cross-examination periods.

Constructive Speeches

First Affirmative Constructive Speech (1AC)	8 minutes
Cross-Examination by 2nd Negative Speaker	3 minutes
First Negative Constructive Speech (1NC)	8 minutes
Cross-Examination by 1st Affirmative Speaker	3 minutes
Second Affirmative Constructive Speech (2AC)	8 minutes
Cross-Examination by 1st Negative Speaker	3 minutes
Second Negative Constructive Speech (2NC)	8 minutes
Cross-Examination by 2nd Affirmative Speaker	3 minutes

Rebuttal Speeches

First Negative Rebuttal (1NR)	5 minutes
First Affirmative Rebuttal (1AR)	5 minutes
Second Negative Rebuttal (2NR)	5 minutes
Second Affirmative Rebuttal (2AR)	5 minutes
Total Preparation Time for Each Team	5 minutes*

Total Time Required for Completion of One Round:	74 minutes

Some tournaments have differing amounts of preparation time; 5 minutes is the time allotted in National Forensic League tournaments, including the national final tournament.

How Do You Know Whether You Will Be Affirmative or Negative?

In each round of debate there is an affirmative team and a negative team. The affirmative team says "yes" to the resolution, while the negative team says "no." Suppose the resolution is "Resolved: The United States federal government should establish a guest worker program for illegal immigrants." The affirmative team must support the resolution, and the negative team must oppose it.

Almost all policy debate competition involves switching of sides, so each team must be prepared to debate both affirmative and negative. You won't know whether you will be affirmative or negative in the first round of the tournament until a few minutes before the tournament begins. The debate *tab room* (meaning the persons assigned by the sponsoring organization to administer the tournament) post a schedule shortly before the round begins. This round schedule lets each team know whether it will be affirmative or negative, which opponent it will debate, the name of the judge, and the room in which the debate will occur.

By the end of the preliminary rounds of the tournament, you will have been assigned to the same number of affirmative as negative rounds. If you do well enough to qualify for elimination rounds, sides are determined in a slightly different manner. If the two teams meeting have not previously met in preliminary rounds, a coin toss determines who is affirmative and who is negative. If you win the coin toss, you are allowed to choose affirmative or negative. If you have already met the team you are assigned to debate, you switch sides in the second meeting.

How Are First and Second Speakers Determined?

Ultimately, it is your debate coach who decides who is the first speaker and who is second. Following are, however, some of the factors used to determine speaker position:

- *Affirmative and negative speaker order can be different*: There is no rule requiring that the debater who is first affirmative also must be first negative. Some coaches choose to have one debater be first when the team is on the affirmative and second when the team is on the negative (or vice versa). Neither is there a rule requiring that a speaker who begins a tournament as first affirmative speaker keep that same speaking position for all the affirmative rounds in the tournament. A debate coach might decide that one debater will be first speaker in some of the debates but then switch to the second position in others (although this would be an unusual choice).

  Most tournament rules allow debaters to switch positions in rebuttals (in other words, the debater who spoke first in the constructive speeches speaks second in the rebuttals). This latter strategy does, however, confuse judges. Teams wanting to use this strategy should ask the judge's permission before the beginning of the debate round to "switch positions" in rebuttals. In the overwhelming majority of debate rounds, debaters keep the same positions in rebuttals as in constructive speeches.

- *Experience:* The more experienced and more persuasive debater should generally be the second speaker. This is true because the persuasive quality of the final rebuttal speech for each team often determines the outcome of the debate.

- *Rate of speech (speed):* The first affirmative rebuttal (1AR) is the most difficult one in the debate. This speaker is called upon to answer thirteen minutes worth of negative attacks (the eight minutes of the 2NR and the five minutes of the 1NR) all in one five-minute speech. If key arguments are left unanswered in the 1AR, it might be almost impossible for the affirmative team to win the debate. Accordingly, the faster of the two speakers might need to go first when the team is affirmative. The same criterion holds true for the negative team. The first negative speaker is expected to place arguments into the debate; the second negative speaker tries to gain maximum persuasive impact for these arguments as the debate progresses.

What Is Preparation Time?

Each team in a round of policy debate has a set amount of preparation time. For National Forensic League (NFL) tournaments, the preparation time is five minutes per team. Many state and local tournaments specify smaller amounts of preparation time, so be sure to check the tournament invitation.

If the preparation time is five minutes, this does not mean the speaker receives five minutes before each speech; it means the team has five minutes of total preparation time. If all five minutes are used before the first speech, no preparation time is left for any of the remaining speeches. In that case, you will be expected to rise to speak immediately after the previous speaker takes his seat. If you are not ready, your speech time still begins immediately.

The strategy in the proper use of preparation time is simple—save as much time as possible for the period just before the team's final rebuttal. As you become more experienced in debate, you will discover that you are able to save most of your preparation time for the crucial last rebuttal.

What Are the Stock Issues in Policy Debate?

The place to begin in understanding the argument structure of policy debate is with the *stock issues*. The five stock issues describe the arguments that the affirmative team must win in order to win the debate. These stock issues are topicality, significance of harm, inherency, solvency, and desirability.

The *topicality* stock issue means the affirmative team must advocate the resolution. In each policy debate the affirmative team must present a plan in its first affirmative constructive speech. The *plan* provides a detailed description of what the affirmative team has chosen to advocate.

Imagine the resolution says that the federal government should "increase public health assistance to sub-Saharan Africa." The affirmative plan might read something like this: "The United States will double its funding for the president's Emergency Plan for AIDS Relief (PEPFAR) with all the additional funding designated for sub-Saharan Africa. In addition, the U.S. will eliminate the current earmark requiring that HIV/AIDS prevention funds be spent on abstinence-based programs."

To be topical, the affirmative plan must fall under the umbrella created by the wording of the resolution. In the previous example, the affirmative plan must propose a U.S. federal government program (not the United Nations or the Global Fund to Fight AIDS, Tuberculosis, and Malaria). Also, the plan must propose a "public health" program for sub-Saharan Africa. There would be a clear violation of topicality if the affirmative plan proposed to give military aid to Africa because the resolution calls for "public health" assistance.

Notice, however, that the affirmative case can be topical without proposing everything that falls under the umbrella of "public health" assistance. The affirmative team can choose whether it wants to deal with HIV/AIDS, malaria, water/sanitation issues, or various neglected tropical diseases. The affirmative team is given considerable leeway to select its own case area so long as it falls within the boundaries created by the wording of the resolution.

On the other hand, the negative team can win the debate if it can show that the affirmative plan falls outside the boundaries of the resolution. It is not enough that the affirmative plan meets most of the words in the resolution; the negative can win on topicality if it can show that the affirmative plan fails to meet even one of the words in the topic.

The *significance of harm* stock issue requires the affirmative team to demonstrate that the present system (or *status quo*, as debaters often call it) has a serious defect at present. The nature and severity of harm required can be judged only in the context of a particular topic. Consider the following examples of harm arguments: a basic human right is now denied; people are sick or dying; the environment is polluted; national security is threatened; or animal rights are ignored. For the affirmative team to win, it must show that something is other than it should be.

Inherency is the stock issue that focuses on the causes of the harm cited by the affirmative. The affirmative team has a responsibility to show why the present system cannot or will not resolve the problems cited in the affirmative case. If the present system is fully capable of solving the problem on its own, there is no reason to enact the affirmative plan.

The two types of inherency are *structural* and *attitudinal*. The strongest inherency arguments focus on some structural defects written into current laws. An affirmative case proposing immigration reform might, for example, point to current legislation mandating the construction of a border fence as an inherent barrier to an effective solution. An affirmative case attempting to preserve the ocean environment might point to current legislation allowing the leasing of the continental shelf for oil drilling. Other inherency arguments might focus on attitudes and show why decision-makers in the present system are improperly motivated to solve the problem. A case dealing with environmental protection might, for example, claim that the Environmental Protection Agency has been captured by corporate interests.

The *solvency* stock issue asks whether the affirmative team has authoritative evidence to show that the affirmative plan will reduce the harm shown in the case. The judge is unlikely to vote for a change if it offers no better solution than can be found in the present system.

Desirability is the final stock issue in policy debate. The affirmative team must be able to show that the disadvantages of adopting the affirmative plan are outweighed by the advantages of doing so. The negative team often argues that the affirmative plan would create problems that would outweigh any slight advantages the plan could offer—such arguments are called *disadvantages*. Suppose the affirmative plan proposes to send more fertilizer to Africa so African farmers can grow more food. The negative team might present evidence showing that more intensive agricultural production in Africa would destroy fragile ecosystems. The affirmative team would, therefore, have to prove that the advantage of feeding hungry people in Africa would outweigh the risk of destroying the environment.

What Happens in Each Speech in Policy Debate?

First Affirmative Constructive Speech: In this speech the affirmative team should present its plan, the reasons this plan is necessary or desirable, and authoritative evidence supporting these reasons. The plan must be presented in a reasonably detailed manner, including such details as who will do the plan (which agency of government) and precisely what will be done.

The reasons offered in the first affirmative speech must present a *prima facie* case. A prima facie case is one that would, at first glance, be sufficient to convince a reasonable person that the plan should be adopted. The normal understanding of this "first face" requirement is that the case must show (with evidence) significant harm, inherency, and solvency. If any one of those three key elements is missing, the affirmative team has not met its burden of placing a complete argument on the floor for debate.

It is important that the first affirmative constructive speech be well organized with clearly labeled observations, contentions, or advantages. Each of the major arguments should be supported by clearly labeled subpoints. The speeches that follow the first affirmative constructive will attempt to follow the organizational structure outlined in the first speech. If the structure of the first speech is unclear, the debate can become quite disorganized.

First Negative Constructive Speech: This speech presents the reasons for opposing the affirmative case. The traditional approach to this task is to have the first negative speaker focus on a direct point-by-point refutation of the first affirmative speech, leaving the second negative speaker to present disadvantages or other *off-case* arguments. It has now become customary for the first negative speaker to present the whole of the negative position, including any topicality positions, harm attacks, inherency attacks, solvency attacks, and disadvantage shells.

The disadvantage *shell* typically involves a short presentation of the essential elements of a disadvantage argument. The entire shell (for a single disadvantage) is often presented in less than one minute of actual speech time. The essential part of a disadvantage argument includes a link (what is it about the plan that would cause this disadvantage?), some uniqueness argument (why would the plan cause the disadvantage any more than does the present system?), a brink argument (why is this the critical point for the disadvantage?), and some impact (why would the disadvantage be worse than the affirmative harm?). Each of the elements of the disadvantage must be supported with authoritative evidence.

During the case attack portion of the first negative constructive, it is desirable that the speaker follow the structure of the first affirmative speech. It is not necessary to attack every part of the affirmative case, but the negative should think carefully about the strategy necessary to defeat the case. Suppose, for example, that an affirmative contention argues that preserving freedom of speech is more important than any other policy consideration. The negative team cannot afford to allow such a decision-rule claim to go unchallenged; with such a standard in place, the affirmative team could quite obviously outweigh the negative disadvantages, no matter what they might be.

Second Affirmative Constructive Speech: The affirmative speaker must respond to whatever the first negative speaker had to say. If the negative speaker presented a topicality attack, that argument must be answered. If disadvantage shells were presented, disadvantage answers must be offered. If the affirmative case is attacked, there must be responses to those attacks. If any arguments are made in the first negative speech that go unanswered in the second affirmative constructive, the negative team will claim that their argument has been *dropped.* Further, they will say that any answer from the affirmative made in rebuttal speeches would be a new argument in rebuttal. The quickest and most decisive way for the affirmative team to lose the debate is to neglect to answer a major argument made by the negative in the first negative constructive speech.

Second Negative Constructive Speech: In the traditional approach, the second negative speaker typically originates the disadvantage attack on the affirmative plan. In modern practice, however, the disadvantages are first presented in the first negative speech. This means the second negative speaker can focus on winning disadvantages by completely answering the attacks on those disadvantages made by the second affirmative constructive speaker. In the typical debate, a second affirmative speaker might make five or six answers to a disadvantage. The second negative speaker might decide to spend all eight minutes of the constructive speech giving extensive answers to each of those five or six responses.

One of the most important strategic concepts for the negative strategy in the second affirmative constructive is called *division of labor.* The second affirmative constructive speaker should work in conjunction with the first negative rebuttalist to properly divide up the second affirmative constructive arguments. The two negative speeches are back-to-back, so no purpose is served by repeating the same arguments in the two speeches. The second negative constructive speaker should communicate with her partner to decide how the arguments will be divided. Suppose, for example, the debate going into the second affirmative constructive contains a topicality argument, some case attacks, and three disadvantages. The second negative constructive speaker might take two of the disadvantages, leaving the remainder of the responses for the first negative rebuttalist.

First Negative Rebuttal Speech: The first negative rebuttalist
should deal with any of the arguments from the first negative
constructive speech that were not covered in the second negative
constructive speech. Successful negative teams learn to make this
decision (concerning who will cover what) before the beginning of
the second negative constructive speech. This procedure allows the
first rebuttalist to use the whole of the final constructive speech as
preparation time for the rebuttal.

First Affirmative Rebuttal Speech: In this difficult speech, the
first affirmative speaker must give brief answers to each of the
important arguments presented in the second negative constructive
speech and in the first negative rebuttal speech. If any arguments
go unanswered, the negative team will rightly claim that the argument has been won by the negative.

Second Negative Rebuttal Speech: The 2NR should focus the
attention of the judge on the key reasons the affirmative plan
should be rejected. In offering these reasons, the negative debater
must depend on arguments that were extended from the attacks on
the case made in constructive speeches.

Second Affirmative Rebuttal Speech: The 2AR should cover all the
issues reviewed by the second negative rebuttalist, plus any important issues from the first affirmative rebuttal the negative team
might have ignored. The final rebuttal provides an opportunity for
the affirmative team to explain to the judge why the affirmative
side of the resolution should win the debate.

THE IMPORTANCE OF THE FLOWSHEET

The *flowsheet* refers to the record debaters themselves keep of the
arguments that have been made in a debate. In policy debate, there
is something called *the burden of rejoinder.* This means an argument made by one team is assumed by the judge to be true unless
and until the other team answers the argument. For example, say
the affirmative team argues "Global warming is the most serious
problem facing the planet." If the negative team fails to answer this
argument in its next speech, the judge will assume that the negative

team accepts the truth of the argument. In the language of a debater, the negative team has *dropped* or *granted* the argument by failing to respond to it.

It is because of the burden of rejoinder that the flowsheet is so important in policy debate. Everyone in the debate round—all four debaters and the judge—keep careful track of the arguments in the order they have been made. The flowsheet becomes the debater's notes for an upcoming speech.

If the debater is flowing on paper (as opposed to on a computer), each group of arguments is placed on a separate sheet. The affirmative case arguments (the ones from the first affirmative speech) go on one sheet. All negative arguments against the affirmative case go on that same sheet. Each subsequent speech in the debate requires a new column on the flowsheet.

Every major off-case argument made by the negative team is placed on a new sheet of paper. If the negative team challenges topicality, each topicality argument is placed on its own sheet of paper. If the negative team offers three disadvantages, each disadvantage is then placed on a separate sheet of paper. In a typical round of policy debate, a complete flowsheet might require eight to ten sheets of paper. Each sheet of paper contains a record of what happened to the argument all the way to the end of the debate.

Keeping an accurate flowsheet requires carefully listening to an opponent's argument. It also requires the use of short labels for arguments. Debaters commonly use the letter *T* to label a topicality argument, *DA* for a disadvantage, *CP* for a counterplan, and *K* for a critique argument. Shorthand symbols quickly evolve for each new resolution. If the resolution uses the term *sub-Saharan Africa*, for example, that will quickly become simply *SSA*.

The following picture might help you conceptualize what a flowsheet looks like. Notice in the picture that each argument is clearly labeled at the top. These labels assist the debater in finding the correct sheet of paper to record arguments while listening to an opponent's speech.

Example of flowing on paper.

Before beginning their speeches, policy debaters usually announce a list of the arguments they are about to make; this list is called a *road map*. A first negative constructive speaker might, for example, say, "I will have two disadvantages, two topicality arguments, and then the case." This lets the judge and the other team know that they will need to have ready four new pieces of paper and then the case flowsheet (which already has recorded the case from the first affirmative speech).

Remember that in the rebuttal speeches there can be no new arguments. Therefore, a road map before one of the rebuttal speeches tells listeners the order for all of their existing sheets of paper. The road map for a first affirmative rebuttal speech might be as follows: "I will start with the case, then the 'Deficit' disadvantage, the 'Substantial' topicality argument, the 'Borders' critique, and then the 'United Nations' counterplan." This alerts the judge and the other team that they should line up the pages of their flowsheet in that order.

Many debaters are beginning to keep their flowsheet on a computer, using spreadsheet software such as Microsoft Excel. If you would like to try this flowing method, be sure the rules of the organization sponsoring the tournament allow the use of a computer during a debate round. NFL rules and the rules of many state associations now allow the use of computers for policy debate so long as the connection to online materials (the Internet, text messaging, e-mail, and so on) has been disabled.

Following is an example of a flowsheet using Microsoft Excel.

Notice also in the following example that the bottom worksheet tabs in Excel have been used to store the various parts of the flowsheet. By clicking any one of these tabs, the debater can quickly switch between the case flow, disadvantage argument flows, and so forth.

If you want to use Excel for flowing, several modifications of Excel defaults are necessary. First, you need to enable text wrap. In its default mode, Excel displays only one line of text within each of its cells. You want to be able to store several lines of text within the same cell. To enable text wrap, follow these steps: (1) Select whole worksheet (Ctrl+A); (2) Select Format Menu: Cells; (3) Click the tab for Alignment; (4) Under Text Control, check the item labeled Text Wrap.

You also need to learn how to create and rename new folder tabs at the bottom of your Excel workbook. You can do this with the following four steps: (1) Use the Edit menu to select Move or Copy Sheet; (2) Click the option to Create a Copy; (3) Right-click the tab name at the bottom of the screen; (4) Select the option to Rename.

	A	B	C	D
1	I. Malaria threatens millions of people in SSA A. Malaria is responsible for millions of deaths in SSA (Lawson '05: 3 millions deaths/year)	1. Treatment of malaria is available and effective in SSA (Miller '05) 2. Most people in SSA have developed an immunity to malaria. (Snow '06)	1. If treatment is so effective, why are there still 3 million deaths from malaria each year? 2. Immunity doesn't help children, which is why malaria is the #1 killer of children in SSA	1. Treatment is being rapidly expanded; the number of deaths is decreasing 2. The Snow evidence said that there are few actual deaths from malaria
2	B. Malaria perpetuates poverty (Lawson '05) (WHO '06)	1. There are many causes of poverty. (Sachs '06) 2. The Lawson evidence says malaria causes only a 1.5% decline in GDP.	1. The fact that there are many causes of poverty doesn't mean we should ignore this cause of poverty. 2. The Lawson evidence says 1.5% PER YEAR, which means about a 15% decline over a decade.	1. The AFF now admits that they can't do anything about many causes of poverty; this means that poverty will be perpetuated even if this single cause is removed. 2. This is still a small amount each year.
3	II. SSA requires international assistance to prevent malaria			
4	A. Prevention is the best hope for eliminating malaria in SSA (Roberts '06) (Attaran '05)	1. Prevention and treatment should be pursued at the same time (Gelletly '07) 2. Prevention is vigorously pursued at present. (Miller '05)	1. Treatment can never eliminate malaria; the fact that prevention has eliminated malaria in other countries shows there is hope. 2. Prevention can be increased.	1. Treatment can eliminate the DEATHS from malaria. 2. One can always increase anything; the point is that there is no inherency: Prevention is already extensively pursued
5	B. Most SSA nations lack the capacity to prevent malaria on their own. (Coetze '06) (Webster '05)	Most SSA countries have their own programs for malaria prevention. (der Gaag '06)	These programs lag behind their potential because of lack of funding and support	Chemicals are inexpensive; Labor is the major issue & SSA countries have an abundant supply of labor
6	III. Present II C. health assistance to			

CASE / "Substantially" T / "Savage;Victim;Savior" K / Bush DA / DDT DA

Example of flowing on the computer.

In the Excel example shown previously, you will notice that several cells contain numerous answers made to a single argument. You might wonder how this is done, considering that whenever you press Enter, Excel automatically moves you to the next cell. The answer is to hold down the Alt key when the Enter or Return key is pressed. By doing so, you can enter as many answers as you want within the same cell.

When flowing on paper, most debaters switch colors to show which team made the argument. If the column represents arguments made by the affirmative team, the ink color might be black. If the column represents arguments made by the negative team, the ink color might be red or blue. How can you do the same color variation in Excel? Follow these three steps: (1) Select the whole column by clicking the Column Letter at Top; (2) Select the Format menu option and then select Cells; and (3) Select the Font tab and choose the color you want.

DELIVERY SKILLS IN POLICY DEBATE

Speech *delivery* refers to the management of the voice and the nonverbal elements of public speaking. Effective public speaking requires the proper management of eye contact, vocal variety, rate of speech, vocal fluency, and gesturing.

Policy debate has been justifiably criticized for its failure to cultivate these skills. The inattention to speech delivery in policy debate is a natural outgrowth of the decision model.

Judges award wins and losses based on the arguments presented and the evidence offered in support of those arguments. Given this logical emphasis, few debate judges are willing to say they voted in favor of the weaker argument but did so because the debaters sounded better. Logical substance should trump style of delivery. In an ideal world, however, a debater would have both substance and style.

So, what are the elements of effective style in policy debate? Judge adaptation should be the guide. Debate is a contest in which a judge's decision is final. How do you know what a judge expects? Often debate tournaments provide *judge philosophy* sheets, allowing debaters to read a judge's own view of how winners and losers are determined in debate. Sometimes the judge philosophies involve answers to standardized questions such as, "What do you think about speed and rate of delivery in debate?" If judge philosophy sheets are available, pay careful attention to what your judge expects and try to adapt to those expectations. If a judge philosophy sheet is unavailable, you might be able to gather information from your coach or from other debaters from your school who have had experience with your same judge. Gather as much information about your judge as you can before the debate round begins. Sometimes judges will answer questions from debaters just before the beginning of the round. You should do whatever you can to adjust your speaking style to match the expectations of your judge.

What about eye contact? Most policy debaters make very little eye contact during the early portions of a debate. All participants—including the judge—are writing the arguments down on their flowsheets. There is little point in looking at the judge if the judge is writing on her flowsheet rather than looking at you. Also, the fact that you are reading your constructive arguments from pre-prepared briefs makes it difficult to maintain eye contact. As the round draws closer to the end, however, eye contact becomes more important. You are no longer making new arguments, but instead trying to convince the judge of the logical power of the arguments already made. In the late rebuttals the judge will still be flowing but will now be paying more attention to you. As any good public speaker knows, eye contact plays an important role in projecting credibility and confidence. The best policy debaters bring all their persuasive powers to bear in the final rebuttals.

What about speed of delivery? Debaters who win consistently are those who go fast when necessary but can also adapt to a judge who does not like speed. Policy debate tends to be fast because of the premium placed on making arguments the other team cannot answer. If one team drops an argument, that argument is considered won by the other team. Accordingly, policy debate becomes a game in which some teams try to make as many arguments as possible within the shortest amount of time; the calculation is that the other team will not be able to get to everything. The resulting speed contest has educational benefits as well as detriments.

One benefit of speed is that debaters are trained to think very rapidly on their feet; they have to process a great deal of information in a short amount of time. A second benefit of speed is the premium placed on word economy. Policy debaters quickly learn to express themselves succinctly. This training in economical expression pays off in the real world. No one enjoys listening to a public speaker who takes ten minutes to say something that could have been expressed in a paragraph or two.

The drawbacks to the *speed-and-spread* methods of policy debate are, however, significant. Outside observers of policy debates sometimes (incorrectly) assume that the activity has little value because the speeches sound to them like mere jibberish. This sometimes causes school principals or debate coaches themselves to discontinue policy debate because they doubt its value as a training ground for public speakers. Many policy debaters themselves get frustrated when they realize that well-reasoned arguments often get lost when attacked with a rapid-fire, brain-dead barrage of responses. Yet this potential weakness of policy debate can also be its strength. The best debaters learn how to sort out persuasive, winning arguments from the chaff that makes up a typical policy debate round. The best policy debaters are able to bring the whole round down to one or two dominating arguments as they approach the final rebuttal. This ability to bring order out of argumentative chaos is a vital skill in real-world decision-making.

FURTHER READING

Burgett, Cynthia. *Policy Debate*. New York: Rosen Central, 2007.

CHAPTER 6

AFFIRMATIVE CASE STRUCTURES IN POLICY DEBATE

Selecting a powerful and well-structured affirmative case is essential to success in debate. Planning to win consistently on the affirmative is comparable in importance to holding serve in tennis. You have important advantages when you are on the affirmative: (1) You have the privilege of selecting the example of the resolution you want to defend, and (2) You have both the first and last speeches in the debate.

CHOOSING THE GROUND

Most resolutions in policy debate provide considerable latitude to the affirmative in selecting an affirmative case. Suppose the resolution is "The United States federal government should substantially increase alternative energy incentives in the United States." An affirmative case could focus on any form of energy meeting the definition of alternative energy—solar, wind, ethanol, hydrogen, nuclear, biomass, geothermal, and so on. If an affirmative team chooses to defend wind power, the whole debate then focuses on whether the expansion of this one form of energy is a desirable option. The affirmative is under no obligation to defend every possible example of the resolution. The following paragraphs discuss some of the strategies affirmative debaters use when selecting an affirmative case.

Fall in love: Are you a true believer in an affirmative case? After you have done considerable research, you might come to believe that a case is simply true. This means you will bring passion to the task of persuading judges to vote for the affirmative option. Although passion won't win rounds by itself, it can be an important part of a winning formula.

Surprise: Will the affirmative case catch the negative team off guard? The negative team might be prepared to debate wind or solar power, but it might never have considered the possibility of cogeneration: having waste incinerators produce electrical power by burning refuse. A *squirrel case*—the term debaters often use for a surprise case—has some significant limitations, however. First, word spreads quickly at a tournament when a new case is winning debates. The surprise often lasts only for one or two rounds before negative teams begin developing a preround strategy for the case. Second, the surprise strategy often backfires. When a negative team doesn't know how to answer an affirmative case, the resulting chaos is not always a good thing for the affirmative. The negative team might reach into its backfiles to find its own strange arguments such as a kritik of reason or de-development good.

Predictability: Does an affirmative case allow you to anticipate the negative attack? This criterion is actually the opposite of surprise. Consider the chess analogy: The best chess players are those who can think several moves into the future. Thinking into the future requires an ability to predict what the other player will do when you make your move. Suppose the affirmative team plans to use a geothermal energy case. A predictable negative response to a geothermal energy case is that drilling holes in the earth will increase the potential for earthquakes. An affirmative team might actually hope for this response because it has evidence that geothermal drilling relieves pressure within the upper earth crust, making earthquakes less likely. This argument is what a debater calls a *turnaround*—or just *turn*. A turn takes an argument made by the other team (increased likelihood of earthquakes) and makes it into another reason to support the affirmative case (decreased likelihood of earthquakes).

Something in reserve: A good affirmative case has advantages on the surface, but even more below the surface. Consider a wind power affirmative case. The first affirmative speech might have based the wind advantage primarily on the need for energy independence—the need to be free from reliance on Middle Eastern oil. Yet numerous other advantages can be called upon to turn various negative disadvantage arguments. The negative might argue that wind power harms wildlife by killing birds that fly into turbines. This argument can be turned by arguing that wind power cuts down air pollution from coal-fired plants, saving far more birds (and other wildlife) than would be killed in turbine accidents. The negative might also argue that wind power undermines the environment by requiring large tracts of land. This argument can be turned by arguing that wind power limits global warming which causes sea-rise, destroying much more land than would be required for wind farms. Or the negative may argue that wind power will increase the price of energy, risking a serious economic recession. This argument can be turned by showing that wind power is actually less expensive than continued reliance on fossil fuels.

Topical: Does the affirmative plan do what the resolution says it should do? Negative teams commonly challenge topicality because they know they can win the debate on this argument alone. Often even obviously topical cases are subjected to topicality challenges. Consider the 2007–2008 national policy topic: "Resolved: The United States federal government should substantially increase its public health assistance to sub-Saharan Africa." You must be prepared to show how your affirmative plan meets every one of the words in the resolution—even seemingly simple terms such as *substantially* or *to*. You might want to propose that the United States take military action to stop the killing in Darfur. Before selecting such a case, however, you must be confident you can prove that U.S. military intervention in Darfur is an example of "public health assistance." If you lose an average of one or more rounds per tournament on topicality, you should consider moving to a more clearly topical case.

DECISION PARADIGMS

What must an affirmative team prove to win the debate? These standards for decision are called *paradigms*. The traditional paradigm is the stock issues, as discussed in Chapter 5.

A stock issues approach is based on a *legal model*. In this legal model, the affirmative team is equivalent to the prosecution. The prosecution must overcome a presumption of innocence. Similarly in the stock issues paradigm, the present system is presumed innocent until proven guilty. How does the prosecution overcome the presumption of innocence? It must prove (beyond reasonable doubt) all the elements of a crime. If the crime is first-degree murder, certain elements of the crime can be established by state law, including opportunity, motive, and premeditation. The prosecution must prove every element of the crime to gain a conviction. Similarly in debate, the affirmative team must win every stock issue to overcome presumption and win the debate. The stock issues of topicality, significance of harm, inherency, solvency, and desirability must all be decided in favor of the affirmative for the judge to award an affirmative win.

A policy-making paradigm is based on a *legislative model*. The policy-making model—also called a *comparative advantage model*—focuses on desirability, asking whether the advantages of change outweigh the disadvantages. This model effectively does away with the notion of presumption. Defenders of a policy-making approach object to the stock issues model as having a conservative political bias. Why, they ask, should there be a presumption against change? Robert Kennedy often used the following quotation from George Bernard Shaw in his speeches: "Some men see things as they are and ask why. Others dream things that never were and ask why not." The legal model provides a presumption of innocence to persons accused of crime as a way of ensuring important civil liberties. But this analogy doesn't properly apply to political decision-making. Why should existing policies be given a presumption of innocence?

Although a compelling case can be made for the policy model, it doesn't really justify doing away entirely with the traditional stock issues. Most judges using a policy-making model still consider topicality an independent voting issue for the negative team. This follows a standard of germaneness required in nearly all legislative sessions. If the topic on the floor is "U.S. public health assistance for sub-Saharan Africa," the chair would normally rule out of order a motion to establish a system of national health insurance for all U.S. citizens. So topicality remains a concern regardless of the paradigm. But what about the stock issues of significance of harm, inherency, and solvency? The significance of harm stock issue focuses on what is wrong now. Is it really possible to show that a totally new approach to helping sub-Saharan Africa is desirable without discussing the human suffering now plaguing sub-Saharan Africa? The inherency stock issue focuses on whether present system efforts are already addressing the problem. Can we meaningfully discuss whether a new approach is desirable without uncovering the deficiencies in the present approach? The solvency stock issue focuses on whether the affirmative plan would truly solve some of the problems cited in the case. Can we discuss desirability of change without showing that the change would work as claimed? The policy-making model simply takes the issues of harm, inherency, and solvency and packages them all within the final stock issue of desirability.

The main difference with a policy-making model is that the stock issues are no longer seen as independent of one another—they are not independent voting issues. Instead, they must be considered as factors in a formula. This formula is essentially as follows: desirability (advantage) = the amount of harm for which the plan can solve – the amount of harm for which the present system can solve. The amount of the affirmative advantage (assuming it is a positive amount) must then be weighed against the disadvantages suggested by the negative team.

It is significant, however, that the policy-making model does away with presumption. If the affirmative team offers a topical affirmative case and shows any excess of advantage over disadvantage, the judge will vote affirmative. The present system carries no presumption of innocence requiring a beyond-a-reasonable-doubt threshold.

The hypothesis testing paradigm is based on a *social science model*. The assumption of the hypothesis testing paradigm is that the debate resolution is like a scientific hypothesis; the affirmative team is offering its affirmative plan in an effort to prove the truth of the hypothesis. In hypothesis testing, the notion of presumption returns in an even stronger form than in the stock issues model. The scientific method would never allow a researcher to suppose the truth of a hypothesis; it must be proven true against all challenges.

In the hypothesis testing model, it is especially important that the affirmative plan offer a topical example of the resolution. One could not prove the truth of a hypothesis (the resolution) by offering an example that is atypical. The need to show that the affirmative plan is typical of the resolution gives rise to a justification argument. Consider the resolution calling for the United States to increase public health assistance to sub-Saharan Africa. The negative team might argue that there is no "justification for increasing HIV/AIDS assistance just in sub-Saharan Africa considering that the disease is also rampant in South Asia." This need to justify terms of the resolution is unique to the hypothesis testing paradigm.

Every argument offered by the negative team should be seen as offering an independent test of the truth of the hypothesis. A researcher in the social sciences would never claim that a hypothesis is true because it has passed a single test; it must be tested against all competing claims. A negative team could prove the hypothesis untrue by winning any one of the standard stock issues.

The hypothesis testing model has one other important implication: it is more forgiving of contradictory negative positions. The function of the negative team is to test the affirmative hypothesis against numerous competing possibilities. Because the negative team is assigned to provide these tests, there is no reason to worry about internal inconsistencies. If any one test disproves the hypothesis, the judge simply declares the hypothesis false. The negative team is under no obligation to support its own hypothesis. This is significantly different from the policy-making model in which the judge assumes that the affirmative policy is to be compared to the negative policy. If the negative team offers an inconsistent/contradictory policy alternative, the affirmative policy is more attractive by comparison. In hypothesis testing, negative inconsistency is forgiven.

There are other paradigms for debate, but the main three are stock issues, policy-making, and hypothesis testing. How will you know which model the judge will apply? In some tournaments you will have access to a written judge philosophy in which the judge describes the paradigm she brings to judging a debate. In other instances, the judge will tell you before the round begins about her expectations and assumptions. In many cases, however, you simply will not know the preferences of the judge until you hear or read the reasons for the judge's decision. Other times the judge will say that her paradigm is *tabula rasa*—meaning a blank slate. In such cases, it will be left to the debaters to determine how arguments should be evaluated.

CASE STRUCTURES

The first affirmative constructive in policy debate is a fully written-out eight-minute speech. You must carefully design the structure of this speech and rehearse it to ensure that it will fit within the time limit. You won't be able to change this speech to have one version for a stock issues judge and another for a policy-making or hypothesis testing judge. As a practical matter, this means your case must address the issues of significance of harm, inherency, and solvency. A stock issues judge would insist that those three stock issues be addressed in the first speech (as would a hypothesis testing judge). On the other hand, a policy-making judge would probably not pay very much attention to the inherency element of your case but would not hold it against you that it was present.

In every first affirmative speech, you present your affirmative plan. The length of the plan can range from one to ten or twelve sentences. In general, the affirmative plan answers the following questions: (1) What will be done?; (2) Who will do the plan?; (3) How will funding—if necessary—be provided? In some instances the plan is very simple (as in cases where you are proposing to abolish some existing policy). In other instances some significant elaboration might be necessary (if, for example, you are proposing the creation of a national health insurance system).

There is no rule saying where in the first speech the plan must be presented. In some case structures, the plan is presented early in the speech, whereas in others it might come near the end.

A *traditional need case* addresses each of the three middle stock issues (significance of harm, inherency, and solvency) in arguments called *contentions*. The significance of harm contention makes a claim about what is wrong now. The inherency contention describes what is wrong with the efforts of the present system to resolve the harm. The solvency contention claims that the affirmative plan will resolve all or part of the harm. Under each contention there are usually sub-contentions, each of which must be supported with authoritative quotations.

Sometimes debaters use the term *observation* in place of *contention*. Even though the two terms mean essentially the same thing, *observation* best fits a situation in which the argument seems especially obvious or indisputable.

Following is an example of a traditional need case structure:

> Plan: The Department of Health and Human Services (HHS) will establish a single-payer national health insurance system such that the federal government will be responsible for all health care payments to health providers. HHS will establish a system of cost controls based upon fair market estimates. Funding for national health insurance will be derived from a tax on all employers.
>
> Contention I: Many Americans lack adequate health care because they are uninsured.
>
> > A. Millions of Americans are not covered by health insurance.
> >
> > B. Millions of Americans forego proper health care because of the lack of insurance.
>
> Contention II: The present employment-based health insurance system is inherently flawed.
>
> > A. Americans who are unemployed will never be covered by an employment-based health insurance system.
> >
> > B. Americans who are self-employed are inadequately covered by an employment-based health insurance system.

Contention III: National health insurance will provide access to health care for millions of Americans.

> A. National health insurance is the most equitable approach.
>
> B. National health insurance best assures quality health care.

A *comparative advantage* case is a superior design for a policy-making paradigm. This case structure can also be managed in such a way that it addresses the concerns of a stock issues judge. There is no rule concerning how many advantages are required in a comparative advantage case—sometimes there is only one advantage. Somewhere within the case structure the three stock issues of significance of harm, inherency, and solvency are addressed. The order in which they are addressed is unimportant so long as they are present.

> Plan: The United States will change its immigration policy with respect to Mexican-American immigrants in the following ways: (1) All Mexican-Americans who can prove that they have been present in the United States for a period of five years will be granted amnesty; (2) The U.S. Department of Labor will establish a guest worker program designed to register Mexican-Americans who are eligible to work in the United States; (3) Social services will be provided to Mexican-American immigrants with funding to be derived from a tax on wages for registered guest workers.
>
> Observation: The present law enforcement approach to immigration control is unworkable.
>
> > A. The construction of a border fence is a failed policy.
> >
> > B. The heavy demand for immigrant workers makes the present system unsustainable.
>
> Advantage I: Amnesty will best protect America against international terrorism.
>
> > A. There are huge numbers of illegal immigrants living in the United States.

B. Terrorists can easily hide among the millions of undocumented immigrants.

C. Amnesty best allows for the documentation and registration of immigrants.

Advantage II: A guest worker program will improve the health of the U.S. economy.

A. There is a growing labor shortage in the U.S.

B. U.S. citizens are unwilling to perform many of the jobs for which guest workers are needed.

C. A guest worker program will improve the health of the American economy while meeting the needs of Mexican-American immigrants.

A third affirmative case structure is a *goals/criteria case*. This type of case works well when the affirmative team believes it can prove that some well-accepted goal would best be met by adopting the affirmative plan. In this case structure, the goal is often presented in an opening observation. Following is an example of a goals/criteria case:

Observation: Access to health care is a basic human right.

A. The Universal Declaration of Human Rights establishes a basic right to health care.

B. Access to health care is essential to the pursuit of happiness.

Plan: The United States federal government will establish a universal health care system based on the British model. Funding will be provided by increasing income taxes.

Contention I: A universal health care system best meets the goal of health care for all Americans.

A. Millions of Americans are now denied access to health care.

B. An employment-based system for providing health insurance is inherently flawed.

C. The British model has demonstrated the capability to ensure quality health care for all.

In each of the foregoing case structures, the affirmative team has addressed the stock issues of significance of harm, inherency, and solvency. What about the other two stock issues (topicality and desirability)? There was a time when affirmative teams were expected to offer definitions of terms in the first affirmative speech. This is no longer a common practice. Instead, the affirmative team waits for the negative team to challenge topicality. If the negative team doesn't offer any topicality argument, the case is presumed to be topical. If, however, the negative team does challenge the topicality of the affirmative case, it is imperative that the affirmative fully answer the argument.

The same procedure is followed for the desirability stock issue (the question of whether advantages outweigh disadvantages). It is up to the negative team to offer disadvantages. The affirmative team must then answer these disadvantages and show they are either untrue or are outweighed by affirmative advantages.

FURTHER READING

Herbeck, Dale. *Paradigms of Debate*. Indianapolis, IN: National Federation of High Schools, 1988.

CHAPTER 7

NEGATIVE STRATEGY IN POLICY DEBATE

Unlike affirmative teams, negative policy debaters cannot script their first constructive speech. The negative team is expected to respond specifically to the example of the resolution advocated in the affirmative case. If the resolution calls for increasing public health assistance to sub-Saharan Africa, the particular affirmative case might focus on HIV/AIDS, malaria, tuberculosis, malnutrition, maternal health, sanitary waste disposal, or numerous other possibilities.

In the typical debate tournament, there is seldom more than twenty or thirty minutes between the time a round pairing is posted and the time the debate is expected to begin. Most of the allotted time is taken up just by moving all the debate materials to the assigned room. This means there will be little time before the round begins for planning a negative strategy. Sometimes just knowing the identity of the affirmative team will disclose the case area. If the affirmative team used a given case in a previous tournament or in an earlier round of the current tournament, the case will likely remain the same. Often, however, the negative team will not know the particular focus of the affirmative case until the first affirmative speech has actually begun.

This uncertainty about the affirmative case area means the negative team must enter a tournament with pre-prepared strategies for all the likely affirmative cases.

FIVE RECOMMENDATIONS FOR BUILDING A NEGATIVE STRATEGY

1. *Advocate something.* You will be more persuasive when you let the judge know what you are for, not just what you are against. If the affirmative proposes federal subsidies for the development of energy alternatives, you can advocate free enterprise solutions. If the affirmative proposes increases in U.S. foreign aid for sub-Saharan Africa, you can advocate international alternatives. If the affirmative wants to expand wind power, you can advocate reliance on nuclear power.

   My suggestion that you should advocate something might sound as if I am telling you to use a counterplan in every debate. That is certainly not my intention. Advocacy can latch onto something the present system is already doing. You can argue that the present system follows a free enterprise approach rather than government subsidization of energy industries. As a negative team, you are advocating this free enterprise approach as a proper choice. The Global Fund to Fight AIDS, Tuberculosis, and Malaria is an existing international program to provide public health assistance in sub-Saharan Africa (and elsewhere). As a negative team, you can advocate this international approach as superior to the U.S. federal government's solution to Africa's problems.

2. *Minimize and then outweigh.* This recommendation means that direct clash with the affirmative case should play a part in your strategy. Many negative teams make the mistake of focusing entirely on their own arguments while ignoring the claims made in the affirmative case. Consider an affirmative contention that millions of persons in Africa are dying from AIDS. The problem of AIDS seems so undeniable that the negative team won't even try to minimize the affirmative case. Instead, the negative focuses on its own deficit disadvantage claim that spending more money on AIDS would

cause economic recession or depression. Why put the judge
in a position of having to weigh millions of deaths in Africa
against an economic depression in the United States? Reduce
the size of the affirmative advantage to an amount the disadvantage can more easily outweigh.

Direct clash with the affirmative case does not always take
the form of denying the affirmative harm. The negative could
offer an inherency argument showing that the problem of
AIDS is being properly addressed by international actors (the
World Health Organization and the Global Fund to Fight
AIDS, Tuberculosis, and Malaria). Solvency arguments could
show that additional U.S. funding for AIDS would not solve
the harm (because of a shortage of health workers in Africa,
for example).

In many instances it is possible to show that the affirmative
harm itself is exaggerated. If the harm is global warming,
the negative might be able to show that the rate of warming
is slow enough to allow natural ecosystems to adjust. If the
harm is that people lack health insurance, the negative might
be able to show that emergency rooms in the United States
provide critical care for the uninsured.

The recommendation to offer direct clash with the affirmative case seems difficult because of the wide range of
affirmative options. In reality, this is less difficult than it
seems. Consider a resolution that calls on the affirmative to
fund energy alternatives. An affirmative team can choose
from a wide variety of energy approaches it will advocate.
Nevertheless, the potential harm arguments are all very
similar. Why would anyone say we must develop energy alternatives? There are really only three potential harm areas: the
need for energy independence (security harms), the need to
save the environment (environmental harms), and the need
for lower energy costs (economic harms). The same pattern
repeats for almost all policy resolutions; there are usually
only two or three possible harm arguments that are specific
to that topic. Although you might not know what particular direction their case will take, you can prepare argument
briefs to minimize all the likely harm claims.

3. *Think backwards from disadvantages.* The best negative teams win debates with powerful disadvantage arguments. For each of your strategies, select a disadvantage or two that can outweigh the affirmative case. Only after you have decided upon the disadvantage(s) should you then pick the other elements of your strategy. Make sure that every other element of your strategy is consistent with your disadvantage(s).

Suppose you have decided you will defeat a national health insurance case with an unnecessary surgery disadvantage. This disadvantage claims that when health care is free, it is overused, leading to increased health problems for Americans. Thinking backward from this disadvantage, the negative team will argue that when people have to pay something for their health care they will use it sparingly—which actually leads to better health outcomes. If the unnecessary surgery disadvantage is going to headline the negative strategy, you don't want the first negative speaker to argue that uninsured Americans can now be treated free of charge in emergency rooms. Such an inherency argument would destroy the uniqueness of the disadvantage. If cost is already a nonissue for Americans seeking health care, why wouldn't the unnecessary surgery disadvantage already be happening? Similarly, the negative team would have to avoid any disadvantage claim that national health insurance would lead to long waiting lines and denial of health care. The negative team must decide whether national health insurance will lead to too much or too little health care.

4. *Limit the number of strategies.* One of the main advantages of being affirmative is that you are debating the same thing in half of your debate rounds. You naturally become more adept than the other team at arguing on ground that is familiar to you. Learn to bring that same advantage to the negative side as well. As a negative team, you should develop two or three basic strategies that will provide options against any affirmative case. Suppose, for example, you are debating the 2007–2008 resolution that the United States should increase public health

assistance to sub-Saharan Africa. After researching this topic, you could have discovered that microfinance is a strategic alternative to government subsidies. Many international actors, including the World Bank and various United Nations agencies, now provide thousands of small loans to persons in developing countries to help them set up businesses and local institutions to meet social needs. Defenders of microfinance argue that it enlivens self-help and avoids the dependency and corruption that inevitably accompanies foreign aid solutions. A negative team could develop an entire strategy around microfinance solutions. Because many international institutions already support microfinance, it isn't even necessary to present a counterplan. The negative can argue that the present system is superior to the affirmative plan because it promotes microfinance-based, self-help solutions rather than dependency/corruption-prone foreign aid schemes. By conducting in-depth research, the negative team can find evidence linking microfinance solutions to many of the case areas likely to be chosen by the affirmative (water purity and sanitation, women-in-development, training of health workers, treatment of homes for malaria prevention, and so on).

The most successful negative teams are those that can succeed in bringing the debate to familiar negative ground. So the affirmative case might be advocating some little-known system for water purification, but the negative succeeds in making the debate about microfinance solutions. Find two or three strategies that work against almost any case. This makes selecting a strategy much simpler. After you discover the affirmative case area, you just choose the strategy that best fits this particular case.

5. *Take what the resolution gives you.* The affirmative team is defending the resolution; you are defending the nonresolution. Every policy debate resolution in the past quarter century has the United States federal government as its agent of action. This locks the affirmative team into defending federal solutions to public policy problems. This leaves considerable leeway for the development of negative strategies. State or local government action can be superior to federal action.

Private enterprise can provide a better way to deal with problems. International actors such as the United Nations, the Global Fund, the World Bank, the International Monetary Fund, the World Trade Organization, or the International Criminal Court might be able to solve problems in a much more advantageous fashion. If these nonfederal-government agencies already have programs underway to deal with the affirmative harm claims, inherency arguments are in order. If no such solutions are underway, the negative team can advocate a counterplan (the subject of Chapter 8).

CHALLENGING TOPICALITY

Most debate coaches recommend that the topicality challenge be presented in the first negative constructive speech. Much of the credibility of the argument is lost if the negative team waits for the second negative constructive speech to issue the challenge. After the discussion has been underway for forty minutes, it is a bit unusual to say that the whole discussion up to that point has been irrelevant to the resolution.

The structure of the topicality challenge should include an argument label, a standards section, and a violation. The main argument label should stipulate that the argument is topicality and should indicate the word or phrase in the resolution the plan fails to meet. Following is an example of a label for a topicality argument: "Substantially: The plan is not topical because it fails to substantially increase public health assistance to sub-Saharan Africa." This label tells the judge and the opposing team that the argument is topicality and that the particular violation claimed will relate to the term *substantially*. The inclusion of the word or phrase being violated is important because some teams make three or four different topicality arguments claiming that the plan violates several words of the resolution. The participants in the debate round must have a way of distinguishing one topicality violation from another; this is typically done by including the word or words being violated in the argument label.

The standards section provides a brief explanation of ways the judge should determine which definition is superior. In most debate rounds, the judge will have definitions from each side supporting its interpretation of the resolution. The topicality standards debate helps the judge assess which definition is the better of the two.

The each-word-has-meaning standard argues that the better interpretation of the resolution is the one that offers an independent role for each of the key terms in the resolution. One should assume that the framers of the resolution placed each word in the resolution for some reason other than to be redundant.

The debatability standard argues that the better interpretation of the resolution is the one that more fairly divides the ground between the affirmative and negative teams. Consider the example of an affirmative case that claims global warming is undermining public health in sub-Saharan Africa. The affirmative plan calls for the United States to sign the Kyoto Protocol and get serious about meeting carbon-dioxide emission reduction targets. The negative team should argue the importance of making a distinction between what is public health and what affects public health. It may well be true that global warming affects public health, but allowing such an effects topicality standard would unlimit the resolution, making it undebatable. By such an effects standard any of the following cases would be topical:

- A nuclear war would undermine public health in sub-Saharan Africa, so the United States should pursue nuclear disarmament.

- An asteroid collision would cause nuclear winter and undermine public health in sub-Saharan Africa, so the United States should pursue a space program designed to intercept asteroids.

- Globalization and trade liberalization increase poverty and ill health in sub-Saharan Africa, so the United States should pull out of the World Trade Organization.

- A worldwide economic collapse would undermine public health in sub-Saharan Africa, so the United States should balance the U.S. federal budget.

- International terrorism, if it continues to spread, will cause violence and death in sub-Saharan Africa, so the United States should expand its campaign against state-sponsored terrorism in the Middle East.

As this list illustrates, an affirmative team could choose any serious international problem and argue that its solution would benefit public health in sub-Saharan Africa. The matrix of affirmative possibilities would be endless. Given the specific wording of the resolution, however, there is no authority for the affirmative team to specify changes in policies elsewhere in the world (other than in sub-Saharan Africa). The affirmative advantage must come from public health assistance to sub-Saharan Africa. A debatability standard on the sub-Saharan Africa resolution requires that the affirmative interpretation of the resolution maintains fair limits on the topic; if any change in U.S. foreign policy is topical, the resolution is undebatable.

Debatability asks whether it would be better for debate (more equitable or fair) to accept the affirmative or the negative interpretation of the terms at issue. This standard usually requires the debaters to show which kinds of cases would be included and excluded by the competing standards. The most debatable definitions are those that create some bright line allowing a reasonable number of cases to be debated. A negative interpretation would be viewed as unreasonable if no cases (or only a few cases) would be topical by such a standard. An affirmative interpretation would be viewed as unreasonable if it would enable hundreds of cases to be debated; the preparation burden created for the negative would be unmanageable.

The most limiting standard suggests that the better definition is the one that is most precise. If the affirmative team provides a definition of *substantially* as tangible rather than imaginary, it would be inferior to a negative definition saying that the word means an increase of at least 90 percent. Whatever one thinks of the latter definition, it is certainly more precise than the vague definition offered by the affirmative. The problem with this standard is that it offers no real explanation as to why precision is better than abstraction. One could define an orange as a piece of fruit in the citrus family that has a diameter of 2.7 inches. This definition is certainly precise, but precision provides no guarantee of appropriateness or accuracy.

The field context standard argues that we should prefer those interpretations of the topic that come from the real-world public policy contexts rather than from dictionary definitions.

The intent to define standard says that definitions are better when they are written for the specific purpose of defining a term. This standard is exactly the opposite of the field context standard; it offers reasons dictionary definitions should be preferred over chance occurrences of words in the field context. Scholars who prepare definitions of words in *Webster's Dictionary* or other dictionaries are writing their definitions after giving careful thought to the question of what should be included and excluded. Efforts to define from the field context are defective because the authors might be using terms in an imprecise manner.

The grammatical context standard argues that a definition is better to the extent that it accounts for the full context of the resolutional sentence. The affirmative team often tries to present definitions for each separate word in the resolution and then add up those meanings using its own creative interpretations. To prevent this sort of creative addition, the negative team suggests the superiority of a definition that places all the words of the resolution in proper grammatical context.

Given the many options, how does the negative team select a standard? Three principles should govern the application of a standard: (1) clarity, (2) correspondence, and (3) simplicity.

The *clarity principle* means the negative debater should be very clear about the standard to be applied to the definitions. This principle is violated when the debater presents two or more standards. What is a judge to do when a debater defends both the intent to define and the field context standards? The first standard says that dictionary definitions should be preferred over natural occurrences in the literature; the second standard claims precisely the opposite. Even when the standards are not contradictory, the presence of multiple standards is confusing, so the judge is left to wonder which of the standards should be given priority over the other.

The *correspondence principle* means the standard should bear a clear relationship to the violation. Negative debaters commonly present topicality standards and defend them to the end of the round but then never apply the standard to the violation to explain why the negative definition is superior to the affirmative definition. The best way to select a standard is to think backward from the violation. If the negative evidence on the violation comes from a dictionary source, the preferred standards would be each word has meaning or intent to define. If the negative evidence on the violation comes from a military expert, the preferred standard would be field context. The debatability standard is applicable at any time the affirmative plan seems especially abusive.

The *simplicity principle* means the standards debate should be kept short and uncluttered by quoting various debate theorists.

Case Arguments

The *burden of rebuttal* is a central concept in policy debate, stating that an argument is assumed to be valid unless the other side offers a rebuttal. If the affirmative case claims the United States will run out of fossil fuels within the next decade, the negative team must offer a rebuttal or the argument is assumed to be correct. The supporting evidence for the claim might have been exceptionally weak, but this won't matter if the negative team says nothing about the argument. The affirmative team will say that its argument is dropped, meaning it is granted by the negative team.

The burden of rebuttal applies equally to the affirmative and negative teams. Suppose the affirmative case claimed illegal immigration destroys the American economy and the first negative speaker responded with evidence showing that illegal immigration actually helps the economy. The affirmative team must offer a response to this argument in the very next speech; otherwise, the argument is won by the negative. The affirmative team cannot resurrect this argument in rebuttal speeches if it failed to answer it in the second affirmative constructive speech.

When a team drops an argument, it does not necessarily lose the debate. It just means that particular argument is conceded to the other team. Negative debaters often choose not to respond to certain portions of affirmative cases. An affirmative team might present a contention (meaning an argument) that the negative team regards as meaningless to the outcome of the debate. For example, say that an affirmative contention states Iran is currently attempting to develop nuclear weapons. The negative team might decide to let this argument pass without a response, calculating that a negative victory does not depend on denying this claim. Accordingly, the negative team must carefully decide which parts of the affirmative case require a negative response. The following paragraphs are designed to provide advice for handling such decisions.

> *Contest decision rules:* Negative teams must listen very carefully to the first affirmative speech for statements that, if granted, would create value systems favorable to the affirmative team. Consider an affirmative claim that ensuring energy independence is vital to the survival of the United States. If the negative team allows such a claim to go unchallenged, the debate might effectively be over. The affirmative team would remind the judge in the final rebuttal that the negative team has agreed that ensuring energy independence is more important than anything else. The negative team needed to contest the decision rule by reading evidence showing how international peace is best ensured by interdependence rather than independence.

> *Minimize harm claims.* You might not be able to deny that harm exists, but you can show that the extent of the harm is exaggerated. Your objective is to lower the amount of the harm to something your disadvantages can outweigh.

> *Think outside the box on inherency.* Negative teams often make the mistake of arguing that the present system is already doing most of what the affirmative plan proposes to do. This is seldom a winning strategy. Consider an affirmative plan proposing to abandon the funding of abstinence-based HIV/AIDS prevention programs in sub-Saharan Africa in favor of condom-based programs. The negative strategy is to win the debate with a politics disadvantage claiming that the Republican right wing would backlash if the policy of promoting abstinence were to be abandoned. The first negative speaker presents an inherency argument claiming the federal government already extensively promotes condom distribution programs in sub-Saharan Africa. This is an exceptionally

unwise inherency argument because it proves the disadvantage is untrue. If the Republican right wing were going to use condom distribution as the basis for a backlash, it should already be happening.

Negative debaters should avoid inherency arguments based on showing that the affirmative plan is mostly already being done. This type of inherency argument won't win the debate by itself because of the difference between mostly and completely. The affirmative team can always show that its plan goes a little beyond the present system. This type of inherency argument serves only to kill the potential of disadvantages. If the plan has already been mostly adopted, how can the negative persuasively argue that really bad things would happen if the plan were to be completely adopted?

The tendency of inherency arguments to destroy disadvantages causes many negative teams to avoid inherency arguments altogether. This is an unfortunate reaction. A better strategy is to present inherency arguments showing that some present system mechanism wholly unlike the affirmative plan is solving the affirmative harm. In the foregoing condom example, the negative can argue that non-U.S. agencies—such as the Global Fund and the World Health Organization—are aggressively promoting condom distribution programs in sub-Saharan Africa. This inherency argument solves the affirmative harm without triggering the right-wing backlash disadvantage.

Challenge solvency claims: Solvency is one of the weakest links in any affirmative case. Solvency attacks fall into one or more of the following categories: insufficient evidence, counter-causality, and workability.

The insufficiency of evidence is the most common defect of affirmative solvency claims. Debaters, whether affirmative or negative, have a *burden of proof* to present evidence in support of their claims. If a debater makes a claim but fails to support it with evidence, the opposing team can refute the argument by simply pointing out the insufficiency of the evidence. Consider an affirmative case dealing with illegal immigration. The harm argument alleges that illegal immigration is a major cause of crime, and the plan calls for additional funding to build an impenetrable border fence. The affirmative solvency evidence must now prove that building an impenetrable border fence will reduce crime. It isn't enough to just assert that a border fence will reduce crime.

Most affirmative teams know they must read evidence in support of their solvency contention. Often, however, a careful reading of the evidence discloses glaring weaknesses. Suppose the affirmative offers the following solvency evidence:

> *States News Service,* June 28, 2007. Online. Nexis. Accessed August 13, 2007. "Now is the time the American people must help us force the Administration to enforce current law and build a border fence," [Iowa Congressman Steve] King added.

This evidence doesn't say a border fence would stop crime; it simply says it should be built. The following evidence certainly comes closer to providing support for the affirmative solvency claim:

> Tyche Hendricks (Staff Writer), *San Francisco Chronicle,* October 27, 2006, p. A1. U.S. Rep. Duncan Hunter, R-Alpine (San Diego County), a longtime fence supporter, applauded the signing, saying the fence will make border communities more secure. "Since border fence construction began in 1996, crime rates in San Diego County have been reduced by more than half, vehicle drive-throughs have been eliminated, and apprehensions have significantly decreased as the result of fewer crossing attempts," he said in a statement.

This evidence says that a border fence in San Diego has reduced crime in that city. Yet opponents of the border fence argue that the partial fences now in use simply shift illegal immigration to other locations—to places where there is no fence. What would happen if the fence existed along the entire border (as proposed in the affirmative plan)? The affirmative evidence doesn't provide an answer. The negative team could present its own evidence showing that a border fence will never stop illegal immigration so long as the underlying causes of illegal immigration remain unaddressed:

> Eunice Moscoso (Staff Writer), *Atlanta Journal and Constitution,* September 20, 2006, p. 1A. Some Senate Democrats said a border fence would cost up to $9 billion and not solve the nation's immigration problem because more than

half of illegal immigrants arrive in the United States legally and overstay their visas. Sen. Edward Kennedy (D-Mass.), who sponsored a broader immigration bill, said that fences will not keep criminals and terrorists out and that the hijackers who perpetrated the Sept. 11, 2001, terrorist attacks did not cross the Mexican border but came to the United States with legal visas. "Enforcement alone is not the solution.... We can build fences, but people will come around them," he said.

Counter-causality is another type of solvency attack. Most public policy problems have multiple causes. The affirmative plan might remove one of these causes, leaving all the others still in place. Consider the problem of global warming. The affirmative plan might impose a carbon tax designed to reduce carbon-dioxide emissions. Yet such a plan would leave more significant causes of global warming untouched:

Richard Hill (Staff Writer), *The Oregonian*, November 2, 1989, p. E1. Methane, however, is particularly worrisome because it is increasing at twice the rate as CO_2 and can trap 20 times more heat than carbon dioxide. "That's the remarkable thing," [Oregon Research Institute professor, Reinhold A.] Rasmussen said. "Carbon dioxide has only increased maybe 20 percent in the last 100 or so years, but the amount of methane in the atmosphere has more than doubled—gone from 700 parts per billion to almost 1,750, so it's a very large increase proportionately."

Workability questions offer another way to attack affirmative solvency claims. Consider an affirmative plan that proposes to increase funding to purchase more antiretroviral drugs for HIV/AIDS sufferers in sub-Saharan Africa. The negative team could argue that providing more drugs will have little effect given numerous workability problems: corrupt governments will prevent the drugs from reaching those who need them, shortages of health clinics and health workers mean that no one will be able to dispense or monitor the drugs, and extensive water and food shortages mean that drugs will not be taken with food as recommended.

CONSTRUCTING DISADVANTAGES

A properly constructed disadvantage has a link, uniqueness, and impact. The link answers the question "Why will the plan cause the disadvantage?" Uniqueness arguments answer the question "How does the present system keep this disadvantage from happening?" Impact arguments answer the question "How serious would be the harm that will result if this disadvantage happens?"

The link argument in the disadvantage must start from something the plan does. The link then attempts to make a logical connection between the plan and the impact of the disadvantage. If the plan substantially doubles the spending for foreign aid to Africa, such spending provides the link for a deficit disadvantage. If the plan funds the use of DDT in indoor residential spraying, increased DDT use provides the link to the DDT-bad disadvantage.

Uniqueness arguments explain why the disadvantage will not happen in the present system. If the disadvantage will happen inevitably (with or without the affirmative plan), the argument gives no reason to reject the plan. Negative teams can defend the uniqueness of the disadvantages in a variety of ways. The best way is to provide evidence showing that the maintenance of the present course of action will prevent the disadvantage.

The final element of the disadvantage is the impact. The impact shows why the disadvantage is significantly harmful. It is not enough to show that the federal budget deficit will be increased, that trade relations with Europe will be strained, that pollution of the environment will be increased, or that civil liberties will be infringed. A properly designed impact argument goes one step further to show why these outcomes are significantly harmful. What bad things will happen to the United States or world economies if the federal budget deficit worsens? Why do we care about straining trade relations with Europe? So what if already high levels of environmental pollution are increased? How important are civil liberties? How big does the impact need to be? If the negative team is to win the debate, the impact must be bigger than the harm claim in the affirmative case.

Negative teams should always be aware that the affirmative team might attempt to turn around either the link or impact to the disadvantage. A *turn* argument attempts to remake the disadvantage into another advantage of adopting the affirmative case. The affirmative team might try to turn the link of a deficit disadvantage by showing that the plan would actually save money, lightening the burden on the federal budget.

An impact turn to the disadvantage would claim that an economic recession would actually be a good thing rather than the calamity envisioned by the negative team. In some debates the affirmative team chooses to defend the position of extreme environmental groups who welcome a recession as a means of cutting resource use throughout the world to preserve rain forests and prevent species extinction. Impact turn arguments are rare because they represent such a high-risk strategy; an impact turn brings the debate wholly to the argumentative ground chosen by the negative team. Many impact turn claims also attempt to defend counterculture positions that some judges would find repugnant.

There are three basic types of defenses against a link turn argument. The first (and best) defense is to link the disadvantage from something the case claims to do. If, for example, the case calls for an increase in the use of DDT to prevent malaria, the affirmative team cannot reverse the link. It has now foreclosed the option of arguing that the plan would actually decrease the use of DDT.

The second line of defense against a link turn is a good supply of negative evidence supporting the original link. If the affirmative team has proposed national health insurance, for example, the negative team might use a federal deficit disadvantage. Undoubtedly, the affirmative team will attempt to turn the link, claiming its national health insurance proposal will end up saving money. If the negative team decides to use a deficit disadvantage, it must have confidence in the strength of its evidence showing that national health insurance will be more expensive than the current system.

The third and final defense against a link turn is a strong uniqueness position, which serves to disprove the inherency for any affirmative link turn. If the negative uniqueness evidence is true, the disadvantage would be avoided in the present system. This means the link turn can never be an additional advantage for plan adoption because plan adoption is unnecessary to prevent the disadvantage. On the deficit disadvantage, for example, the negative uniqueness argument would show that no recession will occur so long as the federal budget deficit stays at or below current levels. Thus, there is no impact to a link turn. If the affirmative team proves that its national health insurance proposal would save money, the disadvantage just goes away.

FURTHER READING

Carlin, Diana, and Walter Ulrich. *Developing and Defending the Negative Position.* Indianapolis, IN: National Federation of High Schools, 1991.

Ulrich, Walter. *Developing and Defending Disadvantages.* Indianapolis, IN: National Federation of High Schools, 1990.

CHAPTER 8

THE ROLE OF THE COUNTERPLAN IN POLICY DEBATE

Debaters should be aware that counterplan strategies are discouraged by coaches and judges in some parts of the nation; be sure to consult with your coach before deciding whether it would be productive to use a counterplan.

The traditional approach of the negative team is to defend the present system. Sometimes, however, a negative team may decide that the present system cannot be persuasively defended; the alternative is a negative counterplan.

COUNTERPLAN REQUIREMENTS

The requirements for a counterplan are nontopicality, competitiveness, and advantage. The *nontopicality* requirement means that the counterplan must defend the nonresolution. The affirmative team offers its affirmative plan as an example of the resolution in an effort to prove the worth of the resolution. If a negative team has advocated a topical counterplan, it has simply given the judge another reason to vote for the resolution.

Nontopicality means that the counterplan must fail to meet one or more words in the resolution. If the resolution calls for "the U.S. federal government to substantially increase its funding for secondary education in the United States," a nontopical counterplan could do any of the following:

1. State governments could substantially increase their funding for secondary education;

2. The federal government could abolish its Department of Education and end all funding of secondary education;

3. The federal government could substantially increase its funding of elementary education.

In each of the foregoing examples, the counterplan advocates an action outside of the resolution.

The *competitiveness* requirement means that the counterplan must "force choice"—it must give the judge a reason to vote against the affirmative plan. Suppose a member of the legislature has proposed the legalization of gambling. During the debate another legislator rises in opposition, declaring that we should instead legalize the sale of marijuana for medicinal purposes. Anyone listening to the debate would quickly recognize that a proposal to legalize marijuana is irrelevant to the question of whether gambling should be legalized—the two proposals do not compete. The lack of competitiveness is demonstrated by the fact that we could easily do both; we could both legalize gambling and legalize the sale of marijuana.

The *advantage* requirement of the counterplan means that the counterplan must be shown to be superior to the plan in some way. If the counterplan merely offers the same level of advantage as the plan, then there is no compelling reason to reject the plan in favor of the counterplan. The counterplan might be superior because it better solves the harm cited by the affirmative. It might be superior because it avoids the disadvantages that the negative team has shown will apply to the affirmative plan. The counterplan might be superior because it has advantages that outweigh the advantages of the affirmative plan.

STANDARDS FOR COMPETITIVENESS

The two widely accepted standards for counterplan competitiveness are *mutual exclusivity* and *net benefits*. Both competitiveness standards answer the question "Why not do both the plan and the counterplan?" Mutual exclusivity says that the plan and counterplan "can not" coexist—it claims that it would be logically impossible to do both the plan and the counterplan. Net benefits say that the plan and counterplan "should not" coexist—it claims that joint adoption of the plan and counterplan would be less advantageous than the counterplan alone.

The mutual exclusivity standard shows some way in which the plan and counterplan are internally contradictory. Consider our earlier example of an affirmative plan proposing to substantially increase federal funding of secondary education and a negative counterplan proposing to ban all federal funding of secondary education. The negative team would argue that the counterplan forces choice because it is logically impossible to increase federal education funding *and* to ban all such funding.

Most counterplans, however, are not mutually exclusive with an affirmative plan. Consider the counterplan to increase state funding for secondary education; this proposal is not mutually exclusive with increasing federal education funding because it would certainly be possible to increase funding at both levels. Similarly, a proposal to increase funding for elementary education is not mutually exclusive with a proposal to increase funding for secondary education.

The most widely used standard for counterplan competition is net benefits. The net benefits standard claims that adoption of the counterplan alone is more advantageous than the adoption of both the plan and counterplan. Why not make this simpler? Why not just show that the counterplan has bigger advantages than the plan? The reason is that such a standard would give no reason to reject the plan. Consider the following situation: The affirmative team proposes to increase federal funding of education claiming that a more highly educated workforce would improve the ability of the United States to compete in the international marketplace. The negative team offers a counterplan proposing worldwide nuclear disarmament, claiming the advantage of avoiding nuclear war. The negative team says that its counterplan has "net benefits" because the advantage of avoiding nuclear war is bigger than the advantage of improving the health of the U.S. economy. Yet this counterplan gives no answer to the question that competitiveness must answer: "Why not do both?" Unless there is an answer to that question, a judge would simply say that the worldwide nuclear disarmament counterplan gives no reason to reject the affirmative plan to increase educational funding. The appropriate way to evaluate net benefits is always to weigh the counterplan alone against the plan plus the counterplan. Would nuclear disarmament alone be more advantageous than nuclear disarmament plus increased education spending? The answer is no; the counterplan gives no reason to reject the plan.

To establish a net benefit, the negative team must present one or more disadvantages that apply to the plan but not the counterplan. In our education example, the negative disadvantage might be federalism—an argument that federal control of education unconstitutionally infringes on the rights of states and localities. Another negative disadvantage might be deficit spending—an argument that any increases in the already large federal deficit will cause serious economic problems. The adoption of the state counterplan could solve the harm of the affirmative case (poor educational performance) while avoiding the federalism and deficit disadvantages. Thus the adoption of the counterplan alone would be more advantageous than the adoption of the plan plus the counterplan.

Some negative teams attempt to establish competitiveness by standards other than mutual exclusivity or net benefits. Philosophical competition is one such standard. The negative team might say, for example, that the plan advocates government regulation whereas the counterplan advocates promotion of private enterprise. But philosophical competition fails to force a choice between the plan and counterplan. There is no reason that competing philosophies can't coexist; the federal government could (and does) regulate business at the same time that it provides small business loans and otherwise promotes private enterprise.

Resource competition is another example of a weak standard. Consider the previous example of an affirmative plan proposing to increase federal funding for secondary education and a counterplan proposing increased federal funding for elementary education. The counterplan doesn't compete because it gives no reason to reject the affirmative plan. Yet the negative team might argue that federal funding for secondary education competes for the same scarce resources as funding for elementary education. This argument makes sense only if the negative team can prove that it is unwise to spend the money to fund both proposals—in other words, the negative team would need to present a federal spending disadvantage. The negative team would need to show why only the affirmative plan would cause this disadvantage. If all this can be proven, the negative team has really shown that the counterplan is net beneficial. A resource competition claim attempts a lazy argumentative shortcut.

The Permutation as a Test of Competition

The word *permutation* means to explore all possible combinations or groupings of a set of options. Affirmative teams often suggest permutations of the plan and counterplan as an illustration of how they could be desirably combined. By offering a permutation, the affirmative team is not really changing its affirmative plan; instead, it is showing why the counterplan doesn't truly compete with the affirmative plan. The permutation offers protection to the affirmative against counterplans, which are only artificially or superficially competitive.

Sometimes negative teams write the text of their counterplan in such a way that it bans the affirmative action; this ban of the affirmative action seems to make the counterplan mutually exclusive with the plan. Consider the following counterplan text:

1. State governments will substantially increase their funding of secondary education in the United States.

2. Federal funding of secondary education will remain at current levels.

The negative team could claim that its counterplan is mutually exclusive with the affirmative plan because it would be logically impossible to both substantially increase federal funding and to freeze it at current levels.

The permutation reaches inside the existing text of the plan and counterplan to show how the essence of the two proposals could desirably coexist. Sometimes an affirmative team will offer several permutations. In the education example, the affirmative could offer the following permutations:

1. Federal and state governments will simultaneously increase funding for secondary education; and

2. The federal government will increase funding for secondary education, but the state governments will determine how the increased funding will be used in their states.

The affirmative team would argue that if it wins that either of these permutations are desirable, then the competitiveness of the counterplan is defeated.

TYPES OF COUNTERPLANS

The *agent* counterplan is perhaps the most common counterplan type. The resolution forces the affirmative team to utilize the agent of action named in the resolution as the agency implementing its plan—in the policy debate resolutions of the past quarter century, this has always been "the United States federal government." An agent counterplan typically proposes an action very similar (or even identical) to the affirmative plan with the exception that the action is taken by someone other than the U.S. federal government. The alternative agent might be the 50 state governments or various international agencies (the United Nations, the World Bank, the Global Fund, and so on).

The *plan inclusive* counterplan (also called an *exception* counterplan) does the affirmative plan for all but some small subset of the population named in the resolution. Consider the 2007–2008 policy debate resolution calling on the U.S. federal government to "substantially increase its public health assistance to sub-Saharan Africa." An affirmative plan might propose a big increase in funding for HIV/AIDS prevention programs in sub-Saharan Africa. A negative counterplan might suggest doing the affirmative action everywhere *except* in Sudan, arguing that increased funding (of any type) for Sudan would be diverted to support genocide in Darfur. If a resolution calls for increasing federal funding of renewable energy alternatives, a negative counterplan could endorse all of the affirmative plan yet propose a ban on funding for wind power (perhaps arguing that too many birds are killed in windmills).

The *process* counterplan proposes to do the affirmative plan through a different procedure from the one specified in the plan. A *study* counterplan suggests that time should be allotted for certain studies to be completed before the affirmative action is taken. On the other hand, a *consultation* counterplan suggests that certain important allies (or domestic interest groups) should be given an opportunity to participate in the development of a proposal. Sometimes a debate resolution locks the affirmative plan into defending a certain procedure. Consider a resolution calling on the federal government to fund research into alternative energy resources, a negative team might counterplan with tax credits (encouraging private investment) as a superior way to achieve the same result.

The *uniqueness* counterplan is used by some negative teams in an effort to establish the uniqueness of a disadvantage. Suppose the negative team has introduced a federalism disadvantage, claiming that federal control of secondary education undermines a primary function of states and localities. The negative team fears, however, that the affirmative will claim the disadvantage is nonunique because of existing federal funding of secondary education. The negative team could eliminate this uniqueness argument by proposing a counterplan to end all federal funding of secondary education.

COUNTERPLAN MECHANICS

How does a negative team introduce a counterplan? First, the counterplan should be presented in the first negative constructive speech. The counterplan should include the following components.

- Counterplan text
- Nontopicality explanation
- Competition arguments
- Solvency or advantage arguments

The counterplan text should follow the same format as an affirmative plan. There should be a written text detailing what will be done, which agency will do it, and how it will be funded and enforced. Often the affirmative team asks to see the text of the counterplan.

The nontopicality explanation identifies the word or words in the resolution that the counterplan fails to meet. Sometimes the negative team reads definitions of the terms in the resolution to establish why the counterplan action lies outside of those terms.

The competition arguments explain the reason(s) the judge should choose between the plan and counterplan. Often the negative offers both mutual exclusivity and net benefits explanations. The mutual exclusivity explanation describes why it is logically impossible to adopt both the plan and the counterplan (the "can not" standard). The net benefits explanation (the "should not" standard) identifies the disadvantage arguments that apply to the plan but not the counterplan.

The solvency or advantage arguments explain why the advantages of the counterplan outweigh the plan advantages. Sometimes the negative team argues that the counterplan can solve the affirmative harms better than the affirmative plan itself. Suppose the affirmative team has proposed increased federal funding of renewable energy alternatives, arguing that the United States must overcome its dependence on oil from the Middle East. The negative team might counterplan with opening drilling in the Arctic National Wildlife Reserve, arguing that this would be the quickest and surest way for the United States to achieve energy independence.

It is not necessary, however, that the counterplan solve for the affirmative harm. The negative could, for example, argue that the advantage of the counterplan outweighs the affirmative harms. Consider the possibility of a negative counterplan calling for the

United States to join an international consortium to promote research into renewable energy alternatives. Such a counterplan wouldn't even pretend to solve for U.S. energy independence. Instead, the negative team could argue that massive government subsidies to U.S. energy companies will violate existing rules in the World Trade Organization against subsidizing domestic industry. The negative disadvantage would argue that domestic energy subsidies would cause a trade war, trigger another Arab oil embargo, and ultimately lead to world recession or depression. By engaging the world community in a cooperative endeavor, the counterplan would avoid an economic collapse while contributing to long-term energy solutions.

DECIDING WHEN TO USE A COUNTERPLAN

Before deciding to use a counterplan, ask the following questions:

- Will the judge accept a counterplan?

- Is the present system indefensible?

- Do inherency arguments offer an alternative to the counterplan?

- Am I confident that I understand counterplan theory?

- Does the counterplan seem intuitively persuasive?

First, does your judge like counterplans? How would you know this? In many tournaments judge philosophies are available to contestants. A common question on judge philosophy questionnaires asks what the judge thinks about counterplans. If you don't have access to judge philosophies, you might be able to ask the judge some questions before the round begins. If you are contemplating using a counterplan, you might simply ask the judge, "What do you think about counterplans?" If you know that your judge isn't comfortable with counterplans, it is simply unwise to introduce one.

Some debaters make the mistake of assuming that lay judges— meaning judges who have not coached or participated in debate—will dislike counterplans. You can make a counterplan seem persuasive to an inexperienced judge by simply explaining that you are opposing the resolution because a superior option is available. The fact that lay judges are unfamiliar with counterplan requirements can actually work to the advantage of the negative team.

A second consideration in choosing a counterplan is whether you are able to defend the present system. On some topics you might be personally convinced that the present system is indefensible. If the topic deals with public health in sub-Saharan Africa, for example, you might feel uncomfortable trying to argue that the present system is doing enough to prevent the spread of HIV/AIDS. If the topic deals with health care in the United States, you might be unwilling to argue that everyone has access to necessary health care. If the topic is renewable energy, you may truly believe that more needs to be done to save the environment. The counterplan option gives negative debaters the freedom to escape from defending the status quo.

A third consideration in deciding whether to use a counterplan is the availability of inherency options. In some debate leagues there is a strong bias against the use of counterplans. Your debate coach might discourage the use of counterplans. Inherency arguments offer a traditional alternative to the counterplan. Consider the example of an affirmative case that attempts to solve poverty in sub-Saharan Africa by substantially increasing U.S. foreign aid. The negative team in this debate wants to advocate the use of a microenterprise solution—the system of giving small loans pioneered by Muhammed Yunus when he created the Grameen Bank in Bangladesh. The power of the microenterprise solution is that it enables self-help, whereas foreign aid promotes perpetual dependence. Many negative teams would choose to advocate a microenterprise counterplan, but it could just as easily be advocated as an inherency argument. Many international agencies (including the United Nations Development Programme, the World Bank, and the International Monetary Fund) are already actively pursuing microenterprise solutions in sub-Saharan Africa. By defending these solutions already underway, the negative team avoids having to defend the competitiveness of a counterplan. In those debate leagues where counterplans are discouraged, learn to use the power of advocating inherency alternatives.

A fourth consideration in deciding to use a counterplan is how comfortable you are with counterplan theory. Experienced affirmative debaters pepper the counterplan with theory attacks, questioning competitiveness and suggesting numerous permutations. Many of these theoretical issues become the subject of questions in cross-examination. Use a counterplan only if you are mentally prepared to manage the theoretical complexities involved.

The final—and most important—consideration in deciding whether to use a counterplan is a question of persuasiveness. The counterplan should be a persuasive alternative to the affirmative plan. Try to characterize the difference between the plan and the counterplan in a single sentence. The plan advocates more government regulation and bureaucracy; the counterplan proposes to use the power of free enterprise. The plan locks sub-Saharan Africans into perpetual dependence on the United States; the counterplan promotes dignity and self-help. The plan strangles experimentation in secondary education by insisting on federal uniformity; the counterplan returns the power to control education to states and localities. Use a counterplan when, by doing so, you can create a persuasive alternative to the affirmative approach.

FURTHER READING

Ulrich, Walter. *Understanding the Counterplan*. Indianapolis, IN: National Federation of High Schools, 1992.

CHAPTER 9

CROSS-EXAMINATION TECHNIQUE IN POLICY DEBATE

In policy debate, each constructive speech is followed by three minutes of cross-examination. This time provides an opportunity for debaters to question sources of support, expose logical fallacies, or undermine the credibility of the opponent's argument.

THE MECHANICS OF CROSS-EXAMINATION

When a speaker finishes his cross-examination speech, that speaker remains at the podium to await questions. The cross-examiner comes to the front of the room to stand beside the podium, and both debaters face the judge during the cross-examination period. The cross-examiner is limited to the asking of questions as opposed to making statements or giving speeches. The cross-examiner has control of the time in the cross-examination period and can, therefore, politely cut off a long answer to ask another question.

Which speaker conducts the cross-examination? The simple way to remember this is that cross-examination is conducted by the person who does not speak next. The first affirmative speaker is cross-examined by the second negative speaker. The first negative speaker is cross-examined by the first affirmative speaker. The second affirmative speaker is cross-examined by the first negative speaker. The second negative speaker is cross-examined by the second affirmative speaker.

What is meant by *open* CX? In some debate leagues, cross-examination has evolved into an informal question-and-answer period during which either member of a team asks questions and answers are given by either member of the opposing team. This practice is specifically prohibited by the rules of some leagues. In debates sponsored by the Texas University Interscholastic League (UIL), for example, teams are disqualified (meaning they lose) if they engage in open CX. In traditional debate practice, questions are asked by one debater and answers are given exclusively by the debater who just completed her speech. Unless you are confident that open CX is allowed in your league, you should carefully follow the traditional debate practice.

THE PURPOSES OF CROSS-EXAMINATION

Just as in the legal system, the key purpose of cross-examination is to undermine the credibility of the opposing side. The means for undermining credibility include the following:

- Exposing contradictions
- Questioning sources of support
- Showing that evidence fails to support claims
- Demonstrating unfamiliarity with relevant facts
- Illustrating an opponent's inability to clarify a position

Contradictory positions commonly occur in policy debate because of the sheer number of arguments that must be answered. Spotting contradictions simply requires careful listening skills and keen intelligence. There are, however, some natural places to look for contradictions. One such place is the intersection between topicality answers and answers to disadvantages. To demonstrate topicality, an affirmative team often has to characterize its plan as making a big change ("substantial" or "significant"), yet to avoid disadvantage links, the affirmative claims that its plan hardly makes any change at all. You can find an example of this type of potential contradiction in Appendix A, "Policy Debate in Final Round." To defeat the topicality argument, the affirmative team says that it will more than double the number of persons serving in AmeriCorps. However, to avoid the spending disadvantage, the affirmative argues that the level of federal spending would barely change.

Affirmative debaters can often find contradictions between negative inherency arguments and disadvantages. Many poorly designed inherency arguments claim that the present system is already doing most of what the affirmative team proposes to do, yet disadvantages claim that if we were ever to do the affirmative proposal, the world as we know it would come to an end. Many inherency arguments undercut the uniqueness of disadvantages.

Some negative disadvantages are especially likely to contradict other arguments. Consider the growth bad disadvantage: this disadvantage claims that increased economic growth will cause environmental devastation, outweighing the temporary advantages of a stronger economy. What would happen if, in the same round, the negative team presented a spending disadvantage with the claim that increasing the federal deficit would cause economic recession or depression? This disadvantage is premised on the assumption that economic growth is a good thing.

Another potential purpose of cross-examination is undermining the source credibility of the other team's evidence. In a typical policy debate, both teams read evidence supporting their positions on nearly every argument. How is a judge to decide which evidence is the more persuasive? Cross-examination can provide assistance to the judge in this regard. Suppose you have read supporting evidence from a professor of government at Harvard University and your opponent has presented opposing evidence described only as "Smith in 2008." You have looked at your opponent's argument brief and, therefore, you know that Jim Smith is the creator of an Internet blog. Cross-examination offers a prime opportunity to weaken the credibility of your opponent's position.

Cross-examination can also be used to highlight the gap between an opponent's argumentative claims and the supporting evidence. Unfortunately, debaters seem to have a natural tendency to over-claim their evidence. The argument label for the disadvantage impact might say, "The next terrorist attack will trigger an all-out nuclear war," but the supporting evidence just says that terrorists are trying to gain access to nuclear weapons. Unfortunately, debaters and judges often just write the argument labels on their flowsheets. Cross-examination offers an opportunity to expose this difference between an opponent's claim and the evidence used to support the claim.

Another way to undermine the credibility of an opponent in cross-examination is by demonstrating unfamiliarity with relevant facts. Suppose that the negative team has presented a spending disadvantage with the claim that any additional federal spending will cause a collapse of confidence in financial markets, plunging the world into recession or depression. The negative brink evidence is from five months ago. Because you keep up with the news, you have evidence that just last week the president signed a multi-billion-dollar supplemental spending bill for disaster relief. You would set up this cross-examination sequence by asking your opponent whether he is aware of the recent supplemental spending bill. Then you would ask about the date of the brink evidence in the disadvantage. The question sequence would culminate with a leading question: "So are you willing to agree, then, that the disadvantage is nonunique?"

A final way to undermine the credibility of an opposing argument is by demonstrating the opponent's inability to clarify her position. Sometimes debaters simply read briefs that have been handed to them, even though they do not themselves understand the argument they are making. With experience, you will be able to recognize these situations. Suppose your opponent has just read a summer institute brief on the biopower kritik from the introduction to Michel Foucault's *The Archaeology of Knowledge*. One of the key quotations reads as follows: "We must renounce all those themes whose function is to ensure the infinite continuity of discourse and its secret presence to itself in the interplay of a constantly recurring absence." A normal human being, having heard this sentence, could only respond with "huh?" Have your opponent slowly read the quotation and then explain in her own words the meaning of the statement.

Although the central purpose of cross-examination is to undermine the credibility of opposing arguments, it has a practical purpose as well—you want to provide preparation time for your partner. In policy debate, the typical preparation time limit is five minutes per team. But the timekeeper (which is usually also the judge) does not start counting down your preparation time until the end of cross-examination. This means that if you use your full time in cross-examination, your partner has three minutes of preparation time that does not count against your allotted five minutes. Accordingly, your partner will not be happy if you choose to end cross-examination after only one minute because the timekeeper will immediately begin subtracting preparation time from your remaining total.

CARDINAL SINS OF CROSS-EXAMINATION

A trial attorney understands that he can turn off jurors by acting like a jerk. The same thing happens within the debate context. Judges are just people—like all people, they will be affected by your demeanor. If you browbeat an opponent in cross-examination, you can make the judge want to vote against you. Nobody likes a bully. Even if you win the debate, the judge is likely to lower your speaker points. You can maintain your likeable image if you stay away from the four cardinal sins of cross-examination.

The first cardinal sin is talking over an opponent. When you ask a question, provide a reasonable opportunity for your opponent to answer. If you are speaking at the same time as your competitor, the judge will not understand either you or your opponent. It is true that the questioner is in control of the cross-examination period, but it sometimes happens that the respondent's answers are overly long. In such circumstances you should be assertive but also courteous. You can interrupt by saying something like "Thanks, I understand your point. But let me ask you this ...." If you have provided a reasonable opportunity to answer and your opponent is simply wasting time, the judge will not blame you for interrupting.

The second cardinal sin is name-calling. Don't label arguments as "stupid," "crazy," or "insane." Treat your opponents and their arguments with respect. Focus on the weaknesses of your opponent's arguments rather than making personal attacks.

The third cardinal sin is refusing your opponent the opportunity to explain an answer. You can ask for a "yes" or "no" answer, but don't turn this request into a demand.

The final cardinal sin is the making of speeches in cross-examination. The cross-examiner is limited to the asking of questions. When you attempt to gain an advantage by making new answers to arguments or presenting evidence, you accomplish nothing other than to demonstrate your inexperience at cross-examination.

Advanced Cross-Examination Techniques

Debaters wanting to improve their cross-examination skills can learn from the tips offered by trial attorneys.

Prefer closed to open-ended questions. A closed question asks for a limited amount of information that can be provided in just a few words. The most limiting type of a closed question is a "yes or no" question: "Will the affirmative plan establish a new federal agency?" But closed questions need not follow a "yes or no" format. A question like "How much will your plan cost?" is also a closed question; it requests a specific unit of information that requires only a few words to provide.

An open-ended question simply provides a prompt to talk without limiting the range of possible answers. Following is an example of an open-ended question: "So what is wrong with relying on oil from the Middle East?" Such a question provides an opportunity to your opponent to reemphasize the points made in the previous speech.

Closed questions have numerous advantages over open-ended ones. First, you can better control the time in cross-examination and because the answers are brief, you can ask many more questions than in the open-ended format. Second, you prevent your opponents from wandering into subject matters of their own choosing. Third, your cross-examination seems well organized and maintains a focus. Although your opponent might answer a closed question with a lengthy, wandering response, the judge will usually see through such methods. By exposing nonresponsiveness, you undermine the credibility of the opposing argument.

Know where you are going before you start. Trial attorneys are told that they should never ask a question to which they don't already know the answer. Consider a situation in which you are trying to undermine the credibility of a source read by the other team. Open this line of questioning only if you know full well that your source is much better qualified than your opponent's source.

Ask leading questions. Leading questions are ones that suggest an answer. The most powerful form of a leading question is what attorney Larry Pozner, past president of the National Association of Criminal Defense Lawyers, calls a "declarative question." A declarative question makes a statement but carries a vocal inflection that identifies it as a question. Suppose you are negative and are trying to establish the link to a spending disadvantage. Consider the following questions:

- Question 1: How will your plan be funded?

- Question 2: So, will your plan be funded from general federal revenues?

- Question 3: Your plan will be funded from general federal revenues?

Question 1 is an open-ended question that threatens to waste time. You should know the answer you want to hear, so suggest it. Question 2 is a leading question. Like all leading questions, it makes it more likely that the respondent will answer in the way you suggest. Question 3 is what Pozner, author of the 2004 book *Cross-Examination: Science and Techniques* calls a declarative question. It creates the most forceful push in the direction of the answer you believe should be forthcoming. Questions that begin with *what*, *why*, or *explain* are almost certain to be open-ended questions, offering to turn over control of the questioning period to the respondent.

Avoid compound questions. The experienced questioner wants to keep the focus on one issue at a time. Consider the following question: "How much will your plan cost, and how will it be funded?" When you ask a compound question, the judge seldom holds the respondent responsible for answering each of the elements of the question. You are really inviting your opponent to set up her own defense of the cost issue.

Focus on facts, not conclusions. Inexperienced debaters think the goal of cross-examination is to trick the opponent into admitting that his case is not inherent, that the disadvantage has no impact, or that he really should concede the debate. Such concessions might happen once in your debate career, but you will waste many a cross-examination period in the search for this type of magic bullet. As Larry Pozner says, "It is far safer to let the jury reach its own conclusions based on the facts rather than demanding that conclusion from a hostile witness."

Bring the results of cross-examination into your speeches. Judges don't keep track of the cross-examination period on their flowsheets. When the judge makes the decision at the end of a round, she does so by tracing key arguments on her flowsheets. If you succeeded in establishing important facts in your cross-examination, you must mention this in your speeches themselves if you expect the cross-examination to have an impact on the judge's decision.

FURTHER READING

Brown, Peter. *The Art of Questioning: Thirty Maxims of Cross Examination.* Macmillan: New York, 1987.

Ehrlich, J. W. *The Lost Art of Cross Examination.* G. P. Putnam's Sons: New York, 1970.

Pozner, Larry S., and Roger J. Dodd. *Cross Examination Science and Techniques, 2nd Ed.* Matthew Bender & Associates: Newark, NJ, 2004.

CHAPTER 10

CRITIQUES IN POLICY DEBATE

Some policy debaters are experimenting with new argument forms, seeking to reject traditional models such as stock issues or the policymaking. The *kritik* (a German term for *critique*) attempts to use various forms of postmodern philosophy to expose destructive assumptions made by the opposing team. This chapter explains these new challenges to the traditional approaches in policy debate and presents strategies for defeating them.

By the time you reach the end of this chapter, you will, perhaps, discern that I am not a fan of critiques or other argumentative techniques for undermining the policymaking focus of policy debate.

WHAT IS THE CRITIQUE?

The critique means something quite specific. The *critique* (critical theory) got its name from German philosophers associated with the Frankfurt School, which explains why it is sometimes identified by the German word *kritik*. The Frankfurt School philosophers (Theodor Adorno, Walter Benjamin, Herbert Marcuse, Max Horkheimer, Jurgen Habermas, and others) shared an association with the Institute of Social Research in Frankfurt, Germany. All the

Frankfurt School philosophers were advocates of Karl Marx's theory of historical determinism. This theory held that the excesses of capitalism will inevitably lead to its collapse, allowing labor—the only ultimate value—to result in the victory of the proletariat over the bourgeoisie. Thus, the future of the world will feature an inevitable replacement of capitalism with communism. The Frankfurt School toiled, however, with the question of why the communist transition, if inevitable, seems to be so slow in coming. One common answer is that capitalist power persists because it has succeeded in masking its oppressive power. Capitalists mask their evil intentions by using progressive symbols, deceiving the workers into continuing to accept their chains.

Consider some U.S.-based examples of masking. Marxists believed that the Great Depression of the 1930s was capitalism's last gasp—it should have represented the death knell of capitalism. Yet Franklin Delano Roosevelt, with his seemingly progressive moves, masked the evils of capitalism by providing temporary jobs through the Works Progress Administration and Civilian Conservation Corps. The creation of the Social Security system further pacified the masses. Keep in mind that Marxists have not given up on the theory of historical determinism—they still believe that communism will inevitably triumph over capitalism. But the transition to communism will come sooner if the prophets of the movement can succeed in unmasking capitalist symbols. Thus, for Marxist theorists, any effort of Western governments to do good can only be for the purpose of masking evil intentions. The critique, therefore, becomes the ultimate good is really bad argument. Anything that the United States federal government does that seems (on the surface) to be good is actually bad because it only serves to delay the inevitable transition to a communist future.

Defenders of various postmodern critiques might argue that their particular theorist has moved beyond the Marxist grand narrative. Yet if you look under the hood, almost every postmodern theorist (Foucault, Derrida, Lyotard, Agamben, Baudrillard, Lacan, Kristeva, Irigaray, Deleuze, and numerous others) unabashedly pursues the Marxist narrative. The purpose of their critique is to unmask the evils of capitalism so that it can more quickly be overthrown.

I draw the connection between the postmodern critique and Marxism not to tar-and-feather postmodern theorists with a Marxist label. Serious scholars should certainly be free to debate the merits of Marxism. I draw the connection so that the debater can understand why postmodern theorists are so concerned with the *unmasking* of motives and assumptions.

The profound skepticism of the postmodern theorist leads to the conclusion that any seemingly beneficent act of U.S. policymakers must have the motive of masking the evils of capitalism. Thus, the seemingly good act becomes bad because it perpetuates the violence and evil of capitalism, giving it an extended life in the United States and undeserved credibility in the recipient countries. Whatever undermines Western power and influence is, therefore, ultimately good. This prompted one of the leading French postmodern theorists, Jean Baudrillard, to make the following comment about the 9/11 terrorist attacks: The entire world wanted the event to happen. In essence, it was the terrorists who committed the deed but it is we who wished for it (as quoted in *The Australian*, Oct. 12, 2004, p. 29).

How Are Critiques Used in Policy Debates?

Consider the following example: An affirmative case calls for a doubling of U.S. public health assistance to help provide safe water and sanitation services in sub-Saharan Africa. The affirmative case, however, uses the language of human rights, arguing that access to safe water is a basic human right. The negative team bases its attack on the savage/victim/savior (SVS) critique made famous by Makau Mutua, a law professor at the State University of New York at Buffalo. According to Mutua in his 2002 book *Human Rights: A Political and Cultural Critique*, the international human rights campaign is nothing but a Trojan horse: the effort of Westerners to recolonialize the savages in Africa and elsewhere. Westerners portray Africans as victims and themselves as saviors.

In Mutua's book, he says that human rights can be seen as a project for the redemption of the redeemers, in which whites who are privileged as a people—who have historically visited untold suffering and savage atrocities against nonwhites—redeem themselves by "defending" and "civilizing" "lower," "unfortunate," and "inferior" peoples (p. 14). Thus, human rights campaigns are really a form of pathology—the pathology of self-redemption.

Simply put, any effort made by the United States to do something good in Africa is really bad because all such efforts advance the cause of capitalist free enterprise. By this logic, saving lives in sub-Saharan Africa is less important than the fact that allowing the United States to pose as Africa's savior will advance the cause of free market capitalism (thus recolonizing Africa). If debate judges are willing to buy this argument, notice how easy winning becomes for negative debaters. The negative team need only prove that an affirmative case is trying to advance human rights (or even just to save lives) in sub-Saharan Africa.

What's Wrong with Critiques?

First, critiques circumvent the logical processes for decision that have made policy debate such a powerful tool for teaching critical thinking skills. The critique doesn't operate within any of the stock issues. It totally ignores harm, inherency, and solvency. It fails as a disadvantage argument because it offers no reason that the affirmative plan uniquely causes the critique. U.S. federal government programs promote free market capitalism regardless of whether the plan is adopted. Many policy debaters and judges have moved beyond the stock issues decision model to policymaking, hypothesis testing, or some other decision paradigm. Yet the critique attempts to operate outside of all such models. In fact, most postmodern critiques attack the very notion of linear logic as an inherently destructive Western mindset.

Second, critiques are internally contradictory—the only thing they are certain about is that there is no such thing as certainty.

Third, critique theorists become unwitting allies of ultraconservative philosophies in Western societies. Postmodernism takes a cynical view toward any efforts to help the poor or downtrodden because these efforts simply mask the deeper crimes of capitalism. Ironically, such postmodern philosophies end up joining forces with ultraconservatives who advocate inaction in the face of misery.

Fourth, the value relativism inherent in postmodern critiques enables despotism and oppression. Most postmodern theorists argue that all value hierarchies are hypocritical—they are merely examples of choice posing as truth. This cynical relativism leads to the conclusion that the Rwandan genocide is really no worse than the imagined violence of free enterprise capitalism. Postmodern theorists Martin Heidegger and Paul De Man defended Hitler's final solution during the Nazi era. Michel Foucault chose to become an enthusiastic advocate of Iran's turn toward Islamic radicalism. In the ideal world of the postmodern theorist, democratic capitalism would be replaced by a Marxist utopia. We have a few examples of efforts to construct Marxist utopias: the Soviet Union, China, Cuba, and the various Eastern European dictatorships. All such efforts have not just failed—they have been remarkable failures.

A final problem with the postmodern critique is the use of nearly incomprehensible jargon. I have taught graduate courses in rhetorical theory where I have assigned students to read the key works of Michel Foucault, Jacques Derrida, Jean Baudrillard, and other postmodern theorists. Even for students with an outstanding background in classical and modern rhetorical theory, it is almost impossible to meaningfully interpret postmodern texts. Yet critique arguments routinely invite high school students to make sense of arguments that confuse many Ph.D. candidates in philosophy.

Perhaps the most remarkable demonstration of the difficulty of understanding postmodern thought is the publication in the Spring/Summer 1996 edition of *Social Text* of an article by Alan Sokal, professor of physics at New York University. Professor Sokal became convinced that postmodern theorists were engaged in an academic fraud: using incomprehensible language designed to confuse others into thinking that it is profound. Sokal tested this theory by constructing a jibberish-filled article for submission to a leading peer-reviewed postmodern journal, *Social Text*. His article was titled "Transcending the Boundaries: Towards a Hermeneutics of Quantum Gravity." Consider the following sentence from his article: "I suggest that pi (π) isn't constant and universal, but relative to the position of an observer, and is, therefore, subject to ineluctable historicity." The language of the article was intentionally incomprehensible, yet it was selected for publication.

Immediately after publication, Sokal revealed the hoax. He tried to convince the editors of *Social Text* to publish his reaction to their decision to publish his article, but they declined to further embarrass themselves.

Alan Sokal and Jean Bricmont, a professor at the University Catholique de Louvain in France, wrote a 1998 book titled *Fashionable Nonsense: Postmodern Intellectuals' Abuse of Science*. This book argues that the language used by postmodern theorists is difficult to understand precisely because it is without meaning:

> What is worse, in our opinion, is the adverse effect that abandoning clear thinking and clear writing has on teaching and culture. Students learn to repeat and to embellish discourses that they only barely understand. They can even, if they are lucky, make an academic career out of it by becoming expert in the manipulation of an erudite jargon. After all, one of us managed, after only three months of study, to master the postmodern lingo well enough to publish an article in a prestigious journal. As commentator Katha Pollitt astutely noted, the comedy of the Sokal incident is that it suggests that even the postmodernists don't really understand one another's writing and make their way through the text by moving from one familiar name or notion to the next like a frog jumping across a murky pond by way of lily pads (p. 206).

What Are Language Critiques?

In a semifinal round of a major college tournament a few years ago, one team read a piece of evidence using the word *blackmail*. The opposing team at that point chose to abandon every other argument in the debate round and launched a language critique argument based on a claim that the word *blackmail* uses a white is good/black is bad stereotype. The negative team won the debate with the argument that the opposing team should be punished for using a word that perpetuates a racial stereotype. In the world of the language critique, the most obvious offenders are teams using racist or sexist language (*policeman* rather than *police officer*, *he* rather than *he or she*, and so on).

The philosophical background for the language critique arises from two primary sources: the Sapir-Whorf Hypothesis and postmodern deconstruction. The Sapir-Whorf Hypothesis refers to the early twentieth-century work of Yale University linguists Edward Sapir and Benjamin Whorf. The hypothesis holds that language structures thought.

Deconstruction—the philosophical brainchild of Jacques Derrida, Paul De Man, and postmodern theorists—attempts to search in the corners of a text (in our case, meaning evidence cards) for indications of cultural biases and presuppositions. Defenders of deconstruction believe that oppressive structures attempt to hide themselves in language but that a careful critic can spot the vestiges of these structures. This explains why a language critique might seem to react to a single chance word or expression in such a vehement way.

Debaters should argue that the language critique chills meaningful dialogue. Consider the following statement from Edward Lucas in the June 9, 1991, issue of *The Independent*:

> The fear that certain words and opinions will bring an unjustified charge of racism chills the intellectual climate. Even at conservative, prosperous Princeton, a survey found between a half and two thirds of undergraduates did not feel they could speak freely in the classroom. What bothers me is that this has become an alternative to critical thought, said Paul Starr, a sociologist at Princeton. With respect to race and gender, there is a climate which inhibits free discussion. (p. 13)

Morris Wolfe, writing in the January 31, 1991, issue of *The Globe and Mail*, likened the language critique to George Orwell's thought police:

> Thought Police, who want it all now, seem worried about every -ism but dogmatism. Their moral terrorism seems indistinguishable from the tactics of a Meir Kahane or a Louis Farrakhan. I find especially offensive the manipulation of students by their faculty and fellow students. As one American professor puts it, You have to let students say the most outrageous and stupid things. To get people to think and talk, to question their own ideas, you don't regulate their speech.

There's far more intolerance these days among the educated than among the uneducated. Isn't it supposed to be the other way around? The tyranny of politically correct thinking is a scary thing.

How Do You Answer a Critique?

When critiques are used, three essential elements come into play:

1. Framework

2. Link

3. Implications

The *framework* for analysis determines the role that the critique should play in policy debate; these arguments are designed to determine the legitimacy or illegitimacy of the critique as a debate argument. Critique opponents should argue that the critique is an illegitimate debate argument.

Link arguments attempt to determine whether the critique has anything to do with the advocacy of the opposing team. In many instances a critique is simply an indictment of the present system, leaving it unclear what the argument has to do with a particular affirmative case.

Implication arguments compare the impact of the critique to other arguments in the round. Even if the critique is true (an ironic term given that most postmodern critiques argue that truth doesn't exist), why should it cause a judge to vote against the opposing team?

Cross-examination time is very important in a debate round when dealing with critiques. Consider, for example, the savage/victim/savior critique described earlier in this chapter. This critique argues that increased public health assistance to provide safe water and sanitation in sub-Saharan Africa should be rejected because the case implies that Africans are victims needing to be saved. This savior metaphor promotes the recolonization of Africa. An affirmative debater can have great fun in cross-examination asking the negative debater to explain the meaning of this critique. Consider the possibilities:

- Please explain how providing assistance for safe water and sanitation recolonizes Africa.

- How many colonies did the United States have in sub-Saharan Africa?

- So, any effort to save lives in Africa should be avoided?

- Are you, then, advocating that the United States should stop all forms of assistance to Africa?

- Are you saying that the governments in sub-Saharan Africa can, without assistance, solve the problem of unsafe water, or are you saying that you just don't care if they die?

- Is the problem with the language or with the act? In other words, is it okay to preserve lives so long as we don't use the word *saved* or *savior*?

- You say that we don't dare refer to sub-Saharan Africans as victims—are you implying, then, that they are themselves to blame for their poverty?

- You say that colonization was responsible for most of the problems plaguing Africa, yet are you now saying that the colonizers have *no* obligation to help address these problems?

The truth of the matter is that most critiques are so counterintuitive that they fall under their own weight if inquisitive debaters can force the proponents of the critiques to explain them. So long as the debate remains at the jibberish level (the reification of social alienation, or we have to choose between Habermasian discourse and the subtextual paradigm of context), the critique is allowed to continue to wear the emperor's new clothes.

FINAL THOUGHTS ON CRITIQUES

Most debate teams who run critiques use the same briefs from year to year, ignoring the specifics of the particular debate topic. Often it is the case that critique briefs were originally written for college debate topics but have now found their way into the hands of high school debaters.

Advocates of critiques will argue that because fiat is only an artificial creation, the outcome of a debate will have no real impact on the world in any case. Critique advocates say that debaters should spend their time in debates worrying only about those things they can directly do something about, namely, their own attitudes toward important subjects such as the evils of capitalism. From this perspective, the political is not as important as the personal. Regardless of the role of fiat, however, debaters should be willing to take some responsibility for their own personal advocacy. Advocates of a savage/victim/savior critique really are saying that it is more important that the United States admit its complicity in colonialization than it is to help the people of sub-Saharan Africa. Opponents of a savage/victim/savior critique really are saying that it is more important to help the people of sub-Saharan Africa than it is to worry about who is to blame for colonialization. Why is it more important to engage in the rhetoric of blaming and guilt assignment than to advocate for helping people who truly are in need?

The intellectual influence of the postmodern critique is on the decline in the academic world at the very time that it seems to be catching on in the debate community. Emily Eakin, writing in the October 17, 2004, issue of *The New York Times*, said the following:

> Mr. Derrida outlived fellow theorists Louis Althusser, Roland Barthes, Pierre Bourdieu, Michel Foucault, Jacques Lacan, and Gilles Deleuze, but signs of theory's waning influence had been accumulating around him for years. Since the early 1990s, the grand intellectual paradigms with which these men were prominently associated—Marxism, psychoanalysis, structuralism—had steadily lost adherents and prestige. The world had changed but not necessarily in the ways some of big theory's fervent champions had hoped. Ideas once greeted as potential catalysts for revolution began to seem banal, irrelevant or simply inadequate to the task of achieving social change. (p. IV-12)

I frequently hear prominent college debate coaches lament what critiques have done to college debate. For high school policy debate, it is not yet too late. Critique debates are still rare events in many parts of the country. Many judges would like an opportunity to vote against critiques, but they have to have substantive answers allowing them to justify their votes. Many users of critiques in high school debates win purely from the shock value of their arguments; they win because the affirmative team is confused and unsure how to answer a critique based in nearly incomprehensible language.

FURTHER READING

Cheshier, David. "Defending Pragmatism as a Defense Against Certain Critiques." *The Rostrum*. March 2002. http://debate. uvm.edu/NFL/rostrumlib/cxCheshier0302.pdf.

Heidt, Jenny. "Performance Debates: How to Defend Yourself." *The Rostrum*. April 2003. http://debate.uvm.edu/NFL/rostrumlib/ cxHeidtcx0403.pdf.

Schwartzmann, Roy. "Postmodernism and the Practice of Debate." *The Rostrum*. March 2000. http://debate.uvm.edu/NFL/ rostrumlib/SchwartzmanMar%2700.pdf.

CHAPTER 11

AN INTRODUCTION TO LINCOLN-DOUGLAS DEBATE

Lincoln-Douglas debate is one-on-one debate, meaning that a student from one school debates a student from another school. Speakers who are affirmative deliver three speeches. The first of these speeches is called a *constructive speech,* so-named because the contestant is constructing his case. The affirmative debater delivers two rebuttal speeches in which no new arguments are allowed. The purpose of these rebuttal speeches is to answer the arguments made by the negative debater and to advance key affirmative arguments.

The negative debater presents two speeches: a constructive speech and a rebuttal. Why does the affirmative debater have three speeches while the negative debater has only two? The reason is that the affirmative side must have both the first and last speech. Also, the negative speeches are longer, meaning both debaters end up speaking for the same total amount of time.

THE FORMAT OF LINCOLN-DOUGLAS DEBATE

A single round of Lincoln-Douglas debate includes five speeches and two cross-examination periods.

Constructive Speeches

Affirmative Constructive Speech	6 minutes
Cross-Examination by Negative Debater	3 minutes
Negative Constructive Speech	7 minutes
Cross-Examination by Affirmative	3 minutes

Rebuttal Speeches

First Affirmative Rebuttal	4 minutes
Negative Rebuttal	6 minutes
Second Affirmative Rebuttal	3 minutes
Total Preparation Time for Each Team	4 minutes*
Total Time Required for Completion of One Round:	36 minutes

Some tournaments have differing amounts of preparation time; four minutes is the time allotted in National Forensic League tournaments, including the national final tournament.

How Do You Know Whether You Will Be Affirmative or Negative?

In each round of debate there is an affirmative debater and a negative debater. The affirmative debater says yes to the resolution, while the negative debater says no. Suppose the resolution is "Resolved: A just society ought not use the death penalty as a form of punishment." The affirmative team must support the resolution and the negative team must oppose it.

All Lincoln-Douglas debate competition involves switching of sides, meaning that each debater must be prepared to debate both affirmative and negative. You won't know whether you will be affirmative or negative in the first round of the tournament until a few minutes before the tournament begins. The debate tab room (meaning the persons assigned by the sponsoring organization to administer the tournament) post a schedule shortly before the round begins. This round schedule lets each debater know whether she will be affirmative or negative, which opponent she will debate, the name of the judge, and the room in which the debate will occur.

By the end of the preliminary rounds of the tournament, you will have been assigned to the same number of affirmative as negative rounds. If you do well enough to qualify for elimination rounds, sides are determined in a slightly different manner. If the two debaters meeting have not previously met in preliminary rounds, a coin toss determines who is affirmative and negative. If you win the coin toss, you are allowed to choose affirmative or negative. If you have already met the debater you are assigned to debate, you switch sides in the second meeting.

WHAT IS PREPARATION TIME?

Each debater in a round of Lincoln-Douglas debate has a set amount of preparation time. For National Forensic League tournaments, the preparation time is four minutes per debater. Many state and local tournaments specify different amounts of preparation time, so be sure to check the tournament invitation.

If the preparation time is four minutes, this does not mean the speaker receives four minutes before each speech; it means the debater has four minutes of total preparation time. If all four minutes are used before the first speech, no preparation time is left for the remaining speech. This means you are expected to rise to speak immediately after the previous speaker takes her seat. If you are not ready, your speech time still begins immediately.

The strategy in proper use of preparation time is simple—save as much time as possible for the period just before your final rebuttal. As you become more experienced in debate, you will discover that you are able to save most of your preparation time for the crucial last rebuttal.

HOW ARE DEBATE RESOLUTIONS SELECTED?

Most Lincoln-Douglas competitions use the national topic selected by the National Forensic League (NFL). These topics originate with the work of the NFL Lincoln-Douglas Wording Committee. In each academic year, the committee carefully words ten possible Lincoln-Douglas resolutions. Those ten topics are then submitted for a vote (now using an online voting procedure) where each NFL member school is asked to choose one of the ten resolutions for each two-month period of competition: September-October, November-December, January-February, March-April, and a topic for the national NFL tournament). The NFL doesn't release a Lincoln-Douglas topic until approximately one month before the debate on that topic is to begin. Each topic is announced on the NFL website (www.nflonline.org).

Although the NFL topics are used in most national and regional debate tournaments, some state competitions specify their own topics. In the state of Texas, for example, the University Interscholastic League (UIL) selects its own Lincoln-Douglas debate topics. Rather than changing the topic every two months, the UIL announces one topic for the fall semester and another topic for the spring semester. The safest way to know the topic that will be used at a given tournament is by consulting the invitation for that tournament. The tournament invitation will indicate that the topic in use will be the NFL September-October resolution, the spring UIL resolution, and so on. The tournament invitations will either list the actual wording of the resolution or let you know the web address where you can discover the wording of the topic.

HALLMARKS OF LINCOLN-DOUGLAS DEBATE COMPETITION

Lincoln-Douglas competition began in the 1970s as an event sponsored by the NFL. The number of participants in Lincoln-Douglas debates now equals or exceeds those in traditional policy debate. In 2007, the Executive Council of the NFL provided a definition of Lincoln-Douglas debate. The following paragraphs are drawn from the NFL's official description of this form of debate.

Lincoln-Douglas debate focuses on a proposition of value. A proposition of value concerns itself with what ought to be instead of what is.

A value is defined as an ideal held by individuals, societies, and governments. Lincoln-Douglas debaters develop argumentation based upon a values perspective. Accordingly, debaters should focus on reasoning to support a general principle instead of offering particular plans or counterplans. Debaters may, however, offer examples to illustrate how a certain value would play out in practice.

The hallmarks of Lincoln-Douglas debate include:

1. parallel burdens
2. value structure
3. argumentation
4. cross examination
5. effective delivery

PARALLEL BURDENS

Parallel burdens means that both the affirmative and negative have the responsibility to show that their side of the resolution is more desirable as a general principle. The affirmative side does not have some absolute standard of proof that it must meet to prove the resolution is always true. The topics selected for Lincoln-Douglas debate are chosen precisely because they are controversial; such questions of value can never be shown to be entirely true or false. Good value resolutions are debatable. Neither debater should be held to a standard of absolute proof. Neither debater will be able to prove the complete validity or invalidity of the resolution. The better debater is the one who, on the whole, proves her side of the resolution more valid as a general principle.

The burden of proof in Lincoln-Douglas debate means that each debater has the responsibility to provide proof in support of the value claims they make. There is no presumption for either side in a value debate resolution. Both the affirmative and the negative debater have a burden of proof.

The burden of clash means that each debater has an equal responsibility to answer the arguments made by the other side. Judges are instructed that they should not reward a debater for presenting a speech that completely ignores the arguments made by her opponent.

The burden of the resolution means that each debater has an obligation to argue the resolution as it is. The question of whether the resolution is worthy of debate is irrelevant to the outcome of a given round of competition. Negative debaters should not be rewarded for arguing some resolution other than the one that has been announced in the tournament invitation as the focus of debate.

VALUE STRUCTURE

Lincoln-Douglas debate centers on a value structure or framework. This value structure serves the function of providing a central focus for the resolution and offering the judge a method for determining or evaluating this central focus. The Lincoln-Douglas framework includes the following elements: a statement of the resolution, definitions of key terms, a value premise (or core value), and a value criterion (or standard).

The affirmative should offer contextual or dictionary definitions that offer reasonable ground for debate. Contextual definition means an implied definition based on the actual usage of the terms. A contextual definition of domestic violence might be a form of child discipline involving verbal abuse. The negative has the option to challenge the affirmative definitions of terms and to offer counter-definitions.

A *value premise* or *core value* is an ideal held by individuals, societies, governments, and so on that serves as the highest goal to be protected, respected, maximized, advanced, or achieved. This means that debaters choose a value that, in their opinions, best captures the essence of the resolution and provide a focus for argumentation.

The value criterion or value standard provides one or more of the following:

1. It explains how the value should be protected, respected, maximized, advanced, or achieved.

2. It measures whether a given side or argument protects, respects, maximizes, advances, or achieves the value.

3. It evaluates the relevance and importance of an argument in the context of the round. Each debater should clearly show the relationship between the value premise (core value) and the criterion (standard for evaluation).

In some debates there are competing value structures, with each side presenting its own value premise and standard. In other instances the negative might agree on the affirmative's value premise but offer a competing standard for evaluation. In still other instances, the negative might accept both the value premise and the standard but show that the negative interpretation of the resolution best meets the standard.

Consider how this framework might apply to the following Lincoln-Douglas resolution: "Resolved: Colleges have a moral obligation to prohibit hate speech on their campuses." The statement of the resolution simply means that the affirmative debater will state the resolution to be debated somewhere early in the first speech. The affirmative might present a definition of hate speech from the *American Heritage Dictionary* as bigoted speech attacking or disparaging a social or ethnic group or a member of such a group. The affirmative could suggest that the core value   the best way for colleges to meet their moral obligation—is safety. The standard for determining whether safety has been ensured is to ask what would best provide freedom from harm for students who are members of minority groups.

The negative debater would also state the resolution, this time with the objective of opposing it. The negative debater might offer a definition of hate speech as speech that disparages other individuals based on such factors as race, social status, culture, or sexual orientation. The negative could argue that the core value—the best value for determining a college's moral obligation—is freedom of expression. The negative standard for determining freedom of expression would be the maintenance of academic freedom and free/open inquiry. Forbidding any speech that disparages other individuals could chill free expression. A student might, for example, disparage members of another race or culture by criticizing the Sudanese for engaging in genocide in Darfur. Ensuring academic freedom may well require preserving the right to criticize another race or culture.

ARGUMENTATION

In Lincoln-Douglas debate, logical support usually goes well beyond the mere use of authoritative quotations. Debaters might use authoritative quotations, and when they do so, they are expected to use academically sound and properly cited sources. Yet the Lincoln-Douglas debater often offers logical support using a wide variety of forms: a student's original analysis, application of philosophy, examples, analogies, statistics, narrative, as well as expert testimony. Because Lincoln-Douglas debate specializes in value hierarchies, a premium is placed on the ability to discuss great philosophical concepts such as utilitarianism, relativism, the categorical imperative, rationalism, existentialism, humanism, communitarianism, and objectivism, among others.

CROSS-EXAMINATION

Cross-examination should be used by the debater to clarify, challenge, and/or advance arguments in the round. Chapter 15 provides additional advice concerning the proper use of cross-examination in Lincoln-Douglas debate.

EFFECTIVE COMMUNICATION

Lincoln-Douglas debate is a form of debate in which public speaking skills are emphasized. Arguments should be worded and presented so they can be understood by a general audience. A high school principal, a member of the school board, or any other intelligent adult should be able to judge a round of Lincoln-Douglas debate. The intended audience is not limited to former debaters, college debaters, or high school debate coaches.

Written communication plays an important role in Lincoln-Douglas debate. Debaters are encouraged to write affirmative and negative cases that are marked by expressiveness, appropriate word choice, and eloquence. The case should employ clear logic and be supported with topical research.

Although the affirmative and negative cases are pre-prepared, they should be delivered expressively, with attention to eye contact, gesturing, and appropriate posture.

A final consideration in speech delivery is civility. Debaters should treat their opponents with respect. Professional demeanor is expected of all competitors in Lincoln-Douglas debate.

Speaker Responsibilities in Lincoln-Douglas Debate

Affirmative Constructive Speech: In this speech, the affirmative debater provides a pre-prepared case advocating the resolution. The speech should state the resolution, define key terms, identify a value central to the resolution (core value or value premise), offer a criterion (or standard) for achieving or measuring the central value, and show why the resolution meets this standard.

Negative Constructive Speech: In this speech, the negative case is presented (usually taking up about half of the allotted seven minutes); then the negative offers answers to the affirmative case. The negative case is a pre-prepared statement opposing the resolution. The negative case should define key terms, identify a value, defend a criterion (or standard) for achieving or measuring the central value, and show why the resolution fails to meet this standard.

First Affirmative Constructive Speech: In this four-minute speech, the affirmative should answer the negative case and then re-defend the affirmative case (answering the attacks made by the negative in the previous speech). No new arguments are allowed in any rebuttal speech, but the debater can offer new evidence in support of existing arguments. Answers to the other debater's arguments do not count as new arguments.

Negative Rebuttal Speech: The negative has six minutes to crystallize the debate, showing why the negative case is superior to the affirmative case.

Second Affirmative Rebuttal Speech: This three-minute speech offers the affirmative an opportunity to summarize and extend arguments in favor of the affirmative case and in opposition to the negative. A premium is placed on a debater's ability to locate persuasive reasons the affirmative case is superior to the negative.

THE FLOWSHEET IN LINCOLN-DOUGLAS DEBATE

The flowsheet refers to the record that debaters themselves keep of the arguments that have been made in a debate. Debaters keep a record of their own arguments and the answers their opponent has made to those arguments. This record is used to organize the rebuttal portion of the debate.

In a typical Lincoln-Douglas debate, the record of the debate consists of two sheets of paper—one for the affirmative case and one for the negative. Each sheet of paper is divided into four or five columns (one column for each successive speech).

Some judges in Lincoln-Douglas debate are *flow* judges, meaning judges who keep their own written record of arguments in the debate. Other judges merely listen to the speeches, jotting down arguments only occasionally.

FURTHER READING

Halvorson, Seth, and Cherian Koshi. *Introduction to Lincoln-Douglas Debate*. 2006. www.nflonline.org/uploads/Main/IntroductiontoLDDebateOnlineText.pdf.

Lewis, Stan. *Lincoln-Douglas Debate: The Basics of Value Argumentation*. Indianapolis, IN: National Federation of High Schools, 2000.

Wiese, Jeffrey. *Lincoln-Douglas: Values in Conflict*. Topeka, KS: Clark Publishing, 1993.

Woodhouse, Cynthia. *Lincoln-Douglas Debate*. New York: Rosen Central, 2007.

CHAPTER 12

VALUE HIERARCHIES AND PHILOSOPHY IN LINCOLN-DOUGLAS DEBATE

Lincoln-Douglas debate focuses on values. Successful debaters must become adept at selecting and comparing values. This chapter provides a brief description of the most common core values in Lincoln-Douglas debate along with a discussion of the standards used for the weighing of values.

CORE VALUES IN LINCOLN-DOUGLAS DEBATE

Freedom: The United States Declaration of Independence held it to be self-evident that liberty is an inalienable right. The Bill of Rights gives detail to numerous specific freedoms: freedom of speech, freedom of the press, freedom of association, freedom to keep and bear arms, freedom of religion, freedom to petition the government for redress of grievances, freedom from self-incrimination, freedom from cruel and unusual punishment, and freedom from random search and seizure. Later amendments to the Constitution added freedom from slavery and freedom for women to vote.

Freedom (or liberty) is not a single value, but a family of closely related values. Any one of the freedoms enumerated in the U.S. Constitution and Bill of Rights could become the core value focus in a Lincoln-Douglas round of debate. All these freedoms describe a system of limited government. The Founding Fathers' commitment to limited government arose from their frustration with the British monarchy. The love of liberty also was informed by the writings of political philosophers such as John Locke, Jean-Jacques Rousseau, and Charles de Montesquieu. In his two *Treatises on Government* (1690), Locke discredits the divine right of monarchy and claimed that "life, liberty, and property" are all natural rights—the loss of any one of those three would mean the loss of the other two. Rousseau's opening line in *The Social Contract* (1762) is that "man is born free and everywhere he is in chains." Rousseau actually proposed a system of preserving civil liberties through the creation of a contract between a government and its people. Montesquieu, writing in *The Spirit of Laws* (1648), advises that personal liberty could best be ensured when government is based on a division of powers and the creation of an independent judiciary.

Safety: All members of the human species have a need for security—the need to feel safe from bodily harm. We want to protect ourselves, our families, our communities, and our nation from violent crime, environmental harm, international terrorism, and attack by another nation. When our safety is at risk, liberty is also likely to be curtailed. In the months following the 9/11 terrorist attacks, Americans were willing to give up numerous liberties because they were concerned about the safety of themselves, their families, and their neighbors. Intrusive searches at airports, government wiretaps, and the detention of immigrants all became routinely accepted. Similarly, people who live in neighborhoods infested with drug crime do not have the liberty to walk the streets at night. Safety needs can, therefore, be seen as essential to the maintenance of liberty.

In *The Leviathan* (1651), philosopher Thomas Hobbes says that safety needs are the very reason people have freely sought out the protections offered by a strong government. Without government, people live in the "state of nature" where there is "war of all against all." In the state of nature, according to Hobbes, life is "solitary, poor, nasty, brutish, and short" (p. xiii). To escape this life-threatening state of nature, people choose to give up significant freedoms to a sovereign (a strong government) to bring order to their world. We create strong police forces, armies, and a system of laws to provide safety for ourselves and our families.

Justice: We would like to believe that a fair legal system would provide equal protection and due process for all individuals, regardless of their station in life. People naturally recoil at the thought that those with money and positions of power can do as they wish while average citizens are held to the letter of the law. Philosopher John Rawls writes in *A Theory of Justice* (1971) that "the principles of justice are chosen behind a veil of ignorance" (p. 12). By this, he means we shouldn't seek to know a person's station in life before we decide which rights an individual should have and which punishments should be associated with a given act.

Suppose your high school has a rule specifying a three-day suspension from school for any student who defaces school property. Would you want your school principal to make exceptions to this rule for students whose parents are prominent in the community? The notion of justice is that laws (and legal protections) should apply equally to all. Justice demands that all people be given what they are due. The Fourteenth Amendment to the U.S. Constitution declares that a state government does not have the right to "deny to any person within its jurisdiction the equal protection of the laws."

Individualism: Many of the values cherished by Americans suggest that a society works best when individuals follow their own natural inclinations. Ralph Waldo Emerson in his "Essay on Self Reliance" (1841) writes, "nothing is at last sacred but the integrity of your own mind." Henry David Thoreau in his famous lecture "On Civil Disobedience" (1849) says, "there will never be a really free and enlightened State, until the State comes to recognize the individual as a higher and independent power, from which all its own power and authority are derived, and treats him accordingly."

Free enterprise is an economic system based on individualism. The Scottish economist Adam Smith argues in *The Wealth of Nations* (1776) that the pursuit of self-interest would lead to socially beneficial results. Smith argued that the unseen hand of the free marketplace will flawlessly determine prices and desirable levels of production. Ayn Rand also saw self-interest as the surest guide to societal well-being. In her 1966 book *Capitalism: The Unknown Ideal,* Rand writes the following: "America's abundance was created not by public sacrifices to the common good, but by the productive genius of free men who pursued their own personal interests and the making of their own private fortunes. They did not starve the people to pay for America's industrialization. They gave the people better jobs, higher wages, and cheaper goods with every new machine they invented, with every scientific discovery or technological advance—and thus the whole country was moving forward and profiting, not suffering, every step of the way."

Community: The polar opposite of individualism is communitarianism. Communitarians believe that human beings are social animals and that the value of community is unduly eroded by an exclusive focus on the individual. Most prominent among contemporary communitarians is Amitai Etzioni, professor of sociology at George Mason University. Etzioni, author of 32 books, writes a 1997 book titled *The New Golden Rule* in which he suggested the following: "Respect and uphold society's moral order as you would have society respect and uphold your autonomy."

Another prominent communitarian is Mary Ann Glendon, the Learned Hand Professor of Law at Harvard University Law School. In her 1993 book *Rights Talk: The Impoverishment of Political Discourse*, Glendon argues that the strident defense of individual rights is destroying the possibility of community:

> Our rights talk, in its absoluteness, promotes unrealistic expectations, heightens social conflict, and inhibits dialogue that might lead toward consensus, accommodation, or at least the discovery of common ground. In its silence concerning responsibilities, it seems to condone acceptance of the benefits of living in a democratic social welfare state, without accepting the corresponding personal and civic obligations. In its relentless individualism, it fosters a climate that is inhospitable to society's losers, and that systematically disadvantages caretakers and dependents, young and old. In its neglect of civil society, it undermines the principal seedbeds of civic and personal virtue. In its insularity, it shuts out potentially important aids to the process of self-correcting learning. (p. 14)

Knowledge: Free inquiry, pursuit of the scientific method, and academic freedom are all important values in Western civilization. At earlier times in our civilization, people were imprisoned or killed for their commitment to the advancement of knowledge. Socrates was forced to drink poison because he caused the youth of Athens to ask too many questions. Galileo was persecuted by the church because of his invention of the telescope and subsequent discovery that the earth rotated around the sun.

The Dark Ages (a period from the fall of the Roman Empire to the early 1500s) was a time when ancient scrolls were burned and learning was actively discouraged. The Renaissance ushered in an era that welcomed open inquiry. The Royal Society of London, one of the early societies devoted to the cultivation of scientific knowledge, adopted as its motto "in the words of no one else." This motto meant that science would be based on experiment, rather than the citation of authority. The commitment to scientific progress has made possible dramatic improvements in human life expectancy, freedom to travel, ability to communicate, and general quality of life.

Academic freedom is important in nonscientific areas as well. In his 1859 work *On Liberty,* John Stuart Mill describes the importance of a "free marketplace of ideas." Mill argues that the best way to discover truth is to allow all ideas to be entered into the public forum. Any effort to shield some cherished ideas from criticism would be counterproductive, producing only "dead dogmas." By allowing all ideas to be placed into competition, truth would best be appreciated.

Most American colleges and universities have pledged a commitment to free inquiry and academic freedom. They do this out of a commitment to the advancement of knowledge. In practice, this means that professors who have met certain threshold requirements for the quality of their scholarship should not be fired based on the unpopularity of their viewpoints.

Beauty: Poet John Keats's poem "Ode on a Grecian Urn" contains the following famous line: "Beauty is truth, truth beauty, that is all ye know on earth, and all ye need to know." The importance of the arts has been recognized as an important societal value since at least the time of the ancient Greeks. The arts inspire creativity and provide an important source of pride and unity for any community. In his speech at Amherst College on October 26, 1963, President John F. Kennedy said the following: "I see little of more importance to the future of our country and of civilization than full recognition of the place of the artist. If art is to nourish the roots of our culture, society must set the artist free to follow his/her vision wherever it takes him/her."

A community loses a great deal when it fails to see the value of music education, art education, or support of theater arts. Each of these types of education can (and has) been defended on the pragmatic grounds that it results in improvements in academic achievement as measured by standardized tests. Yet many educators argue that any effort to justify the arts by pointing to their practical value is misguided. The arts are worthy in and of themselves in the way they elevate the human spirit.

Democracy: The word *democracy* comes from the Greek *demos* meaning "people" and *cratos* meaning "government." Literally, therefore, it means government by the people. Democracy as practiced in some of the cities of ancient Greece meant that rich male landowners gathered to create and enforce laws for all the residents of their cities. This was an imperfect system of direct democracy because only prominent males were allowed to vote. It is referred to as a system of *direct democracy* because all persons entitled to vote gathered in the assembly to create laws.

St. Thomas Aquinas first suggested the idea for our system of modern representative democracy in his 1267 work *De Regno* (*On Kingship*). Aquinas proposed that the best form of government would be one in which the citizens would be represented by "the best and presided over by one." In a representative democracy we elect persons (hopefully "the best" available) who will represent us in a legislative assembly and select one leader who will preside (be president).

The political philosophers who provided the blueprints for America's Founding Fathers were primarily John Locke, Charles de Montesquieu, and Jean-Jacques Rousseau (see the earlier section on "liberty" for a discussion of the particular contribution made by each of these philosophers). The German philosopher Immanuel

Kant added an interesting dimension to the defense of democracy with his 1795 essay "Project for a Perpetual Peace." Kant's argument was that the spread of democracy would promote peace because democracies would not go to war against one another. This democratic peace thesis continues to have many adherents even in the twenty-first century. In fact, President George Bush and Secretary of State Condoleezza Rice have used the democratic peace thesis as justification for America's push for democratic transitions in the Middle East.

Democratic values were enshrined in Chapter 1 of the United Nations Charter with the inclusion of a "right of self determination" among its list of fundamental human rights. Sir Winston Churchill, speaking before the House of Commons on November 11, 1947, said, "Democracy is the worst form of government except all the others that have been tried."

Sanctity of Life: Some Lincoln-Douglas debaters will argue that life itself should be regarded as the highest value. Accordingly, any action that preserves human life should be regarded as worthy and any action that results in the loss of human life should be regarded as unworthy.

Quality of Life: Is life itself more important than the quality of life? Many Americans now complete living wills, declaring that they do not wish to have heroic measures taken to preserve their lives if doing so would mean living with little or no quality of life. Proponents of euthanasia go further than this, arguing that doctors and patients should have the right to terminate life if continued life means unending pain and suffering.

Critics of this view argue that we risk going down a slippery slope whenever we fail to value life itself. After a society declares it acceptable for elderly patients to choose death over continued suffering, the right to die can easily turn into a *duty* to die. Persons with a potentially terminal illness would naturally ponder the question of whether their continued life would be a financial burden for their loved ones.

Privacy: How absolute is the right to be left alone? The U.S. Supreme Court has, in *Roe v. Wade*, used the right of privacy as the basis for declaring that women should have a right to legal abortion early in a pregnancy. Do people have a right to surf the Internet without any government intrusion? Do people have a right to protect their homes and automobiles from being searched by government agents? If we have these rights, how is society to be protected from evils such as child pornography, illicit drug distribution, and terrorist activity?

Self-Actualization: In the hierarchy of human needs proposed by psychologist Abraham Maslow, the highest human need is "self-actualization." By *self-actualization*, Maslow referred to a commitment to achieving one's own mission in life and accepting that mission as an end in itself. Accordingly, a musician is fulfilled by making great music, an artist is fulfilled by making a great sculpture, and a poet is fulfilled by writing poetry. Each person achieves intrinsic worth by striving to realize his potential.

Critics of self-actualization argue that satisfying the self is not the highest value in a good society. The focus on self can produce a form of narcissism that undermines the family and the common good.

CRITERIA (STANDARDS) FOR COMPARING VALUES

Utilitarianism: The principle of utilitarianism (also called *pragmatism*) is commonly explained as valuing "the greatest good for the greatest number." Utilitarianism originated with the English philosopher Jeremy Bentham and his student John Stuart Mill. Bentham, in his 1789 work *The Principles of Morals and Legislation*, argues that an action is right if it promotes happiness and is wrong if it promotes the reverse of happiness. This system of ethics has often been characterized as allowing the ends to justify the means. An action that might at first appear evil could end up being good if it produces widespread happiness.

Joseph Fletcher, a professor of Christian ethics at Harvard Divinity School, added a modern twist to utilitarianism. In his 1963 book *Situation Ethics,* Fletcher argues that one must examine the nature of a particular situation before declaring which actions would be right or wrong. Fletcher, however, replaced Bentham's criterion of happiness with love—one should always do whatever would be the "loving thing." Fletcher based his philosophy on the following six propositions:

1. Only one thing is intrinsically good—love.

2. The ruling norm of Christian decision is love.

3. Love and justice are the same.

4. Love wills the neighbor's good whether or not we like our neighbor.

5. The end justifies the means.

6. Love's decisions are made only in specific situations—they can't be prescribed ahead of time.

Fletcher's book offers numerous examples of ethical dilemmas, allowing his readers to make up their own minds about what would be the "loving thing" to do.

One ethical dilemma involved the decision facing President Harry Truman concerning the use of the atomic bomb on Hiroshima and Nagasaki. This situation involved causing thousands of immediate deaths to shorten World War II and save even more lives. Another dilemma might involve an elderly man who must make a decision about whether to take an expensive medication that might extend his life for a short period of time but would create financial hardship for his family. Fletcher raises questions without really providing answers, but he certainly seems to imply that dropping the atomic bomb and engaging in passive euthanasia could be the "loving thing" to do.

Deontology: The Greek word *deon* means *obligation or duty.* Accordingly, deontologists hold that an action must be based on its intrinsic worth, not based on the consequences of the act. Deontology is the opposite of utilitarianism, pragmatism, and situation ethics. This view argues that good ends can never be used to justify unworthy means.

The German philosopher Immanuel Kant is the most prominent defender of deontology. In his 1785 work *The Groundwork of the Metaphysics of Morals*, Kant explains his notion of the categorical imperative. Kant says that the determination of what is right must be prior to the determination of what is good. One should not justify immoral acts based on a claim that these acts might serve some long-term societal good. In particular, Kant says that human beings must never be used merely as a means to an end.

Consider an example from Fletcher's *Situation Ethics*: A group of Irish immigrants in the 1830s are traveling through Ohio when they spot some Indians and take refuge in a nearby forest. The immigrants have been told that the Indians kill settlers. One woman is holding her sleeping baby but realizes that the baby is about to wake up and cry. As the Indians draw closer, the mother notices that she is suffocating her baby. If the mother keeps her hand over her baby's mouth, she will kill her child. If she takes her hand away, the baby will cry and the Indians will kill the settlers. What should this mother do?

Fletcher seems to imply that the "loving thing," based on his pragmatic calculus, would be for the mother to kill her baby. Immanuel Kant would say that one must always do the right thing at the first instance. It should always be wrong for a mother to kill her own baby. The mother should act to save the child and then take her chances with the consequences. One can never know the future with certainty. Perhaps it is inevitable that the Indians will find the settlers regardless of whether the baby cries. Perhaps the settlers will have sufficient might to protect themselves against an Indian attack. Perhaps the report that Indians always kill settlers is incorrect. The mother must make a moral decision in the present. Can she make the decision to kill her child based on mere speculation that more people might die? Kant would say that the baby should never be viewed merely as a means to an end.

Cost Benefit Analysis (CBA): This method of comparing values is based on economics. It suggests that a good decision-maker enumerates the advantages and disadvantages of any given action before deciding which is best. The decision is made based on an accountant's ledger sheet comparison of costs and benefits.

Most historical accounts say that cost benefit analysis was first proposed by the French economist Jules Dupuit in an 1844 paper titled "On the Measurement of the Utility of Public Works."

Dupuit's paper compares the costs and benefits of building a bridge, where all elements of the decision were to be converted to monetary terms. Modern approaches to CBA retain the balance sheet approach, but a conscious effort is made to factor in both the monetary and nonmonetary considerations.

When considering the benefits of an action, one must consider direct benefits, indirect benefits, and intangible benefits. If you are deciding whether to buy a car, direct benefits might be the saving of time in getting to work or school without having to walk, take the bus, or wait for a ride from a parent. An indirect benefit might be that your parent won't have to take time away from her work schedule to provide transportation for you. Intangible benefits might include the new friendships or dating experiences that could be made possible if you had your own vehicle.

The costs of an action include the direct costs, opportunity costs, and externalities. Direct costs involve the immediate expenditure of resources required by an action. In the case of buying a car, the direct costs would include the monthly car payment, the cost of insurance, the cost of gasoline, and the expense of maintenance.

Opportunity costs refer to the other benefits that are given up by the choice to take the action in question. The question is not simply how much your car will cost, but also what other things you could have purchased with the money you are spending for the car. You might be spending money that could otherwise be used to pay for your college education or for a new computer system.

Externalities are the negative byproducts of an action that are difficult to measure in monetary terms. Environmental degradation is an often neglected externality. By driving an automobile rather than walking, you might be contributing to the pollution of the environment. You might also be less physically fit as a result of your decision to drive rather than walk to school.

B. Guy Peters, professor of American government at the University of Pittsburgh, writing in the seventh edition of his text *American Public Policy: Promise and Performance*, says that cost benefit analysis provides an unsatisfactory basis for political decisions. Peters refers to cost benefit analysis as "the functional equivalent of witchcraft in the public sector" because "there are so many assumptions involved in the calculations, and so many imponderables about the future effects of projects." He says that it is impossible to place an economic value on things like life, health, and endangered species. Cost benefit analysis is worthwhile, according to Professor Peters, only when it is integrated with other forms of ethical analysis.

Cost benefit analysis works best when a very specific plan is under consideration—for instance, a proposal to build a new bridge or a presidential candidate's plan to provide health insurance for uninsured Americans. But Lincoln-Douglas debate doesn't involve the presentation of specific plans or proposals; instead one value is compared to another value in a variety of public policy contexts.

FURTHER READING

Baird, Robert M. *Socrates in the Forum: The Role of Philosophy in Lincoln-Douglas Debate*. Indianapolis, IN: National Federation of High Schools, 1995.

Polk, Lee R., William B. English, and Eric Walker. *The Value Debate Handbook, 6th Ed*. Waco, TX: Baylor Briefs, 2000.

CHAPTER 13

AFFIRMATIVE CASING IN LINCOLN-DOUGLAS DEBATE

This chapter focuses on the mechanics of writing the affirmative case. The steps involved in preparing an affirmative case are analyzing the resolution, conducting research, defining terms, and writing the case.

ANALYZING THE RESOLUTION

A Lincoln-Douglas debater should begin thinking about a resolution by asking two questions:

1. What are the objects of evaluation contained in the resolution?

2. What value should be used to evaluate these objects?

Every resolution contains one or more terms that are the objects to be evaluated. Following is an example of a resolution that contains only one object of evaluation: "Resolved: Human genetic engineering is morally justified." This resolution introduces a single object—"human genetic engineering"—and asks how highly this object should be valued.

Most Lincoln-Douglas resolutions contain two objects of evaluation, and the debater is invited to compare the importance of the two terms. Consider this example: "Resolved: The principle of majority rule ought to be valued above the principle of minority rights." The resolution introduces two objects of evaluation— "principle of majority rule" and "principle of minority rights." The debater is asked to weigh the value of one concept as compared to the other.

The second question to answer about a resolution is which evaluative term should be used in the context of the resolution. Some resolutions provide their own evaluative terms. Consider the following topic: "Resolved: On balance, institutional censorship of academic material is harmful to the educational development of students." The object of evaluation in this resolution is "institutional censorship of academic material." The resolution itself provides the value that is to be weighed; this value is "the educational development of students." This resolution doesn't ask the debater to decide whether educational development is worthwhile—this value is imposed on the resolution. The only question is whether "censorship of academic material" enhances or detracts from "educational development."

Many Lincoln-Douglas resolutions do not impose an evaluative term, leaving it up to the debater to select the value to be used. Consider the resolution "Resolved: An oppressive government is more desirable than no government." This resolution leaves it up to the individual debater to decide which value will be used in determining desirability. The affirmative debater is more likely to choose a value such as safety, arguing that even oppressive governments offer protection from the anarchy that is present in the "state of nature." The negative debater is likely to select a value such as freedom, arguing that anarchy is preferable to tyranny.

Conducting Research

Lincoln-Douglas debaters can productively engage in two types of research: readings in philosophy and news articles dealing with contemporary issues. Top Lincoln-Douglas competitors are conversant with key philosophical concepts such as utilitarianism, the marketplace of ideas, and the categorical imperative. The best way to develop an understanding of what Jeremy Bentham, John Stuart Mill, or Immanuel Kant had in mind is to read some of their original works. Fortunately, such classic works are often freely available on the Internet. If you have difficulty understanding some of these original works, numerous Internet sites offer assistance. Two such sites are *The Internet Encyclopedia of Philosophy* (available at www.utm.edu/research/iep/) and *Assembled Western Philosophers* (available at www.philosophypages.com/ph/index.htm).

The second type of Lincoln-Douglas research examines contemporary news and commentary concerning the debate resolution. One of the reasons resolutions are selected for debate is because they are timely; there is some current controversy that makes a resolution a debatable issue. The best place to begin in conducting research is to locate the current issue that created the value controversy. Consider the resolution used at the NFL national tournament in 2006: "Resolved: In matters of collecting military intelligence, the ends justify the means." This resolution was timely because of the controversy surrounding the military's use of unusual interrogation methods on detainees in the Guantanamo Bay facility.

By doing research on the interrogation methods at Guantanamo Bay, you can uncover justifications for competing values. Defenders of these interrogation methods typically use a utilitarian calculus: making life uncomfortable for one terrorist suspect might uncover information that could save the lives of millions of innocent people. Opponents of forceful interrogation use the term *torture* to describe the methods used by the American military. They say that America lowers itself to the level of the terrorists themselves when it ignores standards of human decency in the treatment of detainees. By conducting contemporary research on the resolution, you can develop a sense of the values advanced on both sides of the controversy.

DEFINING TERMS

The outcome of any Lincoln-Douglas debate is often determined by deciding whether the affirmative or negative examples are more central to the resolution. The framers of Lincoln-Douglas resolutions are careful to avoid words like *always* or *never* in the wording of the resolution. We are not debating whether "life is *always* more important than liberty" or whether "judicial activism is *never* appropriate." Instead, we have resolutions such as the following: "Resolved: On balance, institutional censorship of academic material is harmful to the educational development of students." This means that it should never be enough for the affirmative to show one instance where censorship was harmful (perhaps pointing to an instance where a school board banned the reading of Harry Potter books). Neither would it be enough for the negative debater to point to a single instance where censorship was justified (perhaps referring to a decision of a high school librarian to refuse to subscribe to *Playboy* magazine). This censorship resolution calls for an on-balance evaluation of institutional censorship. Even if the resolution does not contain the words *on balance*, it is understood that the affirmative must prove that the resolution is true in the most important instances; similarly, the negative must prove that the resolution is untrue in the most important instances.

So what does all this have to do with the task of definition? By carefully defining key terms in the resolution, the affirmative can predetermine which things are most essential. Consider the example of the censorship resolution discussed in the previous paragraph. The negative will seek to characterize censorship as the normal decisions teachers and librarians must make in choosing materials. Does a teacher engage in censorship when he decides not to include creationism readings in a biology class? If the affirmative debater allows censorship to be defined as merely choosing what is academically worthy, then the debate is already lost to the negative. Success for the affirmative requires that censorship be seen in the context of school board decisions to ban well-respected books such as *Huckleberry Finn* or Darwin's *On the Origin of Species by Means of Natural Selection*.

The affirmative would prefer a definition of censorship such as the one found in the *Columbia Encyclopedia* as "official prohibition or restriction of any type of expression believed to threaten the political, social, or moral order" (available at www.answers.com/censorship&r=67). The affirmative would point out that the resolution refers to "institutional" censorship, meaning the decision to restrict the material has been made by the school or school board itself, rather than by the individual teacher of a class.

WRITING THE CASE

A good affirmative case begins with a brief attention-getting element. As in public speaking, any good introduction serves three purposes:

- It gains attention.

- It establishes rapport.

- It leads into the body of the speech.

The introduction might gain attention by using an apt quotation, telling a brief story, asking a rhetorical question, or offering an analogy. You can establish rapport with the judge by establishing an appropriate emotional tone and making direct eye contact. Finally, the introduction should lead smoothly into the statement of the resolution, which in this case begins the body of the affirmative speech.

The introduction should be kept short—certainly no longer than thirty seconds. The introduction does not constitute an argument that the judge writes down on her flowsheet, and the negative debater is not expected to respond to the introduction. Accordingly, you cannot afford to spend too much time on the opening.

The next element of the affirmative case is the statement of the resolution. Consider the way in which Taarini Vohra, the 2007 national champion in Lincoln-Douglas debate from The Hockaday School, introduced the resolution:

- "Those who deny freedom to others deserve it not for themselves." Because I agree with Abraham Lincoln, I must affirm today's resolution: On balance, violent revolution is a just response to political oppression.

After the statement of the resolution, the case should provide a definition of the key terms in the resolution. Taarini Vohra provided her definitions with the following two observations:

I. Definitions of evaluative terms

　A. "On balance" is defined

　B. "A" is defined

II. Definitions of objects of evaluation

A. "Oppression" means "the prolonged cruel exercise of authority"

B. "Political" means "the agent of oppression is a government."

C. "Violent revolution" means "considerable or destroying force which is prohibited by law and directed to change the system of government."

Vohra continued developing her case by directly announcing a core value and a criterion for weighing that value:

- The ultimate value: "I value justice as it is the ultimate good implied by the resolution. While there are different conceptions of justice, all are centrally based on the notion of fairness, in that people should be treated as their actions merit. So justice is defined as giving each their due."

- The value criterion: "The criterion is respecting human dignity, which is the innate worth that separates people from objects. Dignity makes justice meaningful because only beings with worth are due something."

The remainder of the affirmative case is structured in key contentions and subpoints. Vohra offered the following contentions, each of which was supported with authoritative quotations and examples:

I. People have an inherent right to violently rebel.

A. An oppressive government has lost the authority to demand allegiance.

B. The right to violently rebel is justified as a form of self-defense.

II. Any revolution to restore rights will include violence.

The final element of the affirmative case is the conclusion. A good conclusion should provide a brief summary and create a sense of finality. Vohra concluded her speech with the following two sentences: "The only potential for justice is to allow citizens their fundamental right to violently revolt. Thus, I urge an affirmative ballot, and now stand ready for cross-examination."

FURTHER READING

Hanes, T. Russell, and Scott Devoid. "Toward a New LD Paradigm." *The Rostrum,* October 2006. www.nflonline.org/uploads/ Rostrum/1006_047_050.pdf.

Luong, Minh A. "Burden of Proof and Presumption in Lincoln-Douglas Debate: A Call for Reform." *The Rostrum,* November 1995. www.nflonline.org/uploads/Rostrum/ debate1195luong.pdf.

CHAPTER 14

NEGATIVE STRATEGY IN LINCOLN-DOUGLAS DEBATE

The negative constructive speech involves two components—the presentation of the negative case and the response to the affirmative case. Unlike the situation in policy debate, the negative does not have the advantage of presumption in Lincoln-Douglas debate. It is not enough for the negative to raise doubt about the truth of the resolution; to win the debate, the negative must show that the resolution is generally untrue.

CHOOSING THE NEGATIVE CASE

The procedure for writing the negative case is nearly identical to the affirmative; the key difference is that the negative case is shorter—generally less than two thirds the length of the affirmative case. The reason for this brevity is that at least one third of the seven-minute constructive speech must be reserved for responding to the affirmative case.

Begin your negative analysis of the resolution by thinking of specific examples in which the resolution would not be true. Consider the following resolution: "Resolved: When in conflict, globalization ought to be valued above national sovereignty." After researching this topic, you would discover that that opponents of globalization focus on three key themes:

- It advantages rich nations over developing countries.

- It undervalues the protection of the environment.

- It produces the homogenization of cultures.

You could focus your negative case on any one of these themes. In each case, consider the value premise that underlies your position. If you are focusing on harm to developing countries, your value premise is likely to emphasize social justice or fairness. Philosopher John Rawls, for example, claims that the criterion for justice is that an action should protect the least advantaged. If you are focusing on harm to the environment, you might choose safety as your ultimate value. The criterion could be that we must always use the precautionary principle, taking care not to undermine the environmental web that sustains life on planet earth. If you are focusing on the homogenization of cultures, you might choose community as your central value, arguing that whatever undermines indigenous culture impoverishes all of humankind.

RESPONDING TO THE AFFIRMATIVE DEFINITIONS OF TERMS

When you are negative, you can choose whether you want to accept the definitions offered by the affirmative or want to offer your own. In some situations you might be confident that you can show the superiority of your case even working within the affirmative's own definitions. Usually, however, you will want to offer counter-definitions and show why your definitions offer a better understanding of the resolution.

Consider the following topic: "Resolved: Democracy is best served by strict separation of church and state." The affirmative has defined *democracy* as "a system of government marked by broad participation." The affirmative claim is that the injection of religious values into government functions serves to marginalize the participation of minority groups. Although the affirmative definition offers one way to view *democracy*, a far more common definition is a system of "majority rule" in which "the will of the majority outweighs the wants of a minority." This resolution does not ask whether separation of church and state is *desirable*; instead it claims that democracy (meaning "majority rule") is advanced by a strict separation of church and state. In this example (and in many other instances in Lincoln-Douglas debate), the selection of definitions is critical to the outcome of the debate round.

RESPONDING TO THE AFFIRMATIVE CORE VALUE

As a negative debater, you must choose whether you want to accept the value premise offered by the affirmative or offer an alternative. Suppose, for example, you are debating the following topic: "Resolved: In matters of collecting military intelligence, the ends justify the means." The affirmative case advocates the importance of safety, arguing that the detention and interrogation of terrorist suspects is the best way to protect against future terrorist attacks. In this affirmative case, the criterion for safety is the uncovering of information that will prevent future terrorist attacks.

You might choose to counter the value of safety by advocating justice and the rule of law. You would argue that it is more important to follow international law, including the dictates of the Geneva Convention, than any benefit to be gained by torturing terror suspects.

Another strategy is to accept the affirmative value—in this case safety—but offer a different criterion for weighing this value. The negative might argue that the standard for safety is to minimize the likelihood of future terrorist acts. By torturing terrorism suspects and maintaining Guantanamo-type detention camps, the United States might actually be radicalizing the Arab street in the Middle East, resulting in the creation of future terrorists.

A final strategy is to accept both the affirmative value and the affirmative criterion but argue that the criterion is best achieved by opposing the resolution. Remember that the affirmative value is safety and the criterion is "uncovering information that will prevent future terrorist attacks." The negative could argue that by its harsh detention of Middle Eastern immigrants, the federal government has lost the cooperation of immigrant communities. Middle

Eastern immigrants living in the United States offer the best hope of uncovering terrorist plots because they are in the best position to spot and report radical Islamists. They will not, however, cooperate with anti-terrorist efforts by providing information if they are given good reason to fear government mistreatment.

EXTENDING ARGUMENTS IN THE REBUTTAL

The length of the rebuttal in Lincoln-Douglas debate offers a key advantage to the negative. The negative has a six-minute rebuttal to respond to an affirmative rebuttal that was only four minutes in length. The negative should use this time trade-off to full advantage.

Carefully write down each argument made by the affirmative in the first rebuttal. As you are doing so, pay careful attention to the arguments the affirmative failed to answer. Not all judges in Lincoln-Douglas debate flow the speeches, so it is up to you to emphasize the importance of the places where you are given a free pass by the affirmative.

Your rebuttal should generally begin by extending your answers to the affirmative case. The decision of whether to follow a complete line-by-line rebuttal format will depend on careful judge analysis. Do you know (either from a judge philosophy sheet or from observing the judge) whether the judge prefers a line-by-line approach? If the judge seems interested only in the big picture, you still will need to create the sense that you are well organized and are responding to the key arguments of the affirmative. If you have a judge who follows the line-by-line arguments on the flowsheet, you should take full advantage by answering fully each of the arguments. By doing so, you make it very difficult for the affirmative to respond because the final affirmative rebuttal is only half the length of your rebuttal speech.

Any good persuasive speaker likes to save the best for last—that would be your negative case. The final few minutes of your rebuttal speech should emphasize the key elements of your negative case, pointing out any items not responded to in the first affirmative rebuttal.

FURTHER READING

Cossette, N. André. "Three Not-So-New Negative LD Strategies." *The Rostrum,* April 1994. www.nflonline.org/uploads/ Rostrum/ld0494cossette.pdf.

Gottfried, Grant. "How to Win at Lincoln-Douglas." *The Rostrum,* December 1994. www.nflonline.org/uploads/Rostrum/ ld1294gottfried.pdf.

Menick, Jim. "Brainstorming on the Hudson: Knowing the Real Issues." *The Rostrum,* January 2006. www.nflonline.org/ uploads/Rostrum/0106_059_060.pdf.

CHAPTER 15

CROSS-EXAMINATION TECHNIQUE IN LINCOLN-DOUGLAS DEBATE

Many of the principles discussed in Chapter 9 also apply in Lincoln-Douglas debate. Yet there are some key factors that make cross-examination unique in Lincoln-Douglas debate.

The delivery focus of Lincoln-Douglas debate means that impressions created in cross-examination are more important than in policy debate. In policy debate, there is usually a certain decision logic that the judge attempts to implement (stock issues, policymaking, hypothesis testing, and so on). In Lincoln-Douglas debate, there is less agreement among judges and participants on a prepackaged decision logic. Judges are typically instructed to reward debaters who are able to demonstrate poise and confidence in public speaking. Cross-examination offers a prime opportunity for debaters to impress (or turn off) a judge.

The fact that only two cross-examination periods exist in Lincoln-Douglas debate makes each of them more important. Each side has only one opportunity to advance its position.

In Lincoln-Douglas debate, unlike in policy debate, cross-examination cannot serve the purpose of providing preparation time for a partner; the person conducting the cross-examination also becomes the next speaker.

CREATING A STRONG IMPRESSION IN CROSS-EXAMINATION

Cross-examination offers an opportunity for you to sell your ideas as well as your personality to the judge. The judge is more likely to be paying close attention to you during the cross-examination period than during any other point in the debate. The interactive nature of cross-examination naturally creates interest. Also, because the judge is not flowing during the cross-examination, you are more likely to be able to make direct eye contact.

Creating a strong impression involves a number of nonverbal components. Your eye contact should be with the judge, not with your opponent. You should stand near the podium but avoid barriers between you and the judge. When you are being questioned, you create a stronger impression by standing free from the podium. You want to come across as forceful and confident without being arrogant or dismissive of your opponent.

KEEPING THE FOCUS ON YOUR OWN ARGUMENTS

Much of what happens in a debate involves a time trade-off. You have only thirteen minutes of total speaking time in the debate, so the six minutes of cross-examination time is significant by comparison. If you allow the focus of cross-examination to remain on your opponent's case, you create the impression that your own case is less important in the debate. When you have control of cross-examination you should try to keep the focus on your case. You can't, of course, make speeches in cross-examination, but you can ask questions that highlight examples supportive of your case.

USING ANALOGIES

The most interesting portions of cross-examination in Lincoln-Douglas debate involve asking an opponent to respond to hypothetical examples or analogies. Both debaters made extensive use of analogies in the 2007 national final Lincoln-Douglas debate on the topic "Resolved: On balance, violent revolution is a just response to political oppression." In the first cross-examination period, James Logan High School debater Bilal Malik used the following sequence in questioning Taarini Vohra from The Hockaday School:

Q: Let's imagine for a moment that I'm being mugged, okay?

A: Okay.

Q: Do you think it's just for me to retaliate against my aggressor?

A: I would say that that is a right of self-defense.

Q: So, it is just?

A: That would be just.

Q: Okay, now would it be just for me to subdue my attacker, tie him up, and proceed to beat him with a baseball bat?

A: The question you seem to be asking ... the answer is a little more complicated.

Q: Sure, go ahead.

A: Okay, when somebody attacks you, every individual has that fundamental right to self-defense. So, what that means is that in a question of justice and what people are due, that right is something that matters, no matter how you implement that right.

Q: Okay, but isn't there some sort of proportionality to self-defense? Like if you steal a dollar from me, am I justified in breaking your kneecaps?

A: Well, my argument is that when an oppressive government uses violence against ....

Q: No, no, no. I'm just asking you a question outside of the scope of the resolution. Is there proportionality with self-defense?

A: The individual is allowed to use violence in response to the oppressor.

Q: So, if I take a dollar from you right now, can you beat me?

A: The problem with your analysis is ... no, I wouldn't be able to beat you.

Q: Why not?

A: The situation you are drawing is not similar to the situation of an oppressive regime.

Q: Okay, but we can say that there needs to be some sort of proportionality in terms of the response to political oppression, correct?

In this exchange, Bilal Malik is trying to set up a key argument of his negative case that violent revolution is a disproportionate response to oppression when nonviolent means are available.

CREATING BURDENS FOR YOUR OPPONENT

Often cross-examination can expose the fact that an opponent failed to support a claim. Perhaps your opponent presented a definition for a term without offering any authoritative support for such a definition. Perhaps the account of a historical event fails to square with your own interpretation of that event. When these weaknesses are pointed out, your opponent will often offer to read supporting evidence in the next speech. If such an offer is not forthcoming, you can ask your opponent to present such evidence. Your cross-examination is productive in the sense that you are creating performance benchmarks that your opponent might fail to meet. Even if the evidence is presented, you have succeeded in changing the time your opponent planned to spend on an argument.

FURTHER READING

Goldman, Robert E. *The Modern Art of Cross-Examination.* Englewood Cliffs, NJ: Prentice-Hall, 1993.

Mann, James L., II. "Cross-Examination in Policy and LD Debate." *The Rostrum,* November 1994. www.nflonline.org/uploads/ Rostrum/pol1194mann.pdf (accessed August 30, 2007).

CHAPTER 16

FORMAT AND SPEAKER BURDENS IN PUBLIC FORUM DEBATE

Public forum debate is, without question, the fastest-growing competitive debate event in America. Public forum adopts popular media debates as its model—formats such as CNN's *Crossfire* and *Capital Gang*, PBS's *McLaughlin Group*, and Fox's *Beltway Boys*. Because CNN founder Ted Turner was one of the early promoters of the event, it was originally called *Ted Turner debate*, although it also went by the name *controversy debate*. In most parts of the country, the event is now called public forum debate.

THE HISTORY OF PUBLIC FORUM DEBATE

This event, launched in 2002, was the brainchild of National Forensic League (NFL) executive council member Donus Roberts of Watertown High School in Watertown, South Dakota. All of the original rule structure and framework was created by NFL executive secretary James Copeland, with assistance from NFL council members Frank Sferra of Mullen High School in Denver, Colorado, and Ted Belch of Glenbrook North High School in Northbrook,

Illinois. They intended to create an event that would appeal to any bright students who wanted diversified activities—the kinds of students who enjoy academic decathlons, model United Nations, or similar contests. The hope was that public forum debate would enable many more high schools to sponsor competitive debate programs. This event lowers entry barriers for participating schools in three primary ways: (1) The topics are ripped from the headlines and change monthly; (2) The media focus helps avoid complicated argument theory or debate jargon; and (3) Any intelligent adult can judge the event (no special training or certification is required).

Donus Roberts predicted that by presenting exciting, current, controversial topics within a lively, brief, dramatic format, adults and the media would be willing to listen and students would be drawn to participate. His prediction proved true: merely five years after the launching of the new event, NFL reported more than 64,000 rounds of competition occurring within a sample two-month period.

PUBLIC FORUM DEBATE FORMAT

Public forum is a team debate event involving two students from one school competing against two students from a second school. Competitors are given the topic for debate only a few days or weeks before the debate tournament. The topic can be something such as "Colleges and universities should be permitted to pay stipends to their Division I athletes." Prior to the tournament, students are expected to prepare brief pro and con statements because they must be ready to debate either side of the topic. For each round of competition, the tournament host provides a schematic listing the teams competing, along with room assignments. The schematic might look something like this:

UNIVERSITY OF IOWA INVITATIONAL

Round 1	Start Time: 6:30 P.M.		
TEAM A	*TEAM B*	*ROOM*	*JUDGE*
Newton AH	Oskaloosa CC	CC 130	Johnson, Dennis
Grinnell FT	Regis GK	CC 132	Griffin, Amy
Tiffin ER	Dubuque GR	CC 141	Masters, Ron
Ankeny DC	Cedar Falls GH	CC 153	Rollins, Steve

GEORGIA STATE UNIVERSITY SEASON OPENER

Round 1	Start Time: 4:00 P.M.		
TEAM A	*TEAM B*	*ROOM*	*JUDGE*
A231	G119	Dahlonega	Alford, Phil
T113	P421	Louden	Nakayama, Tom
V201	A252	Falcons	Myers, Rhonda
N310	M003	Bruster	Bien, Songsook

Following the University of Iowa schematic example, the teams from Newton and Oskaloosa would go to the assigned room to prepare for the upcoming round of competition. This schematic illustrates the practice of using the school name along with the first letter from each debater's last name. Newton AH, for example, might be the team of Jennifer Ables and Jason Herrera. The Georgia State University schematic example illustrates the use of contestant codes, which is also a common practice in public forum tournaments. When codes are in use, the tournament host assigns letters and/or numbers to identify each of the contestants.

The first task in preparing for an upcoming round is the coin toss. The two teams agree on which team will flip the coin and which will call heads or tails. The winners of the coin toss have a choice—they can either choose a side (pro or con) or choose a speaking order (whether they will speak first or last). If the winner of the coin toss opts to select a side, the loser of the coin toss then chooses a speaking order (first or last). If the winner of the coin toss opts to select a speaking order, the loser of the coin toss then chooses a side. As soon as the judge arrives at the room, the debaters should list their names on the ballot showing the sides and the speaker order that have now been agreed upon. The relevant section of the ballot will look something like this:

Team Name/Code: _____ Side: ___   Team Name/Code: _____ Side: ___

Speaker 1: _____   Speaker 2: _____

Speaker 3: _____   Speaker 4: _____

The team assigned to speak first places their names in the places for Speaker 1 and 3 and writes the team name or code as it appears on the round assignment schematic. The side for the team speaking first is written after Side as either Pro or Con. The team assigned to speak last then places their names in the places for Speaker 2 and 4. The whole debate takes approximately one-half hour to complete and involves the following speeches and crossfire periods:

First Speaker - Team A = 4 Minutes

Second Speaker - Team B = 4 Minutes

  Crossfire = 3 Minutes

Third Speaker - Team A = 4 Minutes

Fourth Speaker - Team B = 4 Minutes

  Crossfire = 3 Minutes

Summary - First Speaker - Team A = 2 Minutes

Summary - Second Speaker - Team B = 2 Minutes

  Grand Crossfire = 3 Minutes

Final Focus - Third Speaker - Team A = 1 Minute

Final Focus - Fourth Speaker - Team B = 1 Minute

  Prep Time (per team) = 2 Minutes

What Happens in Each of the Public Forum Speeches?

The 2006 national final in public forum debate pitted the team from Bishop Heelan High School (Sioux City, Iowa) against the team from Marjory Stoneman Douglas High School (Parkland, Florida). The transcript of this debate is presented in its entirety in Appendix C. Students interested in public forum debate should carefully examine this transcript to see how the most successful teams allocate time in their speeches.

The First Two Speeches: Unlike other competitive debate formats, public forum can start out with either a pro or a con speech, depending on the choices made after the coin flip. The first and second speakers persuasively present their pre-prepared four-minute speech (called their *case*), offering reasoned agreement or disagreement with the topic statement. On the topic "Colleges and universities should be permitted to pay stipends to their Division I athletes," for example, the first pro speaker would present a pre-prepared four-minute persuasive speech detailing the reasons paying college athletes would be a good thing. The con speaker would present a pre-prepared four-minute persuasive speech outlining the problems with paying college athletes.

First Crossfire: This refers to a period of open interchange between one member of the pro team and one member of the con team. The second speaker stays at the lectern and is joined by the first speaker (the speaker of the opposing team who has already spoken). The speakers should both stand in the front of the room for this first crossfire. For the next three minutes, the two speakers interact with one another, using probing questions to explore the weaknesses in the opposing argument. Unlike other forms of debate, neither participant is assigned the role of questioner or respondent; both debaters can both ask and answer questions.

The Third and Fourth Speakers: The debaters use these speeches to attack the case arguments of their opponent and to answer any attacks made against their own case. The best speakers demonstrate a persuasive ability to answer arguments made in previous speeches and during the first crossfire.

The Second Crossfire: This interchange (with both speakers standing at the front of the room) occurs between the fourth speaker (who has just finished giving a speech) and the third speaker. This second crossfire proceeds just like the first with the third and fourth speakers asking questions of one another, exploring weaknesses and strengths in the opposing cases. Debaters are encouraged to present dilemmas and explore contradictions in the opponent's positions.

The Summary Speeches: The first and second speakers each give a two-minute speech designed to defend the most important parts of their own case and to highlight the key weaknesses in the opponent's case. Given the time constraint, there is no expectation that the debaters will respond to every point made by the opponent.

Instead, the premium is placed on finding the most persuasive elements of one's own case and the central problem with the opponent's case.

The Grand Crossfire: All four debaters participate in this final interchange (three minutes in length). Everyone remains seated during the final crossfire but should take care that their location allows proper eye contact with the judge(s), audience, and camera (if the debate is being recorded). Customarily, the first question is directed at the team that just ended its summary (asked by the team giving the first summary speech). After the first question, anyone can ask questions of any other participant. In the competitive public forum format, no questions are to be asked by the judge or spectators.

The Final Focus: Speakers three and four present a one-minute restatement of the reason(s) their position is superior and the opponent's position should be rejected. The original public forum rule structure stipulated that final focus speakers could make only one argument (choosing either a strong point in their own case or a weakness of the opponent's case). This rule proved difficult to enforce because it was often impossible to determine when one argument had crossed the border into multiple ones. Recent rule revisions allow debaters to make more than one argument in the final focus, but speakers are encouraged to highlight key strengths and weaknesses. The number of arguments is less important than the persuasive strength of the selected positions. Public forum judges are instructed to ignore any new arguments in the final focus, although it is acceptable for debaters to present new evidence in support of existing positions.

Preparation Time: Each team is given two minutes of total preparation time to use as it chooses. The team could elect to use a portion of this preparation time before its summary speech, saving the balance to prepare for the final focus speech. Experienced debaters, recognizing the importance of the final focus, save all the preparation time for the time just before the final speech. If a team has used all its preparation time, the timekeeper (which is usually the judge) begins the time for the next speech.

The Judge's Decision: Immediately after the end of the round, the judge is asked to be objective and judge the debate on the quality of the arguments made, not on personal beliefs or on the arguments the judge wishes they would have made. The judge is asked to mark her ballot showing who won (no ties allowed) and how each team is rated (on a scale of 20 to 30, with 30 being the best). The instructions for public forum ask the judge to fill out the ballot, explaining a reason for the decision. The decision is delivered to the ballot collection table, but judges in public forum are asked *not* to reveal the outcome of the round to the participants.

TOURNAMENT FORMATS FOR PUBLIC FORUM DEBATE

Most invitational tournament formats involve competition in preliminary rounds and elimination rounds. A typical two-day tournament might involve six preliminary rounds, after which top competitors are seeded into an elimination round bracket. Smaller one-day tournaments might offer three or four preliminary rounds of competition, followed by one or two elimination rounds. A round of debate refers to the half-hour-long argumentative exchange between two teams assigned to debate one another.

Preliminary Rounds: In a typical invitational tournament, the first two rounds of competition are randomly paired, so each team's opponent is randomly selected. Additional preliminary rounds are power-matched, meaning teams are assigned to meet opponents with similar win-loss records. Teams going into round three with two wins meet other teams with two wins.

Elimination Rounds: At the end of the preliminary rounds, the tournament host determines the ranking of each team from top to bottom, based on the number of wins and team ratings in pre-liminary rounds (judges give each team a numerical rating as well as determining a winner and a loser in each round). Because judges are not allowed to give ties, each team compiles a win-loss and speaker point record that can be used to establish a ranking for it. The number of teams qualifying for participation in elim-ination rounds depends on the tournament size; this number is almost always less than half the teams competing in preliminary rounds. Suppose, for example, that 40 teams have participated in preliminary rounds. The tournament host would establish an octafinal bracket, pairing the top 16 competitors against one another. The team ranked 1st would meet the team ranked 16th, the team ranked 2nd would meet the team ranked 15th, and so on until all of the top 16 teams are paired. Two key differences distinguish elimination rounds from preliminary rounds: (1) Multiple judges are assigned to each round (usually at least three judges); and (2) Only the winner of the elimination round participates in the next elimination round (usually the nonadvancing team receives an award showing that it did advance beyond preliminary rounds). The elimination bracket proceeds round by round, culminating in a final round between the top two remaining teams. The winner of the final round wins the tournament.

Who Are the Judges? In most invitational tournaments, the competing teams are expected to provide a judge who is assigned to adjudicate rounds other than the ones in which their own teams participate. In public forum debate, no special training or certification for judges is required. The judge can be any adult who will make a commitment to listen and follow simple instructions for rendering decisions.

Switching Sides: In most forms of competitive debate, contestants are expected to alternate sides from round to round. Only in elimination rounds do contestants in policy or Lincoln-Douglas debate flip a coin to determine sides. Even then, if the contestants have met before in preliminary rounds, they switch sides when they meet in elimination rounds. In public forum debate, however, there is a coin toss in every round to determine side and speaking order. This is true even in elimination rounds when the teams have met before in preliminary rounds. It is, therefore, theoretically possible (though unlikely) for a team to proceed all the way through a tournament debating on the same side of the topic.

National Forensic League Tournament Competition: The NFL district and national tournaments operate a bit differently from invitational tournaments. In NFL *district* tournaments a double-elimination format is used, meaning teams continue to compete until they have lost a second round of debate. The NFL *national* tournament assigns competitors to six preliminary rounds of competition, with each round having two judges. Competitors accumulating at least eight ballots after the six preliminary rounds then go into a double-elimination bracket. Contestants continue to debate until they have received a second loss or until a national winner is determined.

Finding Tournaments in Which to Compete

Most state organizations sponsoring debate competition maintain websites listing approved tournaments throughout the debate season along with the events to be offered at each tournament (see Appendix D for a state-by-state listing of these websites). Many tournaments also allow online registration through the Joy of Tournaments web entry system (www.joyoftournaments.com). The Joy of Tournaments website lists tournaments chronologically for each weekend of the debate tournament season. Coaches and debaters can scrutinize these listings to find tournaments in their local areas on desired weekends.

What if there are no public forum competitions in your local area? You could contact tournament directors in your area to express your interest in starting a public forum division. Most tournament hosts are willing to support new debate events if enough coaches and debaters express interest in competing. Even if no tournaments are available, you can get involved by establishing a practice contest with neighboring schools. After several such schools have established public forum programs, a new tournament can be created.

Public Forum Debate Topics

Who Picks the Topics? The national public forum topic is announced on the website of the National Forensic League (www.nflonline.org) on the first day of each month during the debate season (September through April). For each invitational debate tournament, participants should carefully read the tournament invitation to determine the topic for debate.

FURTHER READING

Cardoza, John A. "California High School Ted Turner Debate: Proposed Judge Guidelines," *The Rostrum*, April 2003. www.nflonline.org/uploads/Rostrum/rr0403califproposedballot.pdf (accessed March 17, 2007).

Copeland, James M. "Secretary James Copeland Responds," *The Rostrum*, February 2003. www.nflonline.org/uploads/Rostrum/pf0203sharpcopeland.pdf (accessed March 17, 2007).

——— "Ted Turner Public Forum Debate: Not Just Another Contest," *The Rostrum*, April 2004. www.nflonline.org/uploads/Rostrum/pf0404copeland.pdf (accessed March 17, 2007). (Donus Roberts, Ted Belch, Frank Sferra)

Durkee, John. "Ted Turner Debate: Establishing the Theoretical Grounds," *The Rostrum*, January 2003. www.nflonline.org/uploads/Rostrum/pf0103durkee.pdf (accessed March 17, 2007).

NFL. "Public Forum Debate," National Forensic League, 2007. www.nflonline.org/uploads/CoachingResources/PFGuidelines.pdf (accessed March 17, 2007).

CHAPTER 17

THE MEDIA MODEL IN PUBLIC FORUM DEBATE

We live in a media age where the fifteen-second sound bite rules. The media orientation of audiences has redefined the practice of persuasion for politicians, public relations specialists, and marketing executives, as well as for educators. Public forum debate was designed specifically for the purpose of helping students become more media savvy. The event's media focus arises from the following elements:

- The format is designed to mirror the one-half hour current events journalistic exchange.

- The topics are ripped from the headlines.

- Participants are encouraged to engage other panel members in a free-flowing exchange.

- Judges are encouraged to value persuasive speaking skills above the sheer number of arguments or the volume of supporting evidence.

So what skills are involved in becoming media savvy? To answer that question, I have consulted the work of Barbara Gibson, an accredited business communicator, who is the founder and president of SpokesComm. The advice in this chapter adapts the recommendations for media spokespersons to the procedures of public forum debate.

It All Starts with Charisma

Audiences are more likely to be persuaded by speakers who make a personal connection with them. Aristotle simply referred to this quality as *ethos*. Many people mistakenly assume that charisma is something you are just born with (or without). But with work and practice, you can improve your believability and likeability. Receiving and adjusting to feedback is an important part of this process. Work at focusing attention on your listener and making your subject matter interesting and accessible. Find some angle on the topic about which you can be passionate—perhaps it is a story of some outrageous wrong you discovered in the course of your research. Passion makes you more dynamic and interesting.

Taking Charge

When you have the floor, it should be clear to everyone in the room that you are in command of your audience. You command attention with your vocal volume, direct eye contact, and confident delivery. During the crossfire periods, you should take advantage of every opportunity to explain, provide an example, or tell a story to illustrate your points. This doesn't mean that you must dominate or monopolize the crossfire exchange; it simply means that you maximize every opportunity.

Keeping It Simple

Your language should be economical, starting with sentences that are short and to the point. The argument briefs you prepare should have two or three reasons in support of each position rather than five or ten reasons. The evidence or example under each of your headings should also be short. Use single-page briefs or even briefs that fit on a single note card. The brevity of the argument brief will serve as a reminder to avoid lengthy responses.

Business communication coach Barbara Gibson emphasizes the importance of eliminating BTC:

> "What? You don't know what a BTC is? Surely that must mean that I am smarter, more in-the-know, cutting edge, than you, mustn't it? Er ... well ... actually, I made it up. You see, I've somehow worked in or with acronym-loving industries for most of my career, including telecommunications and technology. So, in order to hammer home my point that acronyms and insider jargon are Barriers To Communication, I made up my own and began to interrupt the alphabet-speakers with, I'm sorry, but that's a BTC. Or in meetings, I'd hold up a BTC little sign. Since, of course, my acronym had no meaning to anyone but me, the speaker wouldn't have a clue what I was talking about. It was really fun watching them puzzle about it, sometimes try to fake it, and finally ask what a BTC is. And it was the most effective way to get them to understand what they were doing to their audiences."

MAXIMIZING THE NONVERBAL

Most communication texts (whether for public speaking, small group, or interpersonal communication) report the findings of Albert Mehrabian and his research associates in a classic study presented in the 1967 *Journal of Consulting Psychology*. The assumption of this study is that 100 percent of social meaning comes from lexical cues (the literal meaning of words), vocal cues (the way the words are vocally produced), and facial/physical nonverbal cues. Mehrabian found that only 7 percent of meaning comes from the words themselves with 28 percent coming from vocal cues and 55 percent from facial/physical nonverbal cues. If Mehrabian is even approximately correct, then about 90 percent of meaning comes from factors other than the words we use.

The first televised presidential debate occurred in 1960 and was a contest between John F. Kennedy and Richard Nixon. Surveys demonstrated that people who only listened to the debate on the radio thought that Richard Nixon won the debate, while those who watched on television were persuaded that John F. Kennedy won.

Although Nixon presented a great deal of factual support, his eye contact seemed shifty. Also Nixon was visibly sweating during the debate, while Kennedy appeared calm and collected.

Debaters often make the mistake of assuming that nonverbal factors only make a difference at the margins of a judge's decision—that the most important considerations involve the amount of supporting evidence. Media research demonstrates that the opposite is true. Nonverbal factors such as eye contact, confident posture, avoidance of nervous mannerisms, and natural gesturing have consistently been shown to be major determinants of persuasive success.

AVOIDING VOCAL FILLERS

The prototypical problem utterances are *um*, *er*, and *uh*. In actuality, however, other fillers have become more common: *okay*, *right*, *you know*, and *like*. Occasional use of vocal fillers naturally goes along with an extemporaneous delivery style (which is the delivery style appropriate for public forum debate). When the audience starts counting the number of *okays*, however, the problem becomes serious.

Some Toastmaster groups help their members overcome the habit of using vocal fillers by holding up signs whenever a speaker uses a filler word. You might be able to benefit from a similar method in your practice sessions in class.

COMMAND OF THE FACTS

Effective media spokespersons demonstrate an easy command of the facts relevant to their own expertise. There is certainly no alternative to having done thorough research on your topic. The best way to seem to know what you are talking about is to actually know. The extensive crossfire periods in public forum debate create a premium on having facts and examples at your fingertips.

LOSING THE ARROGANCE

Audiences love to root against a bully. Media coach Barbara Gibson reports that "from the hundreds of conversations I've had with PR people, it's clear to me that arrogance is the greatest weakness of most of the corporate spokespeople out there." I can report that arrogance is also a major problem for debaters. Judges will reward you when you show respect for your opponent and a requisite amount of courtesy.

FOR EXAMPLE

Some repetitive phrases should be avoided, but this one should be cultivated. If your opponent asks a question during crossfire, consider starting your answer with this phrase: Let me give you an example …. Examples aid understanding, and it will seem unreasonable for your opponent to insist on a yes or no answer when you are doing your best to explain.

As you prepare for a debate, try to think of examples for every key message you want to communicate. The examples can be real, fictional, or hypothetical (although you should always let your listener know whether the example is real or imaginary).

TELLING A STORY

Storytelling is an important skill in the media age. The goal should be to draw the listener into the story by making sure that it has descriptive detail and a clear moral. As you do research on the current public forum topic, you will probably encounter numerous human interest stories illustrating the importance of each point of view. This is actually a method of support that journalists cultivate; they do so because they know readers want human interest stories. You can make use of this same characteristic of the media as you prepare for your debate rounds.

The policy debater might ignore these human interest stories and record only the statistic or statement of authoritative support. In public forum debate, however, you should pay special attention to the supporting stories.

Framing the Issue

Media messages are all about *framing*, meaning the context from which to view an issue. Tony Palmieri, professor of communication at the University of Wisconsin, Oshkosh, provides the following example in an article titled "The Love/Hate Relationship with the U.S.: Media Framing":

- Story 1: An infant left sleeping in his crib was bitten repeatedly by rats while his 16-year-old mother went to cash her welfare check. A neighbor responded to the cries of the infant and brought the child to St. Joseph's Hospital where he was treated and released into his mother's custody.

- Story 2: An eight-month-old Milwaukee boy was treated and released from St. Joseph's Hospital yesterday after being bitten by rats while he was sleeping in his crib. Tenants said that repeated requests for exterminations had been ignored by the landlord, Henry Brown.

- Story 3: Rats bit eight-month-old Michael Burns five times yesterday as he napped in his crib. Burns is the latest victim of a rat epidemic plaguing inner-city neighborhoods labeled the "Zone of Death." Health officials say infant mortality rates in these neighborhoods approach those in many third-world countries.

Each of the three stories is based on the same set of events. In the first instance, however, the journalist has framed the story in such a way as to highlight the problem of teen pregnancy. In the second story, the journalistic frame focuses on the irresponsibility of landlords. The third story frames the story in such a way as to emphasize the extent of poverty in the United States.

Some students are shocked when they first discover how media framing changes the news. The more important lesson is that framing is both inevitable and unavoidable. Contemporary events must be framed in some way. Skillful debaters learn to use framing to their own advantage.

FURTHER READING

Gibson, Barbara. "SpokesBlog: A Resource for Corporate Media Spokespeople and the PR People Who Support Them." 2007. http://spokesblog.wordpress.com/tag/spokesperson-coaching-tips/.

Kline, Jason. *Public Forum Debate*. NY: Rosen Central, 2007.

Lundstrom, Meg. "Media-Savvy Kids." *Instructor.* November/December 2004. http://content.scholastic.com/browse/article.jsp?id=3776.

CHAPTER 18

STRATEGY IN PUBLIC FORUM DEBATES

Public forum is a lively, audience-centered style of debate. The successful debater must provide logical support without resorting to technical jargon. Also, the time limits—which are much shorter than for other forms of debate—make it impossible to use more than four or five quotations from authority in any one speech. Public forum debate places a premium on a competitor's ability to provide simple yet powerful logical explanations.

ANALYZING A RESOLUTION

Success in public forum debate begins with the proper analysis of the resolution. Policy debaters have only one resolution for the entire year, whereas Lincoln-Douglas debaters keep the same resolution for two months at a time. For public forum debaters, however, the resolution switches each month.

Debate resolutions fall into three types: questions of fact, value, or policy. Resolutions of fact ask whether a statement is true. An example of a resolution of fact is the National

Forensic League (NFL) resolution used in early 2006: "Resolved: That big box retailers benefit the communities in which they are located." Resolutions of fact focus on the past; they ask us to examine historical evidence for the purpose of verifying the truth of a statement about the past.

Resolutions of value ask how highly we should value something or how highly valued one object should be as compared to another. Consider the following value topic: "Resolved: Human genetic engineering is morally justified." Resolutions of value usually focus on the present, asking us to verify or compare the worth of something.

Resolutions of policy ask whether a specified action should be taken. In 2005, the following resolution of policy was used in NFL public forum debate: "Resolved: In the United States, public high school science curriculum should include the study of the Theory of Intelligent Design." Resolutions of policy focus on the future, asking whether a specified action would be more or less desirable. Policy debate resolutions use the word *should* as a way of signaling the focus on future action.

In the first five years of public forum debate, 45 resolutions have been debated (see Appendix E for a list of these resolutions). Of the 45 resolutions debated so far, 71 percent have been policy topics and 29 percent have been resolutions of fact. No true resolutions of value have so far been selected for use in public forum debate.

The resolutions of fact that have been selected for public forum debate generally follow this formula: "x is beneficial to y," "x aids y," "x negatively influences y," or "x positively affects y." Twelve of the thirteen public forum resolutions of fact have followed this model. The only exception is the 2004 topic "Resolved: The United States is losing the War on Terror."

Analysis of any resolution (whether fact, value, or policy) must begin with a definition of the key terms. Consider the topic "Resolved: That big box retailers benefit the communities in which they are located." What is meant by "big box retailers"? To answer this question, do some research using Internet search engines, placing the whole phrase inside quotation marks. Write down the kinds of retail stores that are returned in your search. Wal-Mart seems an obvious example, along with Kmart. Would Sam's Club stores be included? The question is important because many people claim that Wal-Mart harms small businesses. Sam's Clubs, on the other hand, are designed to assist small business owners. Yet would Sam's Clubs be classified as retail or wholesale stores?

Resolutional analysis also requires adopting a point of view and a time frame from which to view the facts. It is impossible to say whether a thing is good or bad, beneficial or harmful, without asking some additional questions. As long ago as 350 B.C. Aristotle, in *The Organon*, referred to these questions as *topoi* (topics). Some topics—called *contraries*—could be paired with their opposites. Students of rhetoric were encouraged to analyze all of the available means of persuasion by thinking through these contraries. The following paragraphs list some of the paired opposites that apply to public forum debate questions.

Short-term or long-term? The things that seem to benefit a community in the short term might end up being harmful in the long term. Communities might benefit in the short term when a new Wal-Mart offers one-stop-shopping and low prices. It might, however, pay a larger price in the long term when small businesses go under, well-paying jobs disappear, and local school districts lose tax revenue.

Economic or cultural? Is it always possible to determine benefits in dollars and cents? Big box retailers can save consumers money yet create a monoculture in which every community soon comes to be the same. Something in the human spirit yearns for diversity; people travel to distant parts of the world just so they can experience cultural variety.

Corporations or consumers? Sometimes the interests of corporations and consumers work at cross purposes. A computer company might hold down its costs by outsourcing its technical support to China. Consumers may, however, have difficulty explaining their problem to a person who is not a native speaker of English.

Employers or employees? Employers could more efficiently go about their business if they didn't have to worry about the numerous regulations of the federal government's Occupational Health and

Safety Administration (OSHA). Employees, however, might be exposed to many more dangerous chemicals if OSHA regulations were lifted.

Young or old? Older Americans would immediately benefit if Medicare would decrease the enrollment fees and co-payments now required for prescription drug programs. Younger Americans would, however, be paying higher payroll taxes to fund the improvements in any drug program for senior citizens.

National or international? Some actions that benefit Americans can disadvantage people in developing countries. The low prices in big box retail stores can come at the expense of child labor or prison labor in China.

Community or individual? Individual rights are often expensive. Ensuring a fair trial for an accused murderer can often cost millions of dollars. A medical malpractice lawsuit can raise the cost of medical care for everyone in the community.

Quantity or quality? Many more Americans could go to college if admission standards were loosened and tuition charges were slashed. The quality of education would, however, suffer as colleges would have to offer remedial courses and reduce spending on equipment and faculty.

Life or liberty? The United States could prevent all the deaths now associated with automobile accidents by banning cars. This savings would, however, come at a great price in reduced freedom to travel.

Economy or environment? The economy benefits from the use of cheap fossil fuels and lax regulation of industrial emissions. Protection of the environment can require just the opposite— shifting to renewable energy and strict regulation of industrial pollutants.

Most of the topics selected for public forum debate have been resolutions of policy. Consider the following example: "Resolved: That the private ownership of handguns should be banned in the United States." Policy resolutions can best be analyzed by using the following stock issues:

- **Significance of harm**—What problems are created by hand-gun ownership?

- **Causation**—What causes handguns to be any more harmful than, say, hunting rifles or kitchen knives?

- **Solution**—Would banning handguns solve the problems?

- **Disadvantage**—Would the problems caused by banning hand-guns outweigh the problems caused by handgun ownership?

Significance of harm: An examination of the harm from handgun use must ask "harm to whom?" The case could be framed around accidental deaths to children, crimes of passion in domestic violence cases, suicide, or victims of violent crime.

Causation: A policy debater's term for causation is *inherency,* but the public forum debater should use language immediately understandable to a general audience. Why is it important to examine causes? The answer is that it helps guide us to appropriate solutions. Suppose, for example, the harm in the pro case on handguns is the accidental death of children. The true cause of these accidents might be the negligence of adults. If handguns are left unloaded or equipped with trigger locks, the harm to children might be avoided short of a handgun ban. Furthermore, if the true cause of childhood deaths is adult negligence, then children can just as easily be harmed by non–gun-related negligence—such as leaving medicines or poisons within the reach of children. To justify a ban on handguns, the pro side needs to show why solutions already available are unable to prevent harm to children.

Solution: Would adopting the resolution solve the problem cited in the pro case? It might be true that handguns are commonly used in suicides, but would a handgun ban help? Wouldn't people bent on suicide simply use other methods?

Disadvantage: Would adopting the resolution create bigger problems than the ones it solves? When handguns are banned, law-abiding citizens will no longer have them, but criminals will continue to be armed. The benefit of lowering the risk of accidental harm to children (or whatever is the harm in the pro case) must then be weighed against greater vulnerability to violent criminals.

BRAINSTORMING

Brainstorming is a technique used to creatively generate ideas on a new topic. You can conduct a brainstorming session with your debate partner, with your whole debate team, or even as a project in your civics class. To maximize the value of brainstorming, you should set a few ground rules:

- All ideas will be written down in plain view of the participants, on a chalk board or white board.

- The goal during brainstorming is quantity, not quality—you will decide later which ideas are worth pursuing.

- Critical comments—even self-critical comments such as "this is probably a dumb idea, but ..."—are not allowed.

- Confine the session in time—fifteen minutes is a good time frame. You want to create the sense that ideas should flow fast and furiously, like popcorn popping. One idea should stimulate others.

Seed the brainstorming session with questions, forming a simple agenda. Use the italicized terms in the previous paragraphs—the ones in the "Analysis of the Resolution" section—to build your agenda. Start by listing each of the key terms in the resolution and asking what they might mean. If the resolution asks whether something is beneficial or detrimental, think through the list of paired opposites. If the debate topic is a resolution of policy, think through each of the stock issues.

After you have finished your brainstorming session, go back through the items on your list to determine the ones that merit research attention. Chapter 3 provides suggestions for managing your research.

WRITING THE CASE

Public forum participants must prepare two speeches: a four-minute pro speech (supporting the resolution) and a four-minute con speech (opposing the resolution). Each speech should be between 760 and 800 words in length.

The speech should begin with a short attention-getting opening, followed by a statement of your position on the resolution. The resolution used in the national tournament in 2006 was "Resolved: The United States should ratify the Kyoto Protocol." Following is the introduction used by Valerie Hobbs, first con speaker for Bishop Heelan (Sioux City, Iowa), the 2006 national champion in public forum debate:

> "The latest in from Peter Roderick, president of Friends of the Earth International, the leading environmentalist group in support of Kyoto: 'I think that everybody agrees that Kyoto is really, really hopeless in terms of delivering what the planet needs, but it's not the sort of nitty-gritty commas and dots in the text of the protocol; it's the symbolic importance.' Well, Peter, we do agree that Kyoto is really, really hopeless, but where you go wrong is that Kyoto is about the nitty-gritty commas and dots; it is about the text."

The speech should then provide reasons you support or oppose the resolution. Each argument should be supported with quotations from authority. The four reasons the Bishop Heelan team offered for opposing the Kyoto Protocol are as follows:

1. The Protocol is ineffective.

   - The Protocol would reduce emissions by only 5.2 percent.

   - The Protocol exempts 134 developing countries.

   - The Protocol provides huge loopholes.

2. The Protocol will have harmful economic repercussions.

   - Abatement costs will be 2.2 trillion dollars.

   - Gasoline prices will be driven up by 66 cents/gallon.

   - Average family income would decrease by $30,000/year.

   - State tax revenue will decrease by 100 billion dollars per year.

   - The Department of Defense will be forced to reduce training exercises and military readiness.

3. Alternatives to the Protocol are available to address global warming.

- The Carbon Sequestration Leadership Forum promotes renewable energy.

- The Energy Policy Act implemented in 2006 provides market-based tax incentives.

4. The scientific community doesn't support the Protocol.

Close the speech with a brief summary and something to create a sense of finality. Bishop Heelan closed its winning con speech with the following sentence: "We refuse to advise you as a judge to vote to ratify a Protocol that compromises the economic stability as well as the national security of the United States."

Before using your opening speeches in a real debate, try them out on your coach and anyone else who will listen and provide feedback. Each time you rehearse the speeches, carefully check the time. Make certain that each speech—both the pro and con speech—will fit comfortably within the four-minute time limit. You should speak at a conversational rate. Resist the temptation to speak more rapidly to make time for an additional piece of supporting evidence.

After you have fine-tuned your first speeches, you are ready to prepare argument response briefs. These response briefs will be used to respond to the arguments made by your opponent. Your goal should be to have a response brief for every argument that you can imagine your opponent might make.

How do you construct the list of possible opposing arguments? Begin by making sure that you could answer the arguments made in your own opening speeches. You will probably face opponents who will make the same arguments you plan to make. Continue your list of possible opposing arguments by examining the record of your brainstorming session. Many of the arguments you considered using in your own first speeches (but ultimately rejected) will probably be made by one of your opponents. When you return home from a tournament, carefully examine your flowsheets to identify any arguments you had not anticipated. Add any such arguments to your list of necessary response briefs.

A response brief in policy debate might be several pages long and include a dozen pieces of supporting evidence. Such briefs have limited usefulness in public forum debate because you would never have time to present more than one or two responses. I recommend that you prepare your response briefs on 4"×6" index cards. For each brief, select your two best responses along with a statistic or short quotation from authority. Provide a complete source for your evidentiary support.

Making Strategic Choices

Every public forum round of debate begins with the toss of a coin. The winner of the coin toss must first decide whether to select a side (pro or con) or a speaking position (first or second). The loser of the coin toss makes the remaining choice.

If you win the coin toss, what should you do? Usually you choose your preferred side. Although the framers of public forum resolutions try to phrase well-balanced topics, there is usually a natural advantage to one side. Even when the resolution is evenly balanced, you probably have more confidence in one of your beginning speeches than in the other. You also might want to consider the reputation of your opponent. You might be aware that your opponent has experienced great success with its pro case. This knowledge might cause you to select the pro position, putting your opponent on its weakest side.

If, however, you have equal confidence in your two cases, you might consider selecting your preferred speaking order. Most public forum debaters, when given a choice, choose to speak second. Speaking second means you have the final rebuttal—the final opportunity to persuade the judge to vote for your side. The only advantage to speaking first is that you are given the opportunity to ask the first question in all three of the crossfire periods. In general, however, the advantage of having the final rebuttal is more important than questioning first in the crossfire periods.

PRACTICE ROUNDS

An important part of success in public forum debate is the development of a proper practice routine. Just as football teams would never consider playing an opponent without extensive practice sessions, so a debate team should plan a practice strategy. If your school has more than one public forum team, you can practice against each other. If neighboring schools have public forum teams, you might be able to set up an after-school scrimmage. If neither option is available, you can practice against one another, with one member of the team in the pro position and the other in the con. This final option is suboptimal, but it is certainly preferable to no practice rounds at all.

Try to find an audience for your practice rounds. You might find social studies or speech teachers who welcome the opportunity to have you do a demonstration debate for their classes.

Whenever you participate in practice rounds, make certain that you begin with a coin toss just as you would in a regular tournament. This provides an opportunity for you to practice being spontaneous, not knowing whether you will be pro or con until minutes before the beginning of the round.

POLICY DEBATE FINAL ROUND

NFL National Tournament 2007

Resolved: The United States federal government should substantially increase the number of persons serving in one or more of the following: AmeriCorps, Learn and Serve America, Senior Corps, Peace Corps, or the United States Armed Forces.

Affirmative: Andrew Baker and Sarah Weiner (Shawnee Mission West, Coach: Ken King)

Negative: Stephanie Spies and Matt Fisher (Glenbrook North High School, Coach: Christina Tallungan)

First Affirmative Constructive Speech: Andrew Baker, Shawnee Mission West High School

I have a few congratulations and thank-you's I'd like to start out today with. The first is for our opponents. I can attest that they have done exactly as much work as we have on this debate issue, and this is going to be a very clash-oriented round. I guarantee to you this is going to be a good debate.

As far as thank you's are concerned, I would like to give my first thank you to my partner, Sarah Weiner. It is one thing to have a debate partner you know is going to make good arguments when necessary. It is a much more rare and valuable thing to have a debate partner you trust both in and out of round. Sarah is literally one in a million and I will miss her greatly next year when I am debating in college. No matter what, it is worth the trip here, that's for sure.

I would also like to thank my friends and family for all the support for me this year. My family and friends have always been there to both celebrate success and support us after a tough loss.

Additionally, I would like to thank our debate coaches. It is one thing to coach a team with arguments and education in mind. It is a far greater accomplishment to coach a team with a goal of making them better human beings. Our coaches do that for us at every turn, and for that we are forever grateful. I think I speak for both Sarah and myself that you are not only our coaches, but you are also our mentors and friends.

My next thank you goes out to the Kansas debate community. Every coach, assistant, debater, and parent is involved in this thank you. When teams were actuating our chances of actually doing well in this tournament, it was tough to determine whether Sarah and I had a fighting chance because of how small our squad was and the fact that we only found out we were attending this tournament a week in advance. Little did our opponents know that whenever they debated us or any other team from Kansas, that they were taking on an entire state. Little did our opponents know that Kansas had set up a war room in which arguments and intelligence were being shared by everyone. Little did our opponents know that Sarah and I were literally flooded with support at all times in this tournament. This unity is something that I have never seen before in the debate community and something that I believe everyone should strive for. Kansas is the reason why we are debating here today. Between the years of competition it has provided for us and the support we've needed when the time was right, Kansas debate has been there.

(Applause). They are apparently still here as well.

I would also like to thank the University of Texas at Dallas, the school I will be attending next year to debate for. They've given us continuous support throughout the entirety of the tournament, and before it even started, really.

Finally, I would like to thank the Executive Committee of the NFL as well as the local host committee for putting the tournament on. It has been extremely well run from our perspective; they deserve our gratitude for doing that. Additionally the sponsors, also the ones behind this debate; we should really be thankful that they can put this tournament on for us. Let's get to the debate now, without further ado.

Observation One is Inherency. America faces a crisis. Specifically, at-risk youth who are the most in need of summer opportunities currently lack access to support. From Shirley Sagawa, visiting fellow at the Center for American Progress and a national expert on child and youth policy, from two days ago, titled, "Summer of Service: A New Rite of Passage for Young Teens," Center for American Progress, accessed online:

"In the 15 years since its enactment, national service has grown from a demonstration program to a large-scale system engaging more than 75,000 Americans. Unfortunately, research shows that the young people who need this sort of experience most are the least likely to be engaged. Disadvantaged teens are far less likely to volunteer than their peers from more advantaged backgrounds, by a 43-to-59 percent margin. However, those disadvantaged youth who serve hold more positive civic attitudes, discussing politics, believing that they can make a difference, and planning to go to college at higher rates than their low-income peers who do not volunteer."

Unfortunately, the Summer Service Act of 2007 is stalled in committee—it has laid dormant for two months and counting. From the Library of Congress, Online accessed 6-21-2007, Title: A bill to Amend the National and Community Service Act of 1990 to Establish a Summer of Service State Grant Program. Latest Major Action: 4/17/2007, and was referred to the Senate committee.

Thus we present the following plan. Plan plank One is administration: the Congress of the United States of America. Plan Plank Two is the mandates: The United States Congress should substantially increase the number of people serving in AmeriCorps by amending the National Community Service Act of 1990 to incorporate the Summer of Service Act of 2007, Bill 7.1128. Plan Plank Three is enforcement and funding: We are guaranteed through normal means. Plan Plank Four is we reserve the right to fiat and clarify our terms.

Our first advantage is Education. First, the Summer of Service would provide college scholarships to underprivileged students who would otherwise be unlikely to receive a college education.

From Sagawa (previously cited), from two days ago, "Middleschoolers who perform a 'summer of service' under the bill would earn a scholarship. At a time in life when students and their families need to begin thinking about college, this feature would positively brand the participating youth as college material—even those who never considered the possibility—and could set these students and their families on a course of saving for college."

And this is crucial to economic growth in two ways. The first is domestic potential: Increasing minority education efforts is critical to create the necessary domestic talent to sustain U.S. economic growth and national security.

From Shirley M. Malcolm, Daryl E. Chubin, and Jolene K. Jesse, American Association for the Advancement of Science and National Action Council for Minorities in Engineering, October 2004, titled "Standing Our Ground: A Guidebook for STEM Educators in the Post-Michigan Era," accessed online:

"The case for diversity has been well articulated. Economists have identified progress as the single most important determining factor in U.S. economic growth, accounting for as much as half of the Nation's long-term growth over the past 50 years. The number-two greatest threat to national security is the failure to invest adequately in science and to ensure that science and math education produces enough young Americans to actually do the science that is needed."

If women, underrepresented minorities, and persons with disabilities were represented in the U.S. science and engineering, and technology workforce, this shortage of skilled American workers could largely be ameliorated. If we do not act now to incorporate the marginalized groups into the workforce, we risk endangering our economic and national security well into the future.

Second, cross-cultural competence: Diversity in academics is critical to cross-cultural competence and critical thinking which is key to U.S. businesses and the economy. From Thomas A. Gottschalk, Senior Vice President and General Counsel at General Motors Corporation, in 2005, from the paper, "Brief of the General Motors Corporation as Amicus Curiae in Support of Appellants," accessed online:

"The ability of American businesses to thrive in the twenty-first century will depend in large measure on our Nation's responses to the increasing diversity of our own populations. To succeed, American businesses must select leaders who possess cross-cultural competence—the capacities to interact with and understand the multiplicity of perspectives held by persons of different ethnicities. Authorities concur that cross-cultural competence is the most important new attribute for future effective performance in the global marketplace. Research confirms students are likely to acquire greater cross-cultural competence in a multicultural academic environment, in which students and faculty of different cultures and races interact, than they are in a homogeneous one, in which cross-cultural communication is a mere theoretical construct."

And finally, economic growth is key to resolve a host of social problems, aid national security, and improve living standards. From Leonard Silk, Distinguished Professor of Economics at Pace University and Senior Research Fellow at the Ralph Bunche Institute, in the *Foreign Affairs* magazine, Vol. 72, Issue 1, 1994:

"Economic hardship is not the only cause of social and political pathologies, but it aggravates all of them, and in turn they feed back on economic development. They also undermine efforts to deal with such global problems as environmental pollution, the production and trafficking of drugs, crime, sickness, famine, AIDS, and other plagues. Economic growth—and growth alone—creates the additional resources that make it possible to achieve such fundamental goals as higher living standards, national and collective security, a healthier environment, and more liberal and open economies and societies."

Advantage Two is Service Learning. First, current national programs towards underprivileged youth utilize an unsuccessful reactionary policy. Implementing the affirmative is crucial to motivating students and building effective communities. From Sagawa, previously cited:

"Young people's experience would be part of a learning plan that helps them connect their service to citizenship. Some students would be so motivated by their experience that they would want to stay involved, some would use their experience in other ways, bringing their greater sense of self-worth, community, teamwork, and other skills to future undertakings. Unfortunately, these kinds of opportunities are the exception, not the rule in America today. Despite the pivotal nature of the early teen years, youth-focused investments tend to emphasize problems, not potential. We spend money telling teens to stay away from drugs; to discourage teen pregnancy. Yet research tells us that giving young people something to say 'yes' to is an essential part of teaching them to say 'no.'"

Community-building through the affirmative is empirically effective. The examples include support for the environment and the homeless and assistance ranging from tutoring the young children to caring for the elderly. The affirmative teaches students to create and examine real problems in their community and build their own projects to help create a better society.

Sagawa, previously cited:

"Not only would students and their families benefit, communities would as well. Existing programs have mobilized middle-school students to manage recycling programs, educate the community about environmental hazards, and tutor young children. In the wake of Hurricane Charlie, the students interviewed, registered, and deployed more than 5,000 volunteers. The kind of awareness, empowerment, and responsibility built through the program could be exhibited by teens everywhere. We could provide a Summer of Service, helping them to put their lives on a positive trajectory and become a vital resource for their communities."

And finally, deteriorating social bonds exacerbate forms of welfare. Only service learning can build an ethic of community that builds connections and resolves the roots of human conflict.

From Jo Ann Mort, the director of communications for UNITE, the national clothing and textile union, titled, "A Place for Us: How to Make Society Civil and Democracy Strong," from 1998:

"Much is at stake today. The economic reality of jobs vanishing at the very moment when we are reaffirming the ideology of work, calling the work ethic our core value in the politics of welfare reform presents a problem. In our civilization, work has endowed human life with meaning, dignity, and status. As work disappears we must look to new ways to define ourselves. Making ourselves good citizens is the perfect route. Democracy depends on them to be educated into civil society, to participate in deliberation, time to service, volunteer for civic activities. Unless we "find new ways to distribute the fruits of non-labor-based productivity, more citizens will become poor in economic and social terms and the system itself will be undermined and destroyed by political instability, and new forms of class wars."

Observation Two is solvency. First, the plan would make community service a rite of passage for students entering high school, transforming young lives and entire communities. Our author is an expert on this subject. From Sagawa, previously cited:

"Legislation would support community efforts to engage young teens in intensive service as a 'rite of passage' during the summer of high school. Research shows that service-learning promotes positive youth development like few other programs can, motivating students to achieve and teaching personal, social, and civic responsibility. By making the summer service experience a 'rite of passage' for young people transitioning to high school, whole communities could be transformed. Using AmeriCorps members and college students to lead the younger students in service offers the dual benefit of keeping costs reasonable and offering positive role models. The Dodd-Cochran-DeLauro bill encourages this staffing model."

And second, each specific aspect of the plan is absolutely key—the children we target are too old for babysitters and too young for jobs. Summer is an especially important time for the plan to occur.

From Sagawa, previously cited:

"The summer months between middle school and high school can be a particularly testing time when children are redefining themselves and in the process making decisions that may well determine who they will be as adults, for better or worse. For working parents, these next several months are a particular challenge. Their kids are too young for paid jobs and too old to be 'babysat.' Economically well-off families can afford a host of summer camps offering learning opportunities from language immersion to lacrosse. But in too many communities, offerings for older youth are limited and prices steep, making summer a time of particular peril."

Thank you, and I'm now open for cross-examination.

Cross-examination of Andrew Baker (Shawnee Mission West High School) by Matt Fisher (Glenbrook North High School)

Q: OK, my first question is, the plan would apply to individuals that have graduated from the eighth grade, and are then moving into high school, correct?

A: Uh, correct. They are middle schoolers, basically.

Q: I don't know about you, but I definitely was not thinking about getting a college scholarship right after I got out of middle school. So, why would these kids be thinking about the economic motivation that would be necessary?

A: Our Sagawa evidence is empirical on this study. It is not only the economic motivation, but it is also the fact that there is a parent pressure on this issue … the kids aren't doing anything.

Q: So, kids aren't doing anything in the summers? When these kids are eighth graders, going into ninth grade, they have nothing better to do in the summer months than serve individuals? This is obviously a summer time in which, for example, kids could play baseball, kids could enjoy long summer days, any episode of the *Wonder Years* has a host of examples.

A: This is all assuming kids are in a well-off economic environment. Our evidence indicates that those people are already well taken care of. Our Sagawa evidence, the last piece of evidence I read to you, says that low-income families, people that are disadvantaged in the status quo, aren't able to pay for those type things.

Q: So, people are driven only by this economic motivation? No one should serve for the benefits of serving? Everyone should just serve because it could help their economic stature?

A: Our argument is that it is beneficial; the parents can realize that as well. It is not a sequitor as to whether it is true. Our argument on the education debate specifically indicates that this $500 they receive will be good for them going to college.

Q: They receive $500? College tuition for one year at an average college is drastically more than $500. I am wondering why the economic stimulus of this summer is that necessary when kids have four years in the future they can get a job.

A: The first piece of Sagawa evidence is empirical and on point on this argument; it indicates that this $500 at a key time in which families aren't even really starting to think about it yet gets them along that track and gets them to acquire more scholarships.

Q: So the economic benefits derived from the plan would occur not only four years for high school, but then four years for college, and then after that these individuals would be in the labor force, correct?

A: Uh, we're claiming that this immediacy of the plan leads to a perception that these people are now getting into college; it makes them college bound.

Q: There is a perception that college enlistment numbers go up even though they will not actually go up for four more years. Which piece of evidence draws that distinction? Please point it out specifically.

A: These children are immediately serving. Our Sagawa evidence in the civil society ...

Q: Could you please point it out specifically? That's all I'm asking.

A: You got it. On the civil society advantage, our evidence from Sagawa evidence indicates that these people will be serving immediately, thus increasing the community's feeling towards what they can and cannot do.

Q: So the U.S. economy is dependent on a $500 stipend being given to eighth graders?

A: No, the U.S. economy is dependent on cultural diversity in our educational systems.

Q: So we need to be critical thinkers and engage more students?

A: Uh, that's kind of our argument. It's specific students that we're looking for.

First Negative Constructive Speech by Stephanie Spies (Glenbrook North High School)

Before I start, there are a few people that we would like to thank. I would like to thank the National Forensic League for hosting this tournament. Vickie Fellers, the Wichita host committee, the generous tournament sponsors, and especially the Colorado College for hosting policy debate as an event at this tournament. And the tab room at Wichita East for putting on such a well-run and fun tournament. Thank you to the esteemed panel of judges for taking your time to adjudicate this important debate. I would also like to thank our coaches: Christina Tallungan, our director of debate at Glenbrook North; our coaches Michael Klinger, Tristan Morales, and Greg Malis; and Max Boldman, a fellow student and friend, who has been extremely helpful to us throughout the year. They have all been instrumental in our success this year and have really made my last year in debate a really memorable experience.

I would also like to thank my parents for always encouraging and supporting me throughout my years in debate and elsewhere, and my partner, Matt Fisher for making my senior year of debate so successful, exciting, and most importantly, entertaining.

I'd also like to thank our opponents, Chris and Sarah from Shawnee Mission West. I'm glad that I get to share my last debate with such a successful and competitive team. Last, but not least, I'd definitely like to thank Wild West World for such a wonderful afternoon of entertainment.

So, the order will be three new offcase positions and then solvency.

First off is topicality. A: the thesis: In order to be topical. In order to be topical, the affirmative must substantially increase the number of persons serving in AmeriCorps. We have definitional support. First, an increase refers to a process and not an outcome. The plan itself must increase enlistment through active recruitment; it can not simply lead to it. This is the Higher Education Funding Council from 2004, accessed online: "'Increase' is used in relation to considerations to be taken into account in the exercise of a function, rather than an objective in itself. An obligation on principal regulators to 'increase' compliance *per se* is unworkable, insofar as it does not adequately define the limits or nature of the statutory duty. The obligation could be considered to be ever-increasing."

And, "substantial" means the increase must be definite. Potential future increases are not topical. *Words and Phrases,* 1964, accessed online: "Substantial means not concealed, denoting that which not merely can be, but is supposed to be, potential, certain, absolute, real at the present time."

B. Violation. The affirmative only passes a bill and offers the option of summer service. It does not actually guarantee that more people will join after the plan.

C. Standards. First, they blow the lid off the topic. There are a huge amount of things that increase the attractiveness of a program to increase recruitment. That creates an impossible research burden for the negative and causes shallow debate.

Rieffel, visiting fellow at the Brookings Institution, 2005, accessed online:

"Eight factors appear to impact the number who perform service: the missions, demographics, employment opportunities, compensation, prior experience, technology, and safety and security. Interest in the overseas service is linked to the tougher job market. The business cycle also affects the supply of older volunteers. In periods of expansion the risks of taking time out for volunteer service are reduced for men and women who are well-established in their careers."

2. They steal our core ground. The best generics are based out of increasing numbers and mandating people serve. Adequate negative ground is key to going in depth on the question of national service.

D. Topicality is a voting issue. It is a prima facie burden to justify that they fall within the bounds of the resolution. If they do not, it is out of your jurisdiction to vote for them.

Next off is the justification argument. The central question posed by this year's resolution is should the United States federal government increase the number of persons in national service. In order to justify an affirmative ballot, the affirmative team must prove that action by the federal government is necessary to solve the significant harm. We believe the affirmative team has failed to justify federal action because the harm isolated by them could easily be remedied if the 50 states, Washington, D.C., and all other relevant sub-national actors should substantially increase funding to secondary schools to establish and maintain policy debate programs. Solving the affirmative's harm without federal action is a more desirable option because it avoids wasteful spending at the federal level. And, expanding NFL style debate would solve for any academic achievement and civic engagement. Russell Hanes, volunteer for the New York and Southern California Urban Debate Leagues in 2007, accessed online in *The Rostrum*:

"The percentage of schools participating in debate has been declining. Educational inequality is something that debate coaches need to confront. A student at a high school without an NFL program is at a serious educational disadvantage. Students most in need of engagement are the least likely to have such options. What is needed from coaches is collective action to address one of the substantive inequalities in education—to give more students the opportunity to participate in NFL through their school. The new strategy must be active, bringing in new schools and helping small programs grow bigger. Equity issues are survival issues for the debate community."

And, debate is the best tool to educate individuals about domestic politics and get people actually involved as informed citizens. Joyner, professor of international law at Georgetown University, Spring of 1999, accessed online:

"Debate can be an effective pedagogical tool for education in the social sciences, helping students understand different perspectives on a policy issue. Debates present the alternatives and consequences in a formal, rhetorical fashion before a judgmental audience, and not mere passive consumers. Students become legal advocates, gaining greater insight into the real-world legal dilemmas, as they realize the complexities of applying and implementing law."

And, educational policies are best handled by the states. Ferejohn, senior fellow at the Hoover Institution and political science at Stanford University, and Weingast, senior fellow at the Hoover Institution and chairman of the Department of Political Science at Stanford, accessed online, 1997:

"Local government officials have inherently better information concerning local conditions and local preferences. Public schools have been viewed as a responsibility of local governments. The federal government is likely to have insufficient information to tailor neighborhood schools to local needs and tastes. Local provision has inherent advantages."

Next off is the federal budget disadvantage. The thesis: the plan increases federal government spending at a time when our budget is already overstretched. At a time when our nation has to fight two wars and defend our homeland, the irreversible spending on the plan is reckless and endangers national security.

First the uniqueness—Bush has just appointed Jim Nussle as the new manager of the Office of Management and Budget—he will continue to hold the line on any new spending.

Gerstenzang, a *Times* staff writer, in July 2007 in the *Los Angeles Times:*

"Bush named Jim Nussle to replace Portman. Nussle has been better known for his strict adherence to conservative budget priorities. As OMB director, he will use his expertise about the budget process to ensure that the taxpayers' money is spent with respect and with restraint."

Link: The plan funds a new national service priority—since the plan cannot be repealed, it becomes a sacred cow in the federal budget and causes duplicative and wasteful expenditure of resources. Brady, Republican representative from Texas, 2006, in his Congressional testimony:

"If Congress were a manufacturing plant, we would manufacture spending. Once we create a federal program, it never goes away. The closest thing to eternal life we'll ever see on Earth is a government program. Not only do they not go away, but Congress clones them. Every federal program duplicates five others. At a time of war, with large deficits, we cannot afford this inefficiency. We need no sacred cows."

The Impact—Wasteful spending on domestic priorities endangers national security abroad with devastating global consequences. Peterson, chairman of the council on foreign relations and deputy of the Federal Reserve of New York, January, 1999 in *Foreign Affairs*, accessed online:

"One need not be a Nobel laureate in economics to understand that a GDP growth is the product of workforce and productivity growth. National defense is the classic example. The West already faces grave threats from rogue states armed with biological and chemical arsenals. None of these external dangers will shrink to accommodate our declining GDP. Leading developed countries will no doubt need to spend as much or more on defense as they do today."

Now the Case. First, the type of academic achievement that they promote is different. It just causes volunteerism of people later in life. It does not cause a positive contribution to the economy.

Second is that there is a very long time frame for children getting involved in tangible GDP growth in the economy. There is no immediate impact from the affirmative on the economy.

Additionally, there is a five-year trend of skyrocketing civil engagement in youth now. Lester, writing for the Associated Press in 2007, accessed online:

"People in this country have been volunteering at record levels in the years following Sept. 11. More than a fourth of the population did volunteer work in 2006 and was heavily influenced by a sharp increase—almost doubling—in the volunteer rates of young people ages 16 to 19. From 9/11 and the devastation of hurricanes has come an unmistakable good: a strong interest in volunteering and community involvement. Volunteerism rates also have increased for most age groups."

And, no one will use the summer. There is no reason why kids in junior high and high school would give up their summers to volunteer in AmeriCorps.

Additionally, civic engagement is high because of Iraq. Ford, contributing writer for *Vibe News,* 2007:

"Students commemorated the largest anti-war demonstration in history yesterday and it marked the anniversary of the largest anti-war demonstration in history. Students at colleges, universities participated in a variety of walk-outs, strikes, teach-ins and protests. Students felt empowered."

And, there is an internal tradeoff. People that normally do AmeriCorps during the school year will hold off until the summer because of the better benefits of the plan. This will actually cause a net decrease in volunteerism and means they can't solve.

Additionally, if people join just for monetary benefits, it is no different from a job. This undercuts the idea of altruism in place of misplaced selfishness and turns their advantages of volunteerism and civil engagement because kids will join AmeriCorps instead of getting true jobs.

Additionally, volunteerism in AmeriCorps is already high. *World Magazine,* 3/10/2007, accessed online:

"Boosted by patriotism in the wake of 9/11, volunteers have flocked to government-sponsored service programs in the last five years. Applications for AmeriCorps' program of placing willing volunteers with established nonprofits have grown by 50 percent since 2004."

I am open for cross-examination.

CROSS-EXAMINATION OF STEPHANIE SPIES (GLENBROOK NORTH HIGH SCHOOL) BY ANDREW BAKER (SHAWNEE MISSION WEST HIGH SCHOOL)

Q: Let's talk about your topicality violation, first. Our first piece of Sagawa evidence indicates that our bill actively recruits middle schoolers who are underprivileged in the status quo. How do we not meet your violation?

A: Our interpretation is that your affirmative has to be ….First to justify your prima facie burden you have to be different, you have to be a change from the status quo. Which means even if these programs are in place, you do not change them. Second is that …

Q: Wait. Hold on one sec. The first Sagawa evidence indicates that in the status quo they are not recruiting people. How is this argument applying?

A: The bill … all of your plan text says that you will enact this bill. It does not actively recruit people to join AmeriCorps, nor does it guarantee that even when you offer this incentive, people will actually take it and join.

Q: Our first Sagawa evidence indicates that the bill does actively recruit people. Where's the violation?

A: Our evidence indicates that an increase refers to a process, not an outcome, and that it has to immediately start with the passage of the plan. Yes, sometime after the bill is passed, after the affirmative, we will start going out and actively recruiting people but it is not an immediate effect of the plan.

Q: So this is more of an immediacy argument than anything else?

A: It's both. It is not a policy that is a definite increase because you cannot guarantee that anyone will accept the monetary incentive offered, especially because it is only $500.

Q: So do we just need to read evidence on this topic that people will join?

A: Not just evidence but you need to have a justification for why an immediate increase in your plan would be a good idea.

Q: OK, let's go to that justification argument next.

A: Sure.

Q: Are you claiming that debate will solve all aspects of our affirmative?

A: Well, debate could solve all of the aspects of your affirmative, but we are also saying that ...

Q: Could?

A: You need to justify your use of the federal government in the resolution.

Q: Awesome. Does debate actively recruit people?

A: Well, our counter advocacy would say that we should actively recruit people into ...

Q: Do you have any evidence proving this argument?

A: Yes, I read two pieces of evidence on this question.

Q: No, evidence indicating that they do or will advocate and that will actively recruit people and that will solve?

A: Well, our argument is that they should do that, and that will solve.

Q: They should do that, but do you have any analysis as to why they should?

A: We are advocating that they should do that.

Q: OK, you are advocating. Awesome. On this economy disadvantage. Our affirmative indicates the economy is already in the hole right now because of a lack of cross-cultural diversity. Did you make any arguments on that debate in the 2AC?

A: Yes, our evidence indicates that it's actually in the tanks because of Iraq and Afghanistan and the administration and the government continuing to spend in supplemental appropriations on the war. Causing ... forcing the government to shift its focus.

Q: So if we're already spending on supplemental appropriations in the status quo, why can't our affirmative just coincide with that?

A: Because you're not sending people to Iraq or Afghanistan.

Q: Right, but if your uniqueness evidence indicates that they will continue spending supplementally, why does our affirmative ...

A: No, our uniqueness evidence indicates that Bush recently appointed a new director of the OMB to hold the line on any new federal domestic spending, because we are so overstretched in places like Iraq and Afghanistan. Your plan would be a shift away from that which would allow Congress to continue, as our evidence says, its lovely idea of continuing to breed new programs.

Q: So what's the brink on this argument? How much money do we have to permanently spend for you to win a link argument?

A: What do you mean? I don't understand?

Q: How much money does our affirmative have to spend for you to isolate a link argument?

A: Your own affirmative provides budgetary support in your plan. That would obviously have to be a lot in order to be a substantial increase.

Q: What's "a lot" mean?

A: What do you mean?

Q: Contextualize "a lot."

A: Our link evidence is a linear link. Every amount of money spent on federal programs ...

Q: Where is that?

A: Sure. Do you want to see it?

Q: Yeah.

A: This piece of evidence (pointing to a piece of evidence on an argument brief). This piece of evidence right here. Every federal program ... "the closest thing to eternal life we'll ever see on Earth is a government program. Not only do they not go away, but Congress clones them."

Q: OK. Thanks.

Second Affirmative Constructive Speech by Sarah Weiner (Shawnee Mission West High School)

Before I begin, I would like to echo my partner and my competitors in thanking the director of NFL, the Executive Committee, the local host committee, the tab room staff, all of the Wichita East volunteers in those yellow shirts who helped us find the elevator every day during the policy tournament. For everyone who has contributed to this tournament, we are eternally grateful. This has been a wonderful experience for both of us and I know I'll never forget it.

I also want to echo our thanks to our coaches who have always been guides to us. I always talk to Mr. King, my head coach, about why he coaches debate and why we do this. The only thing we can come up with is that we just enjoy it. This is one of the best activities I've ever participated in, and I'm proud to stand in front of you today. I also want to thank my debate partner, who is the best debate partner I could ever ask for. I'm going to miss him terribly when he goes to college next year.

Alright, for the order: First topicality, then solvency, justification, and then spending.

First, on topicality: we meet their violation. Our first solvency piece of evidence from Sagawa on 6/20 specifically says that the bill we pass will support legislation to engage youth. The card reads, "legislation would support community efforts to engage young teens in intensive service as a rite of passage during the summer." This legislation would actively recruit teens who are underprivileged; that's the premise of our 1AC.

Additionally, we meet because the intent of our plan is to increase the number of people in AmeriCorps through the Summer of

Service program. There is no abuse on this argument because we do defend that increase, and they have links to all of their disadvantages.

Additionally, the plan would provide 100,000 students into a Summer of Service at a cost of only $100 million. From Sagawa, cited in the 1AC: "Awareness, empowerment, and responsibility could be exhibited by teens everywhere. For $100 million we could provide 100,000 a Summer of Service and $500 in college scholarships." Additionally, there are only 70,000 people in AmeriCorps right now, which means we would substantially increase the number of people in AmeriCorps, by over doubling the number of people in the institution.

She says … Our counter-interpretation is that "increase" is progressive. From *Merriam Webster Online* in 2006: "to become progressively greater, as in size, amount, number, or intensity." And our standards are better. First is limits: No case is topical under the negative interpretation, because people can't immediately be put into any program.

Additionally, we give them more ground, because the only way to immediately increase the number of people in a national service program would be to fiat them in which would kill negative ground.

She says we explode the limits, but this simply isn't true because we do defend our plan and an increase of 100,000 students. And additionally, she would have us actively recruiting people. If you believe that the legislation does not actively recruit people right now, she would have us fundamentally change something in the status quo to make an organization go out and recruit people. There would be no literature base for this which would hurt the negative ground.

Finally, she says that we hurt the core ground because it needs to be mandatory, but "mandatory" was removed from the topic because the framers of the resolution believed that it overlimited it. We are one hundred percent topical; there is no reason for you to vote on it in today's round.

On to solvency. Her first argument is that we just increase volunteers later, but extend our first solvency piece of evidence from Sagawa which is that we actively recruit youth to be in the Summer of Service AmeriCorps program, and extend the Sagawa evidence that says that we would increase by 100,000 youth.

Her next argumentation is that there is a long time frame to the increase in the GDP. But our education advantage solves the economy. Our first Sagawa evidence from two days ago indicates that the Summer of Service would provide college scholarships to underprivileged students who would otherwise be unlikely to seek a college education. Additionally, our Malcolm, Chubin, and Jesse in 2004 evidence indicates that increasing the education of underprivileged students is necessary to increase domestic talent to sustain U.S. economic growth. And finally, our Gottschalk evidence in 2005 indicates that diversity is critical to cross-cultural competence and critical thinking, smarter workers, and a better economy. The status quo is not going to solve the economy. Only our plan can save the economy in the future, which means that you must consider the time frame to be right now.

She says that civic engagement is up in the status quo. But extend our Sagawa evidence, the first piece of inherency evidence says that underprivileged teenagers are not being civically engaged. These underprivileged youth are a key to the economy because we need to bring the underprivileged into economic sectors like science and math if we are going to be competitive in world markets.

She says that kids won't give up their summer, but all of our Sagawa solvency evidence indicates that these students are looking for something to do during the summer and their parents are looking for something as well.

She says that civic engagement is up because of Iraq, but this is answered above, because these youth simply are not being civically engaged.

She says there is an internal trade-off because these children would do AmeriCorps during the summer and not during the year, but AmeriCorps as a program for post-secondary education is a two-year time commitment. This is a unique program within AmeriCorps which is only for the summer. Additionally, our Sagawa evidence indicates that these underprivileged youth would not be doing it during the year—that they are specifically looking for something to do during their summer.

She says that we just make it a job, but we give them a $500 scholarship. Our Sagawa evidence at the top of the education advantage specifically says that this $500 scholarship brands these youth as college potential, something that neither they or their parents would have considered before. It puts them on the path to college. They don't see it as a job, but as an opportunity. Additionally, extend our last piece of Sagawa evidence on solvency which says that these youth are too young to have jobs during the summer anyway.

And finally, she says that interest in AmeriCorps is high, but extend the first piece of Sagawa evidence in inherency which says that underprivileged youth are not civically engaged, and they are certainly not civically engaged in AmeriCorps.

On to her justification argument. First, she has no evidence indicating that we are going to be able to get underprivileged people within the debate realm. Additionally, we solve this civic engagement with our 1AC. We say that teenagers aren't civically engaged right now and underprivileged children aren't civically engaged. If we civically engage them the summer before their freshman year in high school, then once they are in their freshman year they will be more likely to take activities like debate because they will be interested in public issues.

Additionally, we don't need to justify that we are the only way to solve our advantages. We just need to justify the resolution. And we prove to you that we ought to increase the number of people in AmeriCorps through the federal government.

First, the states can't amend a piece of federal legislation, which is what this bill does. And the national infrastructure of the plan is the crucial internal link to all of our solvency claims. From Shirley Sagawa, cited in the 1AC: "A universally available Summer of Service program would help fill this policy gap by helping communities create positive alternatives for young teens. Developing a national system to enable all young people to participate in service as a rite of passage would be possible if the system were built on the existing infrastructure of service and youth programs."

And finally, move on to spending. First, spending now is going to improve fiscal discipline and stewardship in the long term. From the Economic Policy Institute, online, 2003: "Spending proposals will actually improve fiscal stewardship in the long run as we learned during the late 1990s. Faster growth is the surest route to deficit reduction. By using temporary measures to prime the pump of the economy when we need to do so, we can lessen unemployment and improve prosperity while at the same time promoting fiscal integrity."

Also, extend the piece of evidence I read to you on topicality from Shirley Sagawa. It says that our plan would only cost $100 million. Make them prove a brink that $100 in spending would topple the economy. And additionally, it's non-unique because fiscal discipline on AmeriCorps is weak in the status quo. From Alex Wayne, CQ staff, 6/19, "Senate Bill Defies Bush on Abstinence, Spending," *Congressional Quarterly Weekly*:

"The bill is the largest domestic spending measure, divvying up $149.2 billion in discretionary spending among the three large departments it covers, plus several smaller agencies such as the Social Security Administration and AmeriCorps. Bush requested a fiscal 2008 Labor, HHS, Education appropriations bill totaling no more than $140.9 billion in discretionary spending."

And additionally, extend the analysis on the solvency that we solve for the economy faster and our time frame is important. In turn, the plan aids economic growth in two key ways. First extend our Malcolm et al. domestic potentiality evidence. The evidence is so explicit we'll quote it: "The case for diversity is the single most important determining factor in U.S. economic growth." This is because the plan helps resolve crucial worker shortages that can only be restored through domestic education. And second, extend our Gottschalk cultural competence evidence that American competence is key to competing in foreign markets. And our Malcolm, Chubin, and Jesse evidence in 2004 indicates an increase in education of underprivileged kids is necessary to increase domestic talent to sustain U.S. national security. Unless domestic talent is increased by the plan, a terrorist attack will be inevitable. And our turn outweighs their link arguments because our evidence is so specific.

CROSS-EXAMINATION OF SARAH WEINER (SHAWNEE MISSION WEST HIGH SCHOOL) BY STEPHANIE SPIES (GLENBROOK NORTH HIGH SCHOOL)

Q: How long does it take to translate a person that is involved in a summer activity into talent that they can put back into the economy to make us a competitive economy?

A: We say that immediately—as soon as these children are old enough to have jobs they will be giving back to the economy.

Q: Wouldn't it at least take a whole summer?

A: It will take three months of a summer.

Q: So what do you think will have a faster and larger impact on the economy: kids learning to be civilly engaged and then down the line becoming scientists, thus making us more competitive, or spending $100 million on a domestic issue when we are overstretched in Iraq and Afghanistan?

A: We have two answers; first, the last part of your question proves that this is non-unique. We are spending billions and billions of dollars in Iraq and Afghanistan, and we have not seen this collapse.

Q: Right, but not domestically.

A: Additionally, the argument is that ... our Gottschalk evidence indicates that the only way that we are going to maintain economic primacy and competitiveness in the future is to have cross-cultural education now. That means that your disadvantage is going to be non-unique; the economy will collapse unless we do our 1AC. We are the only option to saving the economy in the future.

Q: Wait, I have a question, though. In the future, it will inevitably collapse, this is probably true, but why if students are getting involved in debate are we not allowed to still be competitive without spending money on a domestic issue?

A: Because people ... I don't understand, I mean if your argumentation is that people being involved in debate cross-culturally would increase foreign accomplishments ...

Q: Well, do you have evidence that we wouldn't be able to get lower-income people involved in debate programs?

A: You aren't ... like you don't have a policy for these judges to vote on that would actively recruit the underprivileged into debate.

Q: Oh, I think you misunderstand. Our justification also says that we could have a counter advocacy which allows the federal government to substantially increase people in policy debate programs rather than in national service.

A: It is our argumentation that these people will not go into policy debate unless they are civically engaged. If you didn't care about policy issues, you would not join debate. We get these kids the summer before they begin high school and make them civically engaged. We're the internal link to your argument about involving people in this activity.

Q: But if these kids are not already involved in policy issues, why, oh why would they care about going to college and take your $500 stipend? And why ...

A: That is exactly the argument that our Sagawa evidence indicates. First, parents are looking to do something with these children, but low-income parents can't afford sum-mer camps, and these kids are too young to have jobs. Our Sagawa evidence indicates that this $500 scholarship, which is not going to pay for college, plants the seed in these children's minds that they are college potential and that they should try to save for college.

Q: So, the way to make them civically engaged is to have their parents force them into these summer programs because they know that it will help them get into college along the way? That doesn't seem like something that will promote getting involved.

A: They learn civic engagement through the program. That is the benefit of our first affirmative.

Q: Sure, and you cite a lot of Sagawa evidence indicating that it would be a good idea to do this, but you don't have one piece of evidence that people will actually want to do this. Is that correct?

A: Our Sagawa evidence indicates that we could recruit 100,00 children.

Q: You can do that?

A: Yes.

Second Negative Constructive Speech: Matt Fisher (Glenbrook North High School)

I would just like to reiterate Stephanie's thanks for the support of coaches, our friends, the esteemed judges, our opponents, and our generous sponsors, my parents, the NFL Committee, Vickie Fellers, the tab room staff, and the rest of the host committee for putting on such a well-run tournament. More than anyone, I would like to thank my partner, Stephanie Spies, for her work ethic, joviality, and amusing affinity for Wild West World.

I'll be addressing the spending, or federal budget disadvantage. There will be an overview on that; then I'll be addressing the case arguments.

Our spending argument demonstrates that you should vote negative in any paradigm. The impact to our disadvantage has a shorter time frame than the impact of the case because new spending will immediately threaten our national security priorities. Moreover, our Peterson evidence explains that the danger from overstretching our budgets include nuclear and biological war or terrorism, which is much greater in magnitude than the affirmative harms.

Our disadvantage also complicates the ability of the affirmative to solve the case because a world in which we are in a protracted war against other nations or another terrorist attack occurs, obviously the economy would be detrimentally affected, which 9/11 proves. As a policy-maker, you have an obligation to err on the side of caution as it relates to new government spending. Vote negative to reject the wastefulness of the affirmative. This is Weldon, a representative of Florida in the *FDCH Political Transcripts*, in 2002:

"In this time of uncertainty and war, we have a moral obligation to end the funding of poorly performing agencies and programs. A dollar spent on a program that does not help the people is a dollar we cannot spend on homeland security. It would be unconscionable to fund a poorly performing program when the physical safety of Americans requires that the government take on many additional expensive tasks. Working on behalf of all Americans, with that privilege comes the responsibility to use hard-earned taxpayer dollars wisely and effectively."

The first argument made in the 2AC is a piece of evidence from 2003 saying now is the critical time to stimulate the economy. First, the fact that this evidence is four years old is a reason that you should be highly skeptical of the government's ability to prime the pump of the economy. Second is that this does not assume the affirmative's means of increasing economic growth, but rather it is an economic theory argument that if the government were to cut taxes, for example, that would stimulate economic growth, not if they were able to spend on national service.

The second argument made in the 2AC is that the plan only costs one hundred million dollars. First, that begs the question of the word "only," because that is the entirety of our disadvantage. Second, we disagree with their characterization .... Rather, our disadvantage is predicated on the type of spending they employ as much as the amount. The 1NC Brady evidence explains that new untouchable budget priorities have a spill-over effect where Congress winds up wasting five dollars for every dollar that actually funds the plan. Our Brady evidence is the most qualified source on this issue because he has served multiple terms in the House of Representatives. This argument also proves that the affirmative massively underestimates the amount the plan would cost in real spending, and that the majority of the spending would be wasteful. As a policy-maker, that proves you have an obligation to reject the affirmative.

In the context of AmeriCorps, it is nothing but a wasteful government bureaucracy. This is Sanchez, a fellow at the CATO Institute, in 2003:

"Even its own director described AmeriCorps as 'another cumbersome, unpredictable government bureaucracy.' AmeriCorps doesn't just waste tax money; it diverts private contributions and volunteer time to the programs that bear its imprimatur."

The third argument made in the 2AC is that there is no fiscal discipline now, but first their argument just says that the budget proposal that was recently passed contains a lot of earmarked spending. Our uniqueness evidence takes this into account by saying that Bush's appointment of the new manager of the Office of Management and Budget is able to take into account this earmarked spending and that Bush would veto this spending when it actually came up before him.

Our next argument is that the U.S. economy is growing and is strong now. *Bloomberg News*, accessed online, 2007:

"Federal Reserve Bank of Dallas President Fisher said he expects accelerated growth in the U.S. economy in the second quarter. The economy is powerful."

And, Bush will restrain excessive spending. This is Weisman, June 20, 2007, from *The New York Times*, accessed online:

"The administration has promised a hard line on spending. Bush praised Portman as pressing for keeping spending under control and reducing the deficit. 'He's put Democratic leaders in Congress on notice that I will veto bills with excessive levels of spending,' the president said."

And, even if government spending is high now, that just proves our argument. The majority of that spending is going to national defense, which is important to prevent a litany of catastrophes outlined in our Peterson evidence. The fact that the government is already spending a lot of money is just another reason why a new untouchable domestic spending priority would be dangerous and irresponsible in the current climate.

The fourth argument: they say that they solve the economy faster. First, I don't know if she was kidding on this in the 2AC because they conceded in the cross-examination it would take at least a couple of years, or at the very worst case a summer, so three months, for them to have any positive impact on the U.S. economy.

Their last argument: They say that diversity is critical to the economy. First is that Stephanie will explain that our counter advocacy of debate is able to access why diversity is good. Second is that solving worker shortages is also a long time frame because people who go to college would not be in the labor force until eight years after the plan happens—so there is a very long time frame in solving for the significant harms of the affirmative.

On the cultural competence argument, their Malcolm evidence and their Gottschalk evidence that they are quoting on this, are talking about education such as science, engineering, and math achievements, not a volunteering of time for other individuals. It is that incompetence in science and in math that is more important to future U.S. economic growth. Thus, they do not access an internal link for why any of this is good.

The case arguments: First, please extend Stephanie's first argument in the 1NC that the individuals that volunteer at the time the affirmative plan says they would volunteer, are just more likely to not get a job in the future, but rather to become to become nonprofit volunteers in the future. These individuals do not contribute productively to the economy because they are not a positive increase in the United States' GDP. All of their evidence assumes a world in which individuals go to college and then are motivated to go on into the labor force, but they do not have evidence saying that that is the case. Rather, it is much more likely that these individuals will be volunteering in not-for-profit organizations after the plan.

The second argument in the 1NC is that it is a very long time frame to solving for the economic harms of the affirmative. That was already explained in the arguments on the spending disadvantage. At the very worse case scenario it would take a couple of years, and fine, maybe the plan is a good idea in a couple of years, but not at a time when the United States is fighting two different wars and thus any new spending now would be irresponsible for Congressional policy-makers.

The third argument is that our Lester evidence indicates that five years prove that civic engagement is very high in the status quo. Their Sagawa evidence, which yes, it is talking about lower-income individuals, is talking about that empirically lower-income individuals have not been able to get involved. Our Lester evidence, which is a snapshot of current volunteering and of trends that will continue, is that more individuals are volunteering in the status quo than their evidence takes into account. Yes, maybe when Sagawa is talking about in the 1980s or the early or late 1990s, lower-income individuals were not volunteering as much, but our Lester evidence indicates and our *World Magazine* evidence—which is the last piece of evidence read—indicates that volunteering is across-the-board high in the status quo. Thus people are already engaged.

Next, people will not give up their summers to do this. Their evidence just indicates that parents might be able to pressure these kids, but kids are not thinking about going into college. Maybe parents are kind of thinking about these kids going into college, but $500 is not enough for individuals to jump-start the ideas of their parents because even parents, especially of lower-income individuals who are obviously making lower incomes, would not be able to save up for college over a period of four years. This means that they are not actually able to solve for these harms.

Our Ford evidence indicates that civic engagement is also on balance high in the status quo because of protests against Iraq, our major example.

The internal trade-off argument was not answered by the 2AC correctly, because individuals that currently are volunteering for free are just going to wait until the summer where there is an economic motivation to actually go and get involved; i.e., people would rather get paid for service and get paid for spending their summer doing service than not get paid at all.

CROSS-EXAMINATION OF MATT FISHER (GLENBROOK NORTH HIGH SCHOOL) BY SARAH WEINER (SHAWNEE MISSION WEST HIGH SCHOOL)

Q: On this spending disadvantage, you read a piece of evidence that says that AmeriCorps is a wasteful program, correct?

A: (Nods yes).

Q: But you also read a piece of evidence that says that Bush cuts wasteful spending, and I'm confused.

A: So the plan would be cut by Bush? You don't win.

Q: Why does not Bush cut AmeriCorps in the status quo if it's wasteful spending?

A: Bush has been cutting AmeriCorps. The Sanchez evidence indicates that AmeriCorps' past financial mismanagement caused Congress to institute a lot more oversight over AmeriCorps specifically.

Q: Wait, Congress instituted more financial oversight?

A: Yes, but I know what you are trying to get at. That does not answer our Brady argument, though; our Brady evidence says that when Congress spends on one program it quote, "duplicates it"... actually I think it says it "clones," actually, sorry—clones it to five other programs. Basically identical, and then you're costing ...

Q: I understand that. But if this is such a problem within the present system with national service programs and Bush is taking such a hard line against such programs, then why has Bush not vetoed AmeriCorps, Citizen Corps in the status quo? Where is that evidence that AmeriCorps no longer gets funded?

A: Well, I didn't know that you would be making this argument in cross-examination, so I didn't preemptively read a piece of evidence on this, but Bush throughout his presidency has been cutting national service funding, for example, AmeriCorps triple C program: the National Conservation Corps has been cut even after the wake of Katrina.

Q: OK, and you say that all national service ... like, all domestic programs, are they all bad for discipline?

A: I'm speaking to AmeriCorps. In time of war it is dangerous and irresponsible for policy-makers, even if the ...

Q: Will you show me in your evidence? Cause I know you read a lot of evidence saying that domestic spending is bad, but I would like to see the piece of evidence that indicates spending on AmeriCorps trades off with war spending. Please show me that in a piece of evidence.

A: You have our Brady evidence. I believe it's right here.

Q: Alright.

A: If you could hand me that, I can't reach that far. (reading) "Either way, if Congress were a manufacturing plant, we would manufacture ..."

Q: Where does it say "AmeriCorps" please?

A: That card, you're correct, does not say AmeriCorps; it is speaking to federal programs ...

Q: Let's move on quickly before we run out of time. That's all I needed, thank you.

A: You want me to ... OK. This card is quite good; I don't think you're giving it the credit it deserves.

Q: That probably wouldn't be my job. Let's talk about solvency. You make argumentation that our Sagawa evidence is talking about the 1980s. Where ...

A: Your evidence kind of like any study ever that is citing empirical history is citing empirical history.

Q: Where do you see that within the evidence, because it was written two days ago?

A: (looking at the evidence): "empirical history"... your evidence is relying on statistics ...

Q: Show me where the evidence is relying on statistics from the 1980s.

A: The fact that he's saying he did research means that he's not doing research about the future; he's basing his research on facts that are in the past.

Q: But where do you see any indication in the evidence that that research wasn't done last year?

A: OK, that evidence is older than our evidence that says currently there is volunteering in AmeriCorps that is high.

Q: But is your evidence about underprivileged youth?

A: Our evidence is about across-the-board youth, yes.

Q: Thank you.

First Negative Rebuttal Speech by Stephanie Spies (Glenbrook North High School)

OK, it will be the justification counter advocacy argument and then topicality.

The first 2AC argument is that we have no evidence that we can get underprivileged people into debate. But first is that our counter advocacy would have the states and local governments expand National Forensic League programs to all schools that do not currently have them. This is able to solve a majority of the arguments that the 2AC makes on this because it does not presume that we would still advocate an alternative action to make the affirmative prove that their action is the best for you to vote for as a policy.

Their second argument is that they are able to solve civic engagement best, however, their summer program would not include debate. Do not let the 2AC and the 1AR spin their evidence to say such a thing. Our counter advocacy is able to solve for a few reasons.

First, is our Hanes evidence indicates that low-income people are only not involved civically because of lack of involvement in programs like active educational programs like debate. This is because of educational inequalities inherent in some of the way that debate programs are distributed. The only way to solve would be to expand NFL to all high schools so that anyone could get involved with debate.

Second, is that debate can give college scholarships much more than $500. For example, the Colorado College is giving a generous scholarship to the winner of this very debate. Additionally, debate can cause multiculturalism and cross-cultural diversity because project teams in college such as the Louisville project, Long Beach, Jordan, Kansas City Central, and other programs prove that debate is a key cross-accessed point for diversity. Additionally, the Urban Debate League, which our Hanes evidence speaks to, is able to cross these bridges by discussing the types of low-income barriers when they have debate rounds. Debate also offers middle school programs like Georgia, so you can still get involved in debate even if you are in the younger age group like the plan.

Their third argument is that they do not need to justify anything but an increase; however, they misunderstand our justification argument. The affirmative does not justify that the United States federal government must do the plan, which is what is mandated by the words in the resolution. Instead the states and Washington, D.C., and all relevant sub-actors can adopt policy debate programs. Even if they win that an increase is a good idea to solve civic engagement, they have not proven that as a policy-maker their policy is a better option than our counter advocacy.

Their last argument is that the states are not able to amend legislation, but we're not trying to claim that they can. Rather, we're trying to claim that the states could do policy debate programs and that the federal government does not have to take action to solve for their harms. They have not met the burden of proof that is a prima facie, stock issue burden for the affirmative that they are the only way to solve for their significant harm. Policy debate programs are able to solve because high school NFL programs are at a … any without a high school NFL program is at a serious educational disadvantage, according to our Hanes evidence, and they are less likely to be civically engaged in the future. This actually means that our counter advocacy is able to get people involved in things like AmeriCorps in the future, so we actually solve civic engagement best.

Secondly, debate is the best tool to get school students educated on domestic politics and international relations. Debates focus on role play and research as the 2AC pointed out in her thank you speech, it is the best way to get people involved and educated throughout their high school experience. We become informed citizens that will continue to be involved in politics and be civically engaged throughout out lives.

Now to topicality. Their first argument is that they meet, but they do not have any evidence that says that people will accept the offer after the bill is repealed in their plan. Their evidence all just says that the bill's effect could have recruiting effects on people, but they do not have any evidence that says that low-income people will accept this offer. They have some rhetorical evidence that says that people might do it for this and this reason, but they do not have any definitive and conclusive evidence which says they will cause an immediate and definite increase. Our Higher Education Funding Council evidence says that it is not how you increase, but that you actually cause an increase in the process.

Their next argument is that they defend an increase; however, even if they defend one it is unpredictable for the negative because no definite increase in the plan text means that we do not get links to our generic disadvantages. For example, we should not have to wait until the 2AC actually answers the spending disadvantage to know whether it is a good idea to read it.

Their third argument … their third and fourth arguments are about how many people they would increase by, but they do not have evidence that the bill will definitely cause much of an increase; it says it possibly could, but this still does not guarantee our link. It does say that if they do defend this that it guarantees us our link to our spending disadvantage because it spends so much money.

Their counter interpretation is not superior to ours because our Rieffel evidence says that it allows an unlimited number of things that can increase the attractiveness of a program, such as pulling out of Iraq, AIDS research, and banning "Stop Loss" orders, that are all … that all would result from this.

They say that we overlimit, but we allow for a mandate of an increase as long as it is in their plan text, things like the draft or raising the end strength of a program, are the core of the topic. Changing the status quo is easy; there is plenty of literature in favor of mandating … or changing the status quo. The 1AC evidence proves this. Our evidence is not about mandatory increases.

First Affirmative Rebuttal Speech by Andrew Baker (Shawnee Mission West High School)

I'm really interested in this Wild West World now. It's going to be the topicality debate, the solvency debate, then the justification debate, then the overview on the budget disadvantage, and then the budget disadvantage proper.

On topicality, they just don't go to this argument with enough time in the 1NR. They're not outlining any case that would be topical; their interpretation just doesn't make any sense. Extend across first that we meet. Our Sagawa evidence from two days ago indicates that people will immediately join. It cites the empirical example of when this program was tried during Hurricane Charlie; they're not answering the warrant to our evidence. Additionally, extend across our second "we meet." Their own definition contradicts their argument. It says that a policy must have a goal; our goal is to increase people, meaning we meet this argumentation. That's not answered in the block. Additionally, they're not isolating unique abuse. We still gave them the link to their disad. We straight turned it, though. They're not making any arguments as to why we're not proving the link to their disad. Additionally, extend across the Sagawa evidence from two days ago. It indicates that because Hurricane Charlie being empirically effective, our plan will get in 100,000 people immediately.

Additionally, they're conceding our interpretation that there are only 70,000 people in AmeriCorps right now; we double the size of it ... more than double the size of it. Meaning, we are substantial; they don't have any arguments against this.

They literally spent a second and a half on our counter interpretation. Our *Merriam Webster*'s evidence proves that their "policy to" definition proves that we're topical. They don't answer our argument. This is key to literature because there is no one advocating everybody immediately join AmeriCorps in the context of an affirmative plan text. Additionally, mandatory was removed from the resolution with a justification by the framers meaning there is no unique scenario as to why our case isn't predictable.

The solvency debate: They're simply wrong on this debate. Our evidence indicates that we need to get people out of volunteerism and into the workforce. Only our aff is able to do that and go through a college education. That's our empirical Sagawa evidence. They say that there's a long time frame. Our time frame is now. That's our service learning advantage. We immediately get them in, thus they create cross-cultural diversity within these communities, leading to a better economic stability. They're conceding the argument that an economic collapse is inevitable in the status quo due to this. That evidence is on point, saying that it's the key issue in this debate.

They're also conceding we solve one hundred percent of our second advantage. There is only a risk of solvency and no offense from the negative.

I'll answer all of their "civic engagement up" arguments right now. Our evidence is from two days ago, theirs is one year ago. There is no reason to even evaluate it. Additionally, our evidence indicates that it's up everywhere but what the plan takes, proving it's uniquely key. AmeriCorps is going up across the board, just not in the disadvantaged youth area, meaning our plan is uniquely important. Our evidence indicates that Sagawa is an expert on this issue; kids will want to join and they're not answering the empirical data on Charlie. There is no reason they wouldn't want to give up their summer.

He extends his trade-off argument, but our Sagawa evidence specifically says that these people aren't involved in AmeriCorps in the status quo, so getting them on board would not get off of the other people. There is no reason not to do the plan.

On to the justification argument. Let's listen to what this argument really is, folks. It's a counterplan that isn't competitive. Our argument is from the Sagawa evidence on 6/20 that the federal government is uniquely key. Our evidence cites three warrants that the block is not answering. The first is that this has to be universally available, which only the federal government can do. No debate program can do that because they're different from state to state; that's the 1NR's argument itself. This means that only our aff solves.

Secondly, it's a rite of passage only when it's on the national level. Everyone in the United States would have to do this before they go to college, meaning that it would be the rite of passage that our evidence talks to, leading to cross-cultural diversity—not answered in the block either. Additionally, our third piece of evidence indicates that an existence institution that is banded together is key. Another conceded warrant; there is no reason that the states or a different debate program could do this. Additionally, they have no solvency advocate indicating that people would increase the amount of benefits that are existing.

As for debate programs, we solve for that because when people get involved in service learning that's the best way for them to gain education. Our Sagawa evidence is comparative on this subject.

Under the overview on the fiscal discipline disadvantage. The 2NC makes a critical mistake when he concedes that collapse is inevitable. Our evidence is on point saying that the key issue in this debate is cross-cultural diversity. Additionally, our Sagawa evidence from two days ago indicates that we must pass this plan now or it is completely ineffective. And in the future these people will not graduate from college. Within four years the economy must ... will collapse; we're the only ones with this argument. Additionally, we're solving the impact of the case. They concede our cross-cultural competency argument, which indicates that these different diversities are key to our national security strategy. They have no argument against this, and that's the argument they're citing in the 2NC. Don't go for this at all.

Additionally, our probability comes first. Our evidence indicates that this disad is non-unique. There was discretionary spending on AmeriCorps last month. That's permanent spending; they're not answering this argument. It takes out the entirety of their link. Additionally, a collapse is inevitable. The economy being up right now does not matter in the context of our argument. They concede our turns outweigh because only our argument cites the status quo from two days ago.

Additionally, extend across our EPI [Economic Policy Institute] in 2003 evidence on the line-by-line. It indicates that if we do the plan now because it's a necessity in the future, we can maintain these types of things. Additionally, they're not proving a brink argument. A hundred million now is a drop in a bucket compared to the millions being spent discretionally on AmeriCorps right now.

Additionally extend across our Wayne 6/19 evidence. This is the evidence indicating that Bush has already spent discretionary. They say that this is a bureaucracy in the status quo. Our evidence indicates that this can be solved by putting in cross-cultural diversity. Additionally, this is not impacted or specific to our aff case.

SECOND NEGATIVE REBUTTAL SPEECH BY MATT FISHER (GLENBROOK NORTH HIGH SCHOOL)

OK, I'll be addressing the budget disadvantage, then the justification argument, then the case arguments.

They concede that as policy-makers you have a moral obligation to vote negative if we prove that the plan is an example of irresponsible spending in a time of war. Our Brady evidence read in the 1NC and the evidence read in the 2NC overview on the spending disadvantage indicate that any dollar that the government is not dedicating to the war efforts—the two wars we have going on in the status quo—is a dollar that is not being spent for the American people. Our Weldon evidence said that you need to evaluate this as a prior decision rule question that before you look to any of the tangible benefits of the 1AC in the long run, you need to look at the current situation now. That we have two wars; we need to be spending on homeland security.

Second, is as policy-makers you should vote negative because we have proven that the plan is worse than the status quo, because they concede that there is a long time frame to solving for the economy and that the jobs that they would cause people to join in the future are not good for the nation's GDP anyway.

And third, is the plan is not the type of educational initiatives that their own evidence is talking about. This means that we will win a risk that the plan makes budget deficits worse. They are not allowed to make new arguments in the next speech. If you think that we are winning the debate after the 2NR, you should be very, very skeptical of any arguments that the 2AR, however pretty she sounds, is able to come up with that level the debate out.

Now, their first argument that they make is economic collapse is inevitable. First, that this is factually not true. Our Bloomberg evidence citing the Federal Reserve Bank of Dallas president indicates that the U.S. economy GDP is growing in the status quo. Their evidence for why collapse is inevitable is mostly from 2005 saying that if we do not have more math and science education, collapse of the economy is inevitable, so they do not even access this.

Second is that even if a collapse of the economy is inevitable, the plan does not solve it immediately either. There is only a risk that our justification argument is able to confront economic collapse as well.

Their next argument, they say that four years means the economy will collapse. Yes, there is a long time frame for these individuals getting involved in the workforce. I sound like I am repeating myself already, but it's because they are not getting the message that the individuals that they cause to go to college take at least four years of high school, four years of college, then maybe they will be involved in the labor pool, so thus it is a very long time frame.

Our Peterson evidence indicates that running higher budget deficits at a time of war causes us to not spend on homeland security as much ... the homeland security that is necessary to stop a biological or nuclear war and terrorism, which they concede outweighs the impact to economic collapse anyway because that would just be isolated to the United States domestically, whereas a terrorist attack or nuclear attack would be internationally.

They say that they are able to solve cross-cultural competencies, but debate is able to do that better.

Their fourth argument, they say that there is spending now because of discretionary spending, but that does not answer our arguments. The 1NC Gerstenzang uniqueness evidence and the 2NC Weisman uniqueness evidence on this question indicate that even if there had been more spending and budget proposals, Bush will veto those proposals in practice—means that there is not more spending.

Their next argument they say that spending is not relevant if collapse is inevitable, that was answered above. They say the plan now is critical—also answered above. They were the ones repeating themselves, I guess, a little bit more than I am even.

Their next argument: They say that AmeriCorps is not corrupt, or that there are millions being spent now. Please cross-apply from topicality the fact they said that they literally, quote, "double the size of AmeriCorps." Combine with our Brady evidence that says any expensive federal program ends up being multiplied 5 times over, means that you should be highly skeptical of them being able to save money.

Our Sanchez evidence says that AmeriCorps is a wasteful bureaucracy anyway because money ends up being wasted and inefficiently used. This is a decision rule question that was not answered by the 1AR.

The justification argument: they have not justified that federal action is critical. If you as a policy-maker are promoting policy debate programs, it is better than promoting this service act for just the summer anyway and giving $500.

They make a couple solvency deficits. They say it is not universally available; that's laughable because our justification argument is that we should put debate programs throughout the country. It's not universally accessible now, we're saying it should be. They are thus not justified; the federal government is not critical to solving the harms. The states could also effectively address the significant harms of the 1AC, vis-à-vis establishing policy debate programs.

Second is that states are different in their educational activities already in the status quo. Our Ferejohn evidence indicates that it is bad when the federal government says all state education needs to be the same thing. They are no different than yet another establishment for teachers to have to meet the bar federally.

The next argument: they say a rite of passage is good, but first, the plan is obviously not a rite of passage, it is only for lower-income individuals. Meaning they are now saying that lower-income people need to have some kind of rite of passage that the upper-income individuals do not. This is repugnant and turns their own 1AC claims. And additionally, debate is able to incorporate lower-income individuals anyway.

We do have a solvency advocate. The first piece of evidence read in the 1NC and Stephanie's fantastic explanation in the 1NR why debate is able to give educational benefits and give these cross-cultural contexts such as through UDLs [Urban Debate Leagues] or through project teams. Kids are able to increase their critical thinking, which is also good for the economy.

The case arguments: the plan is not able to put more people into the workforce. The fact that people are volunteering now means that they are more likely to volunteer in not-for-profit organizations in the long run, whereas most debaters go on to be people like lawyers who do contribute productively to the U.S. economy, whereas the volunteers that they are contributing go on to non-profit organizations, which do not boost the U.S. economy.

Second Affirmative Rebuttal Speech by Sarah Weiner (Shawnee Mission West High School)

The order is solvency, then the justification, spending overview, spending proper.

He gets to the solvency debate with ten seconds left in his speech. There is nothing for you to vote on that would compel you to believe that we don't solve for 100% of our case.

Extend our Sagawa evidence which specifically talks about Hurricane Charlie when youth were mobilized under AmeriCorps to engage in community service to solve for the terrible effects of Hurricane Charlie. This is an empirical example of 100 percent solvency that we can get people into AmeriCorps and working.

Also extend also our Sagawa evidence that specifically indicates that putting these children in the Summer of Service AmeriCorps now during the summer are not going to be in service for the rest of their life, but they are going to go to college to become productive members of the workforce.

They read absolutely no evidence, qualifications, or warrants as to why these people would not be going into the workforce. Prefer our specific evidence. Specifically extend our Malcolm et al. evidence in 2005 from the 1AC. This is going to be where you vote in this round. This evidence indicates that the only way to solve for the economy and for national security is for youth to be involved in science and math and science and math education. This science and math education is only developed through our 1AC because we get children looking into college. When they get to college, they will be going into science and math education; this is in the 1AC.

This means that their justification doesn't solve because they only talk about civic engagement in their justification. We say that we have to get children going to college in math and science fields in order to solve.

Additionally, prefer the specificity of our argumentation. We are the only people reading evidence about the specific Summer of Service AmeriCorps program under the justification.

What do you think you are voting on with this justification argumentation? In the 1NC we had to justify the federal government; in the 2NC we had to justify that debate was bad, and now they have a complete counter advocacy in which you as a judge get to say that everyone does debate.

It simply does not mesh. Extend the argumentation that this is a counterplan that simply isn't competitive. People can be in debate and in the Summer of Service program. In fact, extend the dropped internal link argumentation from the 1AR that people are not going to join debate unless if they are already civically engaged. It is our plan that makes these youth before high school want to be civically engaged, want to learn about public policy, which is what is going to get them to debate in the first place.

Also extend the argumentation that this civic engagement has to become a rite of passage for all youth. It begins with the underprivileged youth and it spreads to the rest of the community. Debate is never going to be a rite of passage because every high school student is just not going to take debate. But our Sagawa evidence indicates that by doing our 1AC we can make national service over the summer a rite of passage, which is going to solve for the economy in the future. Additionally, this is going to solve in the future.

They say debate is going to increase its education; that simply isn't true because debate doesn't increase that science and math education.

On to fiscal discipline: fiscal discipline is the only argument in the 2NR that you might be voting on because the justification is theoretically illegitimate and we are the internal link to the justification.

On the overview on the spending, he says that you as a judge have a moral obligation not to do wasteful spending, but our entire 1AC shows you that that is not wasteful spending. Specifically extend the Malcolm et al. evidence in 2005 at the bottom of the case which says, and this is in the 2AC and the 1AR—it's on your flow—that we solve for terrorism because we get people into science and math fields. This piece of evidence indicates that the only way to get people into science and math fields is through our 1AC, and science and math fields is not only key to competitiveness in the future, but also our security from terrorist threats and wars in the future because these are the people who will be developing national security.

We are the internal link to the impact of this disadvantage, because our evidence indicates that our national security and economy will inevitably collapse unless we solve for these problems. We are the only affirmative solving for those problems in the status quo.

On to the line-by-line. They do not answer our Economic Policy Institute in 2003 argumentation that spending now is going to prime the pump and create fiscal stewardship in the long term. This is a direct turn to the disadvantage, which they simply do not answer. Additionally, this is good for national security, which means that it is not wasteful spending.

Then extend our Wayne from 6/19 argumentation. This is why you don't vote on the disadvantage. This says that literally a few days ago Bush approved discretionary spending for AmeriCorps. This is the most specific evidence in this round on this fiscal discipline debate. This discretionary spending is permanent, meaning that Bush did not veto it, which means that the impacts of the disadvantage are either going to happen anyway or terminally non-unique. Remember at the end of the round that we control the internal link to economic collapse because our evidence indicates that it is going to happen in the future and the only way to prevent it is through our 1AC.

By a vote of 7 to 4, the judges in this debate decided that the negative team from Glenbrook North High School won the debate.

LINCOLN-DOUGLAS FINAL ROUND

NFL NATIONAL TOURNAMENT 2007

Resolved: On balance, violent revolution is a just response to political oppression.

Affirmative: Taarini Vohra (Hockaday School, Coach: Stacy Thomas)

Negative: Bilal Malik (James Logan High School, Coaches: Tommie Lindsey, Jr.; Robert Marks; Randall McCutcheon; Tim Campbell; Chris Marianetti; and Justin Hinojoza)

AFFIRMATIVE CONSTRUCTIVE SPEECH: TAARINI VOHRA, HOCKADAY SCHOOL

Before we begin, I want to thank the National Forensic League for this incredible opportunity and for my debate education over the past four years. Thank you to the Lincoln Financial Group, whose sponsorship of this tournament and great league have made this learning possible. Thank you to the NFL President Billy Tate, Executive Secretary Scott Wunn, and the NFL Executive Council for their tireless dedication. Thank you to the LD tournament chair, Pauline Carochi, as well as Vickie Fellers, Dalvin and Becky Yager, and the entire Derby/Wichita Steering Committee for making this tournament an unforgettable one. And to the city of Wichita, Kansas, we appreciate you opening your doors to us. I'd also like to congratulate my opponent as well as all of the other competitors who've made this a wonderful experience.

I owe much appreciation to many members of our community for helping me grow, not only as a debater, but more significantly as a person. To John Crews, Mike Bietz, and Jo Vaughn, your confidence in me has helped me develop a faith in myself. To my coaches, Stacy Thomas and Tom Evnen, your endless guidance has taught me to always approach challenges in life with perseverance, compassion, and humor. To my Hockaday teammates, for always supporting me as my family away from home—thank you. But most importantly, to my grandfather, mother, and father for their infinite love, support, and understanding. And for always giving me the strength to achieve my goals. To my sister Shivani, you are my best friend and I love you. I will always be grateful to have shared the memories of my last debate tournament with you. And finally, thank you to God for his blessing and guidance in my life and hopefully in the years to come.

With that, I would now like to present my affirmative case.

"Those who deny freedom to others deserve it not for themselves." Because I agree with Abraham Lincoln, I must affirm today's resolution: On balance, violent revolution is a just response to political oppression. To clarify, I'd like to offer two observations.

Observation one explains the evaluative terms: The qualifier "on balance" requires an evaluation of general principles. In addition, in the phrase a just response, "A" according to the *Random House Dictionary* means "not any particular one." Given these operational terms, the question for today's debate is if violent revolution should theoretically be included among the legitimate responses to oppression, not if it is the correct response in an isolated situation or categorically the best option.

Observation two explains the nature of political oppression.

Oppression is defined by the *Oxford English Dictionary* as the "prolonged cruel exercise of authority." The modifier "political" makes the agent of oppression a government. Political oppression goes beyond the restriction of rights because even just states must restrict some degree of autonomy for social welfare. Additionally, all societies can pass bad laws, but if the people have avenues to fix these mistakes, then the system isn't politically oppressive since citizens ultimately have control. Politically oppressed people are denied political rights and thus do not have legal recourse. So oppression has two components: A) it is arbitrary, and B) it is without checks.

Finally, Ted Honderich, philosophy professor at University College London, defines violent revolution as an act of "considerable or destroying force [which is] prohibited by law and directed to change the system of government."

I value justice as it is the ultimate good implied by the resolution. While there are different conceptions of justice, all are centrally based on the notion of fairness, in that people should be treated as their actions merit. So justice is defined as giving each their due.

The criterion is respecting human dignity, which is the innate worth that separates people from objects. Dignity makes justice meaningful because only beings with worth are due something. For example, it would be absurd to discuss what my water bottle is due. To respect human worth, citizens must be allowed to exercise their fundamental rights. My case will prove that making the choice to violently revolt is one of these fundamental rights, and as such, an affirmation is required to validate people's dignity and recognize this due course of action.

Contention One: People have an inherent right to violently rebel. Subpoint A: An oppressive government has lost the authority to demand allegiance. Governments are formed to protect innate rights, and in return, people grant states a monopoly on coercive force. All social contract theories which explain the existence of the state are founded upon this idea.

An oppressive government not only fails to fulfill its obligations but proactively uses the rule of law to abuse its people, turning the social contract on its head. The power given over to the state no longer safeguards citizens but becomes a weapon of persecution.

In these circumstances, the state forfeits its right to monopolize violence. The right returns to the people, who may now reclaim this force as their due power. It is crucial to note here that the resolution prescribes parameters for when violence is just, and those are when it is a response to the oppression initiated by another agent. So, an affirmation isn't an overarching endorsement of violence but recognition of its legitimacy as a check on certain social conditions.

Subpoint B: the right to violently rebel is justified as a form of self-defense. Historically, despotic regimes have killed their citizens. This is the norm, not the exception. Political historian R.J. Rummel proves this in his book *Death by Government*. His research shows that 262 million people were slaughtered by their rulers worldwide from 1900 to 1987. He summarizes: "[This] figure far exceeds the 34 million battle deaths thought to have resulted from the international and civil wars during the same period."

Rummel identifies 218 regimes that committed democide during this time period and adds that the murder rates are assuredly underreported since oppressive leaders try to hide their death tolls. Thus, empirically oppression threatens lives. To further this point analytically, any right you have in an oppressive regime is bankrupt because it is granted solely on the state's whim. Your life is always threatened since your dignity can be stripped at any time, making all rights insecure. Oppressive rulers by definition no longer exercise control legitimately and thus physical coercion becomes commonplace, making violence against the state a proportional response. Every person has the right to self-defense when threatened. Just as we cannot condemn the individual use of violence when assaulted, we cannot condemn citizens who use violence for their collective benefit. Both criminals and the oppressor have willfully created a situation in which justice is achieved at their detriment.

With these subpoints in mind, violent rebellion is proven in two distinct ways to be an inherent right. As a liberty due to people, an affirmation is already supported since the link to justice is clear. However, I will move to my next level of analysis, which addresses the practical objections often raised to revolution.

Contention Two: Any revolution to restore rights will include violence. Even the two most renowned nonviolent uprisings had some violent support. The Indian Independence effort was sparked by the Sepoy Mutiny, a bloody rebellion against the British. Similarly, Malcolm X and the Black Panthers provided the threat of violence that enticed the state to take Martin Luther King seriously during the civil rights movement. King even warned U.S. officials that if they ignored peaceful resistance, they would risk bloody riots, making the fear of violence a powerful negotiating tool. Nonviolence only has any hope of working when targeted against states that are otherwise democratic and worry that a crackdown would undermine their liberal ideology. On balance, this is simply not true of oppressive regimes. Even political philosopher Hannah Arendt, who is an advocate of nonviolence, admits this failure and states: "If Gandhi had met with a different enemy—Stalin's Russia, [or] Hitler's Germany, instead of England—the outcome would not have been decolonization, but massacre and submission. England had good reasons for restraint as they enjoyed domestically the blessings of constitutional government." A negation guarantees perpetual violations of human dignity since the oppressed people have no pure avenue for change. The only potential for justice is to allow citizens their fundamental right to violently revolt. Thus, I urge an affirmative ballot, and now stand ready for cross-examination.

FIRST CROSS-EXAMINATION PERIOD: CROSS-EXAMINATION OF TAARINI VOHRA (HOCKADAY SCHOOL) BY BILAL MALIK (JAMES LOGAN HIGH SCHOOL).

Q: Let's imagine for a moment that I'm being mugged, OK?

A: OK.

Q: Do you think it's just for me to retaliate against my aggressor?

A: I would say that that is a right of self-defense.

Q: So it is just?

A: That would be just.

Q: OK, now would it be just for me to subdue my attacker, tie him up, and proceed to beat him with a baseball bat?

A: The question you seem to be asking ... the answer is a little more complicated.

Q: Sure, go ahead.

A: OK, when somebody attacks you, every individual has that fundamental right to self-defense. So what that means is that in a question of justice and what people are due, that right is something that matters, no matter how you implement that right.

Q: OK, but isn't there some sort of proportionality to self-defense? Like if you steal a dollar from me, am I justified in breaking your kneecaps?

A: Well, my argument is that when an oppressive government uses violence against ...

Q: No, no, no. I'm just asking you a question outside of the scope of the resolution. Is there proportionality with self-defense?

A: The individual is allowed to use violence in response to the oppressor.

Q: So if I take a dollar from you right now, can you beat me?

A: The problem with your analysis is ... no, I wouldn't be able to beat you.

Q: Why not?

A: The situation you are drawing is not similar to the situation of an oppressive regime.

Q: OK, but we can say that there needs to be some sort of pro-portionality in terms of the response to political oppression, correct?

A: Well, I just want to make sure there is a distinction in terms of proportionality.

Q: OK, that's fine.

A: When we talk about proportionality, all I'm saying is that if an oppressive government uses violence against the people, the people are just in using violence in retaliation.

Q: OK, that's fine. I'm kind of curious. I don't know what this has to do with your case, but can you name me a violent revolution that produced a democratic government?

A: Sure, I can actually name three.

Q: OK, go ahead.

A: The American revolution, the Romanian revolution, and ...

Q: OK, wait, let's stop there. The American revolution, right? After the American revolution—isn't it true that one, blacks weren't allowed to vote, that two, women weren't allowed to vote, and that three, if you didn't have property, you weren't allowed to vote?

A: That may be true, but it definitely set us on a path towards a democracy.

Q: So your argument is that the violent revolution that we had in America was justifiable because eventually we used non-violent methods to fix our problems?

A: I never mentioned the word "nonviolent."

Q: But how did we get rid of civil rights or how did we gain civil rights for African-Americans?

A: We gained civil rights for African-Americans in the Civil War after the American Revolution, which was a use of violence.

Q: So there was no segregation or anything?

A: Pardon?

Q: There was no segregation after the Civil War?

A: There may have been, but as I demonstrate ...

Q: Wait, wait, so ... your argument is that there may be harms out of violent revolution, but it's OK to ignore them?

A: If you'd let me finish my answer ...

Q: Go ahead.

A: What I explain in the second contention is that even with the issue of segregation, Martin Luther King used the threat of violence and the reason that the state was able to take Martin Luther King seriously was that the Black Panthers and Malcolm X had already enticed the state to do so.

Q: OK, thank you.

Negative Constructive Speech: Bilal Malik, James Logan High School

I'd like to take a minute to thank everyone who has helped me get this far. Moments like this are very rare and I think that given the rarity it's important to acknowledge everyone who has helped me get this far. I was thinking about this yesterday and I realized that since the early stages of my debate career, debate has been really good to me. I have been surrounded by people that I wanted to emulate. For example, my two former coaches were two former national champions, Adam Preiss and Oscar Shine. And from them I learned that if they were willing to put in hard work into me all I had to do was to follow through. I also want to thank some of my former teammates, people like Michael Joshi, Bonan Zhou, Paul Baldo, and my current LD coach, Justin Hinojoza. Justin, I hope that this is proper compensation for all of the red-eye flights and the caffeine that we drank together. And, also, I want to thank my family as well for their love and support and the NFL for providing me with this opportunity. I also think it is important for me to thank my second family, the James Logan High School forensics teams. I know that they care for me because all of them are here sitting in the audience listening to two teenagers talk about morality for 45 minutes. Also I'd like to thank Mr. Lindsey, the head honcho of the family at James Logan High School. I don't know what words I can find to explain how grateful I am for him and what he does for his students. A few years ago a student explained that even when we don't put 100 percent into ourselves, Mr. Lindsey puts 110 percent into us. So thank you for everything you've done for me Mr. Lindsey, and I hope that I can make you proud.

So with that, I'm going to read over the negative case and then go on to refute the affirmative.

Nonviolence is the answer to the crucial political and moral questions of our time—the need for mankind to overcome oppression and violence without resorting to oppression and violence. Because I agree with Dr. Martin Luther King Jr. that violence is not the answer, I negate the resolution that "on balance, violent revolution is a just response to political oppression." Since the resolution questions the justness of violent revolution, the highest value for the round must be justice, defined as giving each their due. All humans are fundamentally due basic rights and liberties, the clearest of which being the freedom from unjustified harm. We would never condone that an innocent person be subjected to a violation of freedoms, just as we would object to excessive sanctions meted out for petty crimes. Human beings, as the ultimate component of morality and justice, are intrinsically due dignity and respect. This is why it is permissible to use violence to fend off a dangerous mugger, but I am not justified in torturing her after she has been subdued. By causing unnecessary harm I have fundamentally disrespected the rights and humanity of the person I attack. Respect for individuals, thus, requires that we attempt as much as is humanly possible to refrain from bringing about unnecessary suffering. Thus, the value criterion for justice is the prevention of unnecessary suffering.

It is the thesis and sole contention of the negative that violent revolutions produce unnecessary suffering because of the existence of nonviolent alternatives. First, nonviolent change increases the power and popularity of the revolution. Refraining from violence grants the revolutionaries the moral high ground, which aids in recruiting additional revolutionaries. This allows nonviolent revolutionaries to co-opt the vast power of the military. Ultimately, soldiers are just people and when they are shot at, their natural inclination is to shoot back. But historically, nonviolent movements have posed the military with a moral dilemma that often helps the nonviolent revolution. For example, in the recent Ukrainian revolution, soldiers were sent to break up a massive nonviolent protest. However, the soldiers were persuaded by the revolutionary's motives and tactics and promptly joined what became known as the Orange Revolution, which successfully overthrew an illegitimately elected leader. Violent revolution, on the other hand, escalates the violence of the state by giving it grounds to argue that its violence is meant to prevent chaos and safeguard the peace.

Second, by engendering sympathy amongst the general population and the oppressors, revolutionaries force everyone to focus on the message rather than the act of violence itself. The oppressive government is seen to be all the more oppressive for its use of violence against the nonviolent. And indeed, in recent history, the vast majority of successful rebellions have been nonviolent. Peter Ackerman and Jack Duvall, writing for the International Center for Nonviolent Conflict, explain that "in 50 of 67 transitions from authoritarianism in the past 35 years, according to a recent study by Freedom House, it was not violent rebellion but nonviolent civic resistance that was the pivotal force." Nonviolence, with its dedication to reason and democracy, is the only method of rebellion which can ever hope to establish a just state based on democratic ideals. The implication of the negative case is twofold. First, even if you believe that my opponent's criterion is the weighing mechanism in the round, I meet it better because I provide that end without looking to unnecessary suffering. Additionally, you can vote negative based solely on the negative case. I'm not [just] providing an alternative. I'm providing an alternative that doesn't have to harm people. If we can choose between violence and nonviolence, we always have to choose the latter. Otherwise, we are going to be harming the rights of innocent people.

Now let's move on to the affirmative case. There's something really important to understand about the affirmative case. She's talking to you about how violent revolution can be necessary, but that doesn't explain why it's justified. For example, we can agree that sometimes killing is necessary, but we always say that killing is not justified. In self-defense it might be necessary, so the conclusion, then, is that killing is permissible. In the same way, violent revolution is permissible. So even if my opponent is winning every single argument on her side of the flow, you're still going to vote negative because she's not proving the burden of the resolution. She's proving to you that violent revolution is permissible in certain situations, not that it's justified. Additionally, you can look to her definition of political oppression. There is a problem. While there are definitely severe cases of political oppression, my opponent fails to take into account the totality of the resolution. For example, in the year 2000 in Florida, some people were not allowed to vote. That was political oppression, but it clearly was not harsh enough to call on the citizenry to pick up weapons and dismantle the government. There are clearly nonviolent methods, so you ought to err on the side of caution and vote negative because at least that way we don't allow violence to be a tool in the arsenal of a revolutionary.

Then you can look to the argument that she makes in the second contention, and this is very important. She says that the threat of violence is tantamount to violent revolution. This doesn't make sense because if the framers of the resolution wanted to talk about the threat of violent revolution, then they would have inserted the word "threat." So I would argue that the threat of violent resolution is not a way that you can affirm the resolution.

Additionally, the threat of violent revolution exists when you vote negative as well. We classify it as unjust, but people can still threaten the government with violent revolution.

Now you can look to her standard. There are a few problems with her standard. The first problem is that she's telling you that we're only looking at whether or not violent revolution as an idea is justifiable. But if we know that violent revolution is going to produce harms, then we wouldn't say it's justifiable. We know the history of violent revolution. We know that it harms innocents and it is generally unsuccessful. Given this knowledge we can't say that violent revolutionaries are idealistically charging in and all innocent deaths are incidental. By knowingly engaging in acts that produce undesirable results, the revolutionaries intend to do harm.

Additionally, she contradicts herself, and this is very important. She says in her criterion that we need to respect human dignity, but violent revolution necessarily requires violating human dignity in the long run (oh sorry) in the short run, to have long-term benefits. For example, we're going to have to hurt innocent people to have some benefits at the end of the day. Moreover, this criterion is ends based. She has the burden of proving that violent revolution can actually succeed; otherwise, you never know whether or not she is respecting human dignity.

First, the use of violence, especially by ideological revolutionaries, tends to produce what is euphemistically referred to as collateral damage. This is the argument I made earlier. Insofar as violent revolutionaries have this idea that the ends justify the means, they are allowed to violate innocents' rights.

Second, violent revolution tends overwhelmingly to produce undemocratic and oppressive regimes. The problem with violent revolutions is that the revolutionaries do not put down their guns. While violent revolution may be an expedient means of removing the government from power, it also establishes a culture in society in which extra-political methods are an adequate means of creating social change.

Finally, Peter Ackerman and Jack Duvall explain that because of the nature of the state, violent revolution is unlikely to succeed: "In a contest of violence against violence, the superiority of the government has always been absolute. People who choose guns and bombs as the way to rise up will find that the regimes they attack have far more experience in such contests." This means that at the end of the day, violent revolution will not be successful, so she won't be protecting human rights.

Then you can look to her first contention. While she is talking about the social contract, she forgets that the social contract doesn't allow for the innocents and their rights to be trampled upon. Revolution is justified, but violent revolution is not. We can always prefer nonviolence, so you always prefer the negative.

Second Cross-examination Period: Cross-examination of Bilal Malik (James Logan High School) by Taarini Vohra (Hockaday School)

Q: Ready?

A: Uh huh.

Q: So against the affirmative case you talk about Florida as an example of political oppression. And you agree that the resolution is a question of on-balance, general principles, right?

A: I understand that you are going to make the argument that this is one example. My argument, however, is that nowhere in the affirmative case do you prove that political oppression always or on balance has to be violent.

Q: OK, but just answer my question, please. So, would you say that Florida is the norm for political oppression?

A: No, but I also would say that the political oppression ...

Q: So it's not the norm for political oppression?

A: Can I answer the question?

Q: Sure.

A: OK, I would say that the examples of political oppression that you cite in the case are not the norm for political oppression. So, likewise, if you're going to reject my example of what political oppression is, we ought to reject yours as well, because it's also one-sided.

Q: OK. Now let's go to the negative case. You talk about the idea that if there is unnecessary suffering involved, that's unjust.

A: Right.

Q: OK. But let's say that a lifeguard on duty sees a child drowning in the ocean or a pool or wherever they may be, and tries to save that child's life. Perhaps the lifeguard fails. But was the attempt to try and save that life unjust?

A: I don't see how any unnecessary suffering was created there.

Q: Well, I just want to know would that be unjust?

A: Trying to help people is a good thing, Taarini.

Q: So, that's just?

A: It's a good thing, yes, it's just, but I don't see why that creates unnecessary suffering.

Q: OK, and now, your criterion is the prevention of unnecessary suffering?

A: Right.

Q: So necessary suffering then is just?

A: No, it's permissible. That's the argument that I made against the affirmative case, and it's also in the negative case.

Q: But in your own criterion analysis, which has to have a connection to justice, you talk about unnecessary versus necessity. So …

A: Taarini, justice is not a binary. If something is unnecessary, that doesn't make it necessary. It could also be permissible. I spent a lot of time against the affirmative case explaining why that is true.

Q: So then why if something is unnecessary is that unjust?

A: Because it is creating unnecessary suffering.

Q: That was simply a repetition of my question. My question ...

A: No, no, no. It is the answer to your question because there is never necessary suffering. If it's is unnecessary suffering, it's unjust. If it's necessary suffering, it's permissible.

Q: Why?

A: I explained that we have this general norm that killing is wrong. We never say that killing is justified. We say that killing is permissible in certain situations, which is what you bring up in your case in terms of self-defense.

Q: So you would say, then, that an act of self-defense is simply permissible, it is not just.

A: Yeah. I wouldn't want to tell my kids that killing is justified.

Q: So, when somebody is assaulted on the street and is protecting their life, they are unjust in doing so.

A: No, they are committing a permissible act.

Q: Sure, but you're saying that permissibility is different from justice.

A: But that doesn't make it injustice, we can call it "ajust." (Audience laughter). Dude, guys, language is fluid, I can make up whatever.

Q: In terms ... OK, so, then what are the necessary conditions for justice.

A: I don't know what the necessary conditions are. My argument is that you're not meeting the condition that if you're creating unnecessary suffering, it is unjustified. I have to negate the resolution.

FIRST AFFIRMATIVE REBUTTAL SPEECH BY TAARINI VOHRA (HOCKADAY SCHOOL)

Let's go to the negative criterion. His criterion is the prevention of unnecessary suffering. And as we discussed in cross-examination, it has a clear link to justice, which means that if he's preventing necessary suffering, that would be unjust. When he uses his own words "necessary" and "unnecessary" within in his criterion, he himself is establishing a link between what would be necessary suffering and justice. However, my opponent fails to draw a distinction in how we determine what is necessary suffering. In the affirmative case, since we both agree that justice is defined as giving each their due, if human dignity and preserving human dignity is a necessity in terms of achieving justice, then it is just. But he also fundamentally mishandles the affirmative criterion when he fails to explain that if violent revolution is a fundamental right, then it respects individuals' dignity, and thus it is a due thing to the people. He has fundamentally mishandled that.

So, the reason you care about preventing unnecessary suffering is due to a conception of human dignity, and the way we protect human dignity is through the protection of fundamental rights.

So then you can go to the affirmative case. First of all, he says that I only explain why it is justified and not necessary. The problem is that if it is necessary in order to achieve justice, it is a part of justice and thus is just.

So then we can go to observation two, which is the part where we talk about what political oppression is. He says that I am not encompassing for the totality of the resolution. The problem is in cross-examination he tells me that his example of Florida is not the norm of what political oppression is. Rather I would say that political oppression is where people have no political rights so it is both arbitrary and has no checks.

But when you get to Contention One, Subpoint B, I give you analysis by Rummel that says 218 regimes worldwide say that political oppression is killing of its citizens, which is clearly "on balance," meaning that political oppression is violence against its own people. So, what that means is that back up into the criterion, if I respect human dignity by showing that violent revolution is a fundamental right, then it is just. He only makes a few answers to it, two of which say that if violent revolution produces harms and it harms innocents then it's unjust. But in cross-examination, I asked him if a lifeguard were to try and save a life and may fail in saving that life, the action of trying to save that life was still unjust? Meaning that the end consequences of an action are not what determines the justness of an action, but rather the action in and of itself. So he's defeated his own arguments to my criterion with his concession in cross-examination. All of his other arguments talk about how violent revolution violates human dignity in the short term and that violent revolution doesn't actually succeed. But remember I don't have to show you whether it succeeds or not, simply whether or not violent revolution is a fundamental right.

So this is where you are going to come to Subpoint B, which is conceded completely. Remember that Rummel says that politically oppressive regimes use violence against their people and kill their own citizens. Which means that every individual who has the right to self-defense, which is a fundamental right, is transferred to the collective body of citizens as a right to self-defense against an oppressive regime. Meaning that it is just for individuals to protect themselves using a violent revolution.

But then we can go to the negative case itself. There are a couple of problems with it, most of which are responded to by the second contention of the affirmative case which he mishandles badly. He only makes two answers: one that it doesn't make sense if we are talking about the threat of violence. But remember that the threat of violence only matters because violence itself will be used ultimately. And second, that we can still use the threat of violence in the negative world. In the negative world, because he is saying he is preventing unnecessary suffering through nonviolence, at the point where nonviolence is only effective through the use of violence, then it is just through a violent revolution, which is specifically what my second contention outlines. But both in terms of Gandhi and Martin Luther King, the only reason they were successful is because of violent revolution. His own analysis explains in the Orange Revolution that that was within a democratic regime which on balance is not an oppressive government and that nonviolence was only pivotal. It was not the only thing that allowed the revolution to be successful. Thus, I affirm.

Rebuttal Speech by Bilal Malik, James Logan High School

The order is going to be the negative case and then the affirmative case.

Taarini is very persuasive, but don't let her eloquence cloud your judgment. She's completely mishandling the negative case. To the criterion "prevention of unnecessary suffering," she explains that there is a clear link to justice. If something is unnecessary it's unjust, which means that if it's necessary it has to be justified. That's not true. Justice is not a binary. If something is unnecessary, the other thing doesn't necessarily have to be necessary. Remember, I provided a lot of analysis against this. I told you against the affirmative case, that we know that killing is unjust. We never say that killing is just. Rather, in certain situations we say that killing is permissible. Her response to this argument was that if it's necessary it is just, because it's necessary. If you pay attention to her argument, it is very circular. It says that the warrant for the claim is the claim itself. There is no reason to believe why necessity has to equal justice. I'm telling you that necessity means that it's permissible. We would never say that it's justified to kill people. Rather, it's permissible to kill people in certain situations.

Then she says that I don't explain what unnecessary means. In the context of the resolution, I explain that a violent revolution is unnecessary because it creates harms that don't need to be there, then that means it is unnecessary and as a result, it is unjust. So I do explain the unnecessary factor.

So let's go to the first contention. Her responses are wholly unresponsive. The first contention explains that the reason why nonviolence works is because it increases the popularity of the revolution. This, A) gives the revolutionaries the moral high ground and B) allows the revolutionaries to co-opt the military, which is a benefit that can only be captured by the negative ballot. This is explained through the analysis that I provided about Ukraine. In Ukraine they were having a peaceful revolution. Soldiers noticed the peaceful revolution and instead of shooting the revolutionaries, they joined their movement. Which means that we can co-opt the military through nonviolence. So not only does it reach the same ends, but it is also more beneficial because it allows us to invert the government from the inside.

Then go to the second point I make. I tell you that sympathy forces people to focus on the message and not the action. This is not responded to at all. I explained that oppressive governments are seen to be all the more oppressive when governments are attacking a vulnerable people. This means that the sympathy is on the side of the revolutionaries.

Also, remember the Ackerman and Duvall analysis that she is never refuting. Fifty of the 67 transitions were nonviolent in the past 35 years, which means that nonviolence is an alternative. So here's how you are going to sign your ballot. You are going to realize that while violence might work, it is not necessary because we have nonviolent methods. On balance, 50 out of 67 transitions were nonviolent. So you already have an empirical warrant as to why you are going to vote negative. Do not let her make new responses; do not let her elaborate as this is my last speech.

Now let's move on to the affirmative case. The next easiest place to vote negative is based off of this idea of permissibility. Remember, her only warrant as to why necessity equals "just" is because it is necessary. That is very circular. There is no warrant that she provides to you. I'm providing you with an example and I tell you that insofar as killing is always unjust, we would say that killing is permissible in self-defense. You can sign the ballot right now because she is not providing you with an adequate response as to why there is not a difference between permissibility and justice.

Then you can look to the response I made against political oppression. She says that my example I agreed to is not the norm. But that was the point. There is no reason to believe why her example, or her analysis of political oppression, always being violent is true. We ought to err on the side of caution because voting negative doesn't mean that violence cannot be used. It just means that we are not going to allow revolutionaries to have the blank check of violence in their arsenal. Rather, we ought to look at specific scenarios and then affirm the resolution. Violence hurts innocent people. It's a very important issue. We shouldn't treat it delicately. Insofar as voting affirmative means that sometimes we would be justifying violence when it is not needed, you ought to vote negative. This was not adequately refuted, so you have a third voting issue for the negative side.

Then you can go to her criterion of respecting human dignity. She says that the example she gave in cross-examination and the way I answered the question means that all the responses don't matter. She's wrong, because in the example she tells you that the lifeguard is trying to save the life of the child. The problem, however, is that he doesn't know that he is going to fail. Violent revolutionaries do know that they are going to fail because violent revolutions don't succeed. Remember this is explained by the Ackerman and Duvall analysis that explains that the military prowess of the state is much stronger than that of the revolutionaries. She is never refuting this analysis. So if I know that a certain action would require me to trample over the rights of innocents and I also know that I'm going to be unsuccessful, how can I ever say that it's justified for me to partake in that action?

Additionally, I would argue that she's not refuting the analysis that violent revolution tends overwhelmingly to produce undemocratic regimes. Remember that the problem with violent revolutions is that the revolutionaries do not put down their guns. She gave you the example of the United States being an effective revolution. But that's not the case. After the American revolution, only people that owned property, that were white, that had blond hair and blue eyes were allowed to vote. Blacks were enslaved, women were not allowed to vote, until nonviolent methods were used. Which means that you need the negative side to have any sort of political change.

So, she has the burden of proving that violent revolutions are actually effective, otherwise she's not going to be protecting rights. Additionally, remember I told you she is contradicting herself and this is something she is never refuting. This is another easy place to sign the ballot for the negative. Insofar as she is saying we should respect human dignity and insofar as violent revolution requires us to trample over human dignity, there is no way that she can win the round. She is never refuting this analysis. This is a very easy way out and a very easy way that you can sign the ballot for the negative.

So at the end of the day, it becomes clear that I am winning the round. I am not only proving that violent revolution is unnecessary, I am also proving to you that the affirmative case doesn't affirm. And even if it did affirm, I'm meeting it better than she does. So now you have all the reasons you need to negate the resolution. Thank you.

Final Affirmative Rebuttal: Taarini Vohra, Hockaday School

Let's go to the negative criterion. The problem is that he's still fundamentally mishandling my main argument about necessity and justice. He keeps saying that I don't have a warrant. The problem is that the warrant is very clear. If something is needed, is a necessity of justice, is a part of the process of getting to justice, then it is something people are due, and thus it is just. That is not circular. That is saying that in the process of getting to justice, if there is a step in that process that is just. What that means is that if a violent revolution is a step in terms of getting to justice, it is a fundamental right, and it preserves human dignity because it is a fundamental right, then it is just. He is never responding to that argument.

In terms of his criterion, remember that he is saying preventing unnecessary suffering is just, meaning that the converse would be true: preventing necessary suffering would be unjust. That means either if necessity has nothing to do with justice, his criterion is not linked to justice, so none of the negative case matters, or, that there is an intrinsic connection between necessity and justice as I have discussed. So, what that means is that ... and finally remember I told you that the only reason we care about preventing unnecessary suffering is because of a conception of human dignity. That means you are going to be looking at the affirmative criterion.

Also, my opponent has never addressed the fact that a fundamental part of preserving human dignity is respecting individuals' fundamental rights. So if I show that violent revolution is a fundamental right, then it is something that the people are due, and thus it is just.

That being said, now let's go to the definition of political oppression. He keeps articulating that I'm not showing what "on balance" political oppression is. But as the Rummel analysis states, in 218 regimes worldwide, political oppression is something which is arbitrary, has no checks, and that people are killed. That is very clearly "on balance" what political oppression is. His argument of Florida is not the norm; it is the exception. It should not be considered in terms of what "on balance" is.

So that being said, we can now go to the Contention One, Subpoint B of the affirmative case and remember that the right to self-defense is something that every individual is due in response to violence. So the right to violently revolt is therefore something that each individual is due against an oppressive regime. Thus it is just and it is a fundamental right of the people. This is the first clear affirmative voting issue; it links back to a conception of human dignity.

But then also remember his only other arguments are that I end up harming innocents and that it doesn't work. Remember that we are not looking to the end results, just as the lifeguard doesn't look to the end result of his action; he's only looking to the means of his action. But finally, remember that violent revolution will be successful because all revolutions in order to end oppression have to either include violence or the threat of violence as Contention Two shows. It has been conceded. What that means is this is the second affirmative voting issue. The only way to end oppression and give individuals their due and to end suffering is through a violent revolution because it is the only thing that gives a revolution credence. So that means on the negative side you are guaranteed oppression, whereas on the affirmative you have the potential for human dignity. Thus, I urge an affirmative ballot.

By a vote of 9 to 4, the judges decided that Taarini Vohra from the Hockaday School won this round.

PUBLIC FORUM FINAL ROUND

NFL NATIONAL TOURNAMENT 2006

Topic: The United States should ratify the Kyoto Protocol.

Con: Valerie Hobbs and Michelle Schmit (Bishop Heelan, Coach: Elizabeth Dalton)

Pro: David Nadle and Jennifer Goldstein (Stoneman Douglas, Coach: Diane McCormick)

Valerie Hobbs, Bishop Heelan (First Con Speech)

THE LATEST IN FROM PETER RODERICK, PRESIDENT OF FRIENDS OF THE EARTH INTERNATIONAL, THE LEADING ENVIRONMENTALIST GROUP IN SUPPORT OF KYOTO

"I think that everybody agrees that Kyoto is really, really hopeless in terms of delivering what the planet needs, but it's not the sort of nitty-gritty commas and dots in the text of the Protocol, it's the symbolic importance." Well, Peter, we do agree that Kyoto is really, really hopeless, but where you go wrong is that Kyoto is about the nitty-gritty commas and dots; it is about the text. The Protocol in itself is ineffective for the following three reasons.

First, if every country in the world followed the Kyoto Protocol to a *T*, the Protocol would reduce carbon-dioxide emission by only 5.2 percent; 5.2 percent will stop warming by one-twentieth of one degree Celsius in the next 50 years.

The Hoover Institute summed up those pathetic numbers by noting that even ten Kyotos would be ineffective in the long-term goal of solving global warming.

Secondly, the Kyoto Protocol exempts 134 developing countries, most notably China and India. China and India are predicted to produce 85 percent of the future increase in carbon-dioxide emissions. According to the National Interest, Kyoto parties were unable at their 2006 meeting to persuade developing countries to join a post-2012 commitment period. The Protocol is so preoccupied with the past that it ignores the future. Third, the Protocol arbitrarily sets limit reductions behind 1990 levels, which provides huge loopholes for countries such as Russia. Since the collapse of the Russian economy, the country's carbon-dioxide emissions have dropped more than 30 percent below 1990 levels. Russia's limits are set as though the collapse never occurred, meaning that Russia can actually increase their current emissions levels by 30 percent under the Protocol. With these flaws in the Protocol, all emissions goals the United States achieves now will be undone by Russia, China, and other developing countries. So now that we know what the Protocol won't do, it's time to address what it will do.

The certain economic repercussions as a result of the Protocol are enough to put anyone in a bad mood. We don't expect you to catch all of these numbers; just notice that they're all bad. The overall abatement costs stand at 2.2 trillion dollars according to the *Journal of Science*. These costs will be felt by the American family. By 2010 the Wharton Economic Forecasting Association estimates that 2.7 million jobs will be lost. Food prices will increase by 11 percent, medical expenses by 14 percent, electric bills by 55 percent, and home heating costs by 70 percent. If you're complaining about the gas prices now, just wait until Kyoto ups them 66 cents a gallon. The Heritage Foundation estimated that the average family would be forced to make do with $30,000 less between now and 2020. Kyoto comes at the price of unemployment, poverty, and struggle for the American people. State tax revenues will decrease by 100 billion in 2010, negatively affecting state programs such as education initiatives. To put this in perspective, UN statistics state that half the U.S.'s yearly cost of Kyoto could buy clean water, sanitation, health care, and education for every single person in the world. Moving on, national security takes a hit as well. The U.S.'s largest consumer of energy is the Defense Department. Only one-third of the necessary cuts to the department would reduce tank training by 328,000 miles per year; flight training by 210,000 flying hours; and naval training by 2,000 days at sea, according to the Pentagon. It reduces military readiness by adding up to six weeks of time needed to deploy in a crisis. Allowing the UN control over U.S. military is unacceptable.

There are already viable alternatives the United States government has enacted to address global warming. For example, the Carbon Sequestration Leadership Forum is a multilateral agreement in which the U.S. has invested $20 billion to support the advancement of environmentally friendly technology.

The Energy Policy Act implemented in 2006 provides market-based tax incentives to encourage the private sector to choose wind and solar power, clean vehicles, clean coal technology, and renewable biofuels. Market-based incentives have fueled the capitalistic nature of the American economy for years and should continue to do so.

Kyoto did the extent of what it is capable of; it put global warming on the international agenda. But even the scientific community is not backing it. Over 15,000 scientists signed a petition urging the U.S. government to reject the Kyoto Protocol and any other similar proposal. According to Bruce Swami, a law professor, a 30 percent decrease in carbon-dioxide emissions in the next four years is simply laughable. We refuse to advise you as a judge to vote to ratify a Protocol that compromises the economic stability as well as the national security of the United States.

David Nadle, Stoneman Douglas (First Pro Speech)

Before I begin I would like to first start off by thanking the Schwann Company and the Lincoln Financial Group and furthermore the National Forensic League and all of its sponsors. I would also like to thank Ted Turner personally for creating this event and sponsoring it. Finally, I would like to congratulate our opponents for making it this far in debate. Also, my partner and I would like to thank Diane Ramirez and Bradley Hicks, our coaches, who supported us as well as our team. Finally, I would like to thank God—it's Friday.

While the Kyoto Protocol originally began as an environmental treaty, it has become so much more, changing not only countries' economic perspectives, but society's as a whole—precisely why my partner and I stand in affirmation of today's resolution—Resolved that the United States government should ratify the Kyoto Protocol. First, we must look to the United States' potential to improve its international relations.

The United States has truly damaged its international credibility by refusing to officially act upon global warming. By ratifying the Kyoto Protocol, it would be doing just that. According to Margaret Walsh from the European Union Commission on Environmental Affairs, the United States' position is worrying and the United States needs to be prepared for negative implications, both economically and politically. Sam Williams of *The New York Times* on April 6, 2006, states that foreign companies no longer do as much business with the United States companies because foreign companies are under Kyoto Protocol restrictions whereas United States companies are not. And this is directly seen with a 68 percent reduction in foreign investment in United States removal technology sector, most specifically from the European Union as I previously mentioned. Furthermore, the European Union has also stated that it has already begun and will continue to remove its half a billion person market from the United States because of its failure to comply with the Kyoto Protocol. If we were to sign the Kyoto Protocol, it would improve international relations and furthermore allow the United States to revive its foreign investment. Next, we must look to the successes of the Kyoto Protocol in the United States already. My partner and I believe that there are economic models showing both the benefits and the cost of the Kyoto Protocol if we were to implement it in the United States. However, the best way to understand how it would truly affect the United States is to see how it already has affected the United States. The International Council for Local Environmental Initiatives, or

ICLEI, has stated that the United States Conference of Mayors, an organization of over 168 mayors from 37 different states, has already helped 17 major United States cities reduce their emissions below 1990 standards to the Kyoto Protocol ones, but furthermore saved 725 million dollars across the board because of cheaper energy costs. Patrick J. Michaels of the Cato Institute in September 2002 states that California, Massachusetts, New York, and other states, representing 46 percent of the U.S. population, have already worked to implement the Kyoto Protocol. These programs have all been successful in the United States both economically, but more importantly, environmentally. Finally, we must look to the benefits for the United States from developing countries such as India and China. Developing countries, as we all know, are not legally bound under the Kyoto Protocol to reduce their emissions. According to the Energy Information Administration, 40 percent of India's and 43 percent of China's emissions are solely due to United States companies and the manufacturing that they do within those countries. Economist William Nordhaus of Yale University expands upon this by saying that their not having to reduce their emissions can actually work in the best interest of the United States through something known as the clean development mechanism or CDM, which are projects that the United States can implement inside of India and China to reduce their emissions. As a result, those reduced emissions will count toward the United States' Kyoto Protocol goal. The benefits of this are twofold: It will allow United States companies inside India and China that are doing manufacturing to be introduced to this greener, cheaper technology, the benefits of which already been seen from the energy bills of the United States Conference of Mayors cities, as I mentioned saving 725 million dollars. And second of all, it will allow the United States to reduce its trade deficit with China and India, currently at 202 billion and 68.5 billion dollars, respectively, over the next five years. My opponents talked about developing countries being counterproductive; however, that's even more reason to affirm, because then the United States could join on and use this clean development mechanism to reduce their emissions. In retrospect, as we look back on today's topic and whether or not the United States should ratify the Kyoto Protocol, my partner and I stand in affirmation because of the potential to improve international relations, because of the success of the Kyoto Protocol in the United States already, and then finally, because of the benefits for the United States from developing countries such as India and China. Thank you.

FIRST CROSSFIRE

Hobbs: Okay, my first question to you is that you start out by saying that Kyoto started out as an environmental treaty yet nothing in your case links to the environment. So what exactly does Kyoto do for the environment?

Nadle: Well, I'd shown you in my case the fact that the United States Conference of Mayors cities that have already implemented it have been extremely successful in lowering their emissions. Furthermore, my partner will elaborate on the fact that countries across the board have lowered their emissions. But looking toward your case ...

Hobbs: Well, can I have any statistics on how much they have been lowered? Or ...

Nadle: Well sure, I'd shown you that United States Conference of Mayors cities, according to ICLI, has lowered them to Kyoto Protocol standards, which would be 7 percent below 1990 levels, and then my partner will further elaborate on what other countries have done also to be successful. But I have a quick question for you ...

Hobbs: One more quick follow-up question: How much has that affected the temperature?

Nadle: How much that's affected? Again, my partner will bring up more statistics showing the environmental benefits. But I have a question for you. You bring up various economic models, but is it not true that instead of using various economic models of what could happen in the future, it's better to look to what's already happened with the Kyoto Protocol?

Hobbs: Okay, so let's look at what has already happened. You talk about this Mayor's Commission, and yet we have statistics that say that the Mayor's Commission is nonbinding. It's mostly to do ... and we also have evidence that shows it might be of a more a political agenda than anything because it's nonbinding and it says that they want to abide by Kyoto, but it really does not provide the limits that Kyoto does. It gives them absolutely no time frame in which to implement them, and that's where the economic harms come in, is the time frame. Trying to do this in four years is absolutely ridiculous.

Nadle: But has that four years already occurred?

Hobbs: No ... it's from 2008 to 2012.

Nadle: And the United States Conference of Mayor's cities have already met those levels, correct?

Hobbs: You haven't given me any statistics that they have. Seattle, who started this commission, they haven't had anything done to their city. They haven't had any reports since 2002, and if they were so eager to boast about this, you would think that they would.

Nadle: Actually, recent reports from Greg Nickels, the mayor, shows that they've reduced their emissions by 60 percent already since the implementation of the Kyoto Protocol.

Hobbs: But they have no official report to back that up because an official report hasn't been done since 2002.

Nadle: It was an official report done by the United States Conference of Mayors, not the city of Seattle specifically. But again, let's look to your national security point. You again talk about the fact that the United States is not exempt; however, are you aware that the Kyoto Protocol does specifically exempt militaries from emissions?

Hobbs: It doesn't; it specifically exempts unilateral UN sanctioned actions, which doesn't include training or unilateral actions such as the war in Iraq or the war on terror.

Nadle: Are you aware of what the Montreal Convention was in 2005? In that convention, what they were able to do was the United States was able to negotiate ... and furthermore, Congress stated that they do not want the United States to be bound with their military, and they were extremely successful.

Hobbs: They weren't extremely successful; they proposed the draft to the United Nations, which got rejected; that was to exempt all militaries, not just the United States. None of the militaries are exempt except for UN-sanctioned multilateral action, which the United States is not currently involved in.

Nadle: Do you have any questions for me?

Hobbs: You talk about the developing countries and you say that we don't want them to reduce so that America can invest in them. Can you explain that to me?

Nadle: Well, first of all, my partner is going to show you information that they actually are reducing emissions, but furthermore ...

Hobbs: What steps are they taking? I would like for you to present them to me.

Nadle: They are actually putting in cleaner coal mines, but what I would like to show you ... [time was up] May I finish answering the question? ... that if we were to implement the Kyoto Protocol we could use the CDMs to reduce their emissions.

MICHELLE SCHMIT, BISHOP HEELAN (SECOND CON SPEECH)

Are all of my judges ready? First, I'll address their case and then return to my own. Their very first point talks about the potential to improve international relations, but we must understand that the tension that is currently in the global community has nothing to do with the Kyoto Protocol. Actually, it more centers on the global war on terrorism. You can't act like something as small as the Kyoto Protocol is actually going to take away all those tensions that result and come from something entirely different. So to make that direct correlation is probably pretty incorrect. They also talk about foreign companies and how the investments are not going very well. Actually, according to the EBA the investments have risen 11 percent in 2003 and in 2004 foreign investments in the United States were actually higher than our investments in other countries. So our foreign investments aren't really looking that poor. What you also must look to, they talk about a 68 percent reduction in renewable technology. The fact of the matter is that these things can be fixed through market-based incentive. For example, if our companies actually realize that on the global front they are not as competitive, then the profit-driven motive of the capitalistic economy is clearly going to solve for that factor. It has worked in the United States for the last 200 years, and I'm not sure why it would not work now. Secondly, they talk about how current models essentially—the Conference of Mayors is what they really focus on—show the actual benefits and costs. First you have to remember that's only 17 cities. But furthermore, the Conference of Mayors does not actually hold the businesses or the people of their cities to any binding agreements. The Kyoto Protocol is binding and has a timetable; the Conference of Mayors does not. Therefore, there is a huge difference and you cannot really compare the two. If they have no timetable—the timetable is the exact problem. We only have four years to do these drastic measures, and the fact of the matter is that the small businesses that can't afford it can't get it done in four years. So you can't compare something that has no timetables and is not legally binding to anybody within the cities to the actual Kyoto Protocol—that simply is not fair.

Then they talk about how we can use CDMs to help China and India. Well, first of all, China and India need to be willing to help themselves. They talked about how China is actually reducing coal, but this comes from 2006: it's out of Beijing, it says that China is planning 562 new coal-fired power stations, nearly half the world total of plants. So clearly, China is really not doing that good on their own and why are we responsible for China's emissions? We would also like to point out that in the *National Interest* in the Summer 2006 edition it says that China and India at the 2006 meetings in Bonn, Germany, are entirely unwilling at this point in time to sign and ratify Kyoto post-2012. So come 2012, the Kyoto Protocol is looking like it is not in a very strong state anyway and if you don't have those 134 developing countries on board, it's really becoming much less of a global solution because you just took out 134 out of 160—those numbers are not very impressive.

They also stated that Congress—this refers to our military exemption point—don't worry about it because Congress said that our military should be exempt. Well, it's nice that Congress said that, and I do agree with Congress—they are right. The UN has not said that, and they are not allowing our military to be exempt. It comes at a huge cost in national security. The Pentagon is saying that it will require up to six weeks longer to deploy in a crisis because their training cannot go on as it does right now because of the carbon-dioxide emissions of our training. The U.S. military is not exempt and that's a huge problem that needs to be handled before we just take rash decisions and ratify the Kyoto Protocol.

Going back to sum up our case a little more. What we have talked about and looked to first is the fact that the Kyoto Protocol doesn't solve. If it doesn't solve, I would see that as a huge problem and notice they didn't produce any ways that it does solve. It's going to change our temperature by one-twentieth of one degree Celsius according to Steve Mock as well as according to the Hoover Institute. Scientists are deeming that laughable; they say it has absolutely no impact on the climate. If it has no impact and it has all of these repercussions, why exactly would we be compelled to ratify it? It exempts the developing countries and they're not going to get on the bandwagon post-2012, so they will remain exempt. Russia can actually increase their emissions levels by 30 percent under the Kyoto Protocol—it's so biased against the United States. The economic repercussions—you have to understand those 2.2 trillion dollars in abatement discounted over decades—that isn't federal spending, that's spending that comes out of the American people's pockets. That's spending that's going to increase our daily prices of gas, food, medical. You are allowing something that doesn't even solve to be put into place and it's going to increase our poverty level while decreasing our standard of living. I have a huge problem with that. There are other ways to do this. We have a capitalistic economy; we can do it through market-based incentives. The United States government is already investing in cleaner technology, and that would be just as effective.

JENNIFER GOLDSTEIN, STONEMAN DOUGLAS (SECOND PRO SPEECH):

Alright, are my judges ready? Opponents? First, I'll discuss our case and then move on to our opponents'. We do affirm today's resolution to affirm the Kyoto Protocol for four main reasons. We've seen it—as my partner had mentioned—it would improve U.S. international relations. We've seen its success in the United States. And because of the benefits reaped through utilizing India and China.

In addition to these points, I maintain that the longer we wait to join the Kyoto Protocol, the larger the loss in profit margins for our businesses. According to the Center of Environmental Evaluation on September 25, 2005, renewable energy will supply 14 percent of the world's needs by 2020 and 40 percent by 2040. Seeing these trends, the United States stands to gain or lose a significant amount of money. With the Kyoto Protocol, I'm showing a definitive gain. General Electric, for example, in April 2006 reported that because of changes and enhancements in their green research and development, revenues are expected to double by 2010. Jonathan Coller of the Department of Applied Economics in Cambridge showed how Denmark through its early—keyword *early*—investment in wind technology reaped substantial profits. Essentially, if a country wants to invest in greener technology, they are going to invest in countries with Kyoto Protocol restrictions, rather than countries outside of these obligations like the United States because these restrictions lead to the development of the most efficient technology the U.S. doesn't have the incentive or pressure to create themselves.

Now let's look to our opponent's case a little bit. Their first point talks about how the Kyoto Protocol is ineffective and how CO_2 even under best results will only result in only a one-twentieth degree in climate change. And what Oxford University says is that this is amazing. They compare changing climate change like reversing the direction of a train. You have to slow the train down, stop it, then reverse. So if we're ready for the first step of an actual climate change protocol—reversing the process—I'd say that's a significant step. Furthermore, you can look to Jason Schrogen, a professor of finance and economics at the University of Wyoming, who said that without the Kyoto Protocol, temperature will rise 2.5 degrees Celsius and with it will rise 1.5. We're here about reversing climate change, but it's not just going to happen overnight. Our opponents give you several other options that the United States has explored; however, none of these provide for an overnight climate change. If the Kyoto Protocol is already changing climate, that is more reason to affirm.

Then they talk about exempting developing countries, and we can really combine this with my third point, which told you how CDMs in developing nations will help them reduce their emissions and help us reduce our trade deficit with those countries. Countries like China stand to give us a substantial benefit while also reducing their own emissions and others around the world. Currently, according to the United Nations, there are 800 such projects and we've clearly seen success. The Intergovernmental Panel on Climate Control has followed the world over and has seen a net decrease of emissions by 5.9 percent; we're looking at results here, not hypotheticals. And finally, they talk about Russia. However, Russia is a false … the whole market of the Kyoto is a false market. You need sellers and you need buyers. If Russia is a seller, then there are more buyers in the market and the whole market gets more valuable. So that's why Russia essentially doesn't matter.

Now their economy point. They tell how you need to look to all their statistics because … it's just … they're all bad. Well, we have some bad news for our opponents in the fact that we have statistics saying that the Kyoto Protocol can actually gain. The Department of Energy showed that we will actually save $585 billion in less gas usage. The average consumer will spend $567 to make the transition, but that they'll save a net $1,978. The U.S. Senate Committee on Commerce, Science, and Transportation showed how the GDP will increase by .4 percent in 2010 to .9 percent by 2020 and that will save 1.4 million jobs. Basically, we need to look at this holistically. There are estimates on both sides supporting both sides of the resolution. But what's happening now in the Conference of Mayors shows you that it will work in the United States—that under the exact same standards we see results. We're not offering you hypotheticals; we're offering you reality, a $725 million savings per year as a reality under the exact same protocol. So that's why you're going to affirm because we're offering you definite results.

Now under their national security point: we said that the National Center for Policy Analysis on August 6, 1998, showed us that the House of Representatives passed the Defense Authorization bill 420 to zero, which said, "no provision of the Kyoto Protocol will restrict the procurement, training, operation, or maintenance of U.S. troops." The Senate has said this and also it doesn't make sense if the United Nations wants us to ratify a treaty that they're selectively going to say the United States only has to restrict their military. That simply doesn't make sense. We're not restricting solely the United States military. We're saying that all militaries are exempt from the Kyoto Protocol; it's in the actual transactions.

As far as India and China goes, we've already seen in the transcripts that India and China made no motions to say that they would pull out of the climate treaty. That doesn't make sense when they stand to gain so much from these climate treaties through these CDMs. Honestly, in the transcripts, China stood up and said they've a point of information and then they stayed silent, so I have no idea what my opponents are talking about.

As far as scientists go, they say that we can't reduce CO_2 realistically. The Kyoto Protocol addresses over six greenhouse gases, and in fact, methane is found to be 23 times more potent than CO_2, and we're having success reducing methane, which is specifically what the Conference of Mayors focuses on. Our opponents are offering you a narrow scope of this resolution. They're saying that selectively the UN is going to put restrictions on certain countries that they want to join the Protocol. They're saying that selectively, even though 800 projects have been implemented according to clean development mechanisms to get countries to profit, it's somehow suddenly not going to work. They're saying that okay, we already have these standards in the United States, but somehow they're not going to work in the future. They're not offering you a holistic view of this resolution. We're offering you economic benefits. We're offering our businesses a chance to flourish in a new greener technological era, which is a false market in which we can stand to gain from. We only offer you benefits on the affirmative side of the resolution. We're admitting that it will take an initial transaction cost. Anyone who wouldn't admit that is lying. What we're telling you is that a net gain will result from this resolution, and that's what you want to affirm. You want to give our businesses a chance to compete; you want our deficit with India and China to decrease; and you want to give our country a chance to see the benefits on a 100 percent global scale that we've seen in select cities. Overall emissions have reduced worldwide according to the Intergovernmental Panel on Climate Control, the IPCC, the official measurer of this. That is why you want to affirm today's resolution.

SECOND CROSSFIRE

Schmit: Okay, now, you talked about how in '98 the House passed it, and I'm supposed to be impressed by that, but you do realize that the '98 measure when the House passed it, what they were doing was passing a resolution against the Kyoto Protocol because our military is not exempt underneath the Kyoto Protocol and that's one of the huge reasons that we have not ratified it as of now.

Goldstein: Alright, well, I already told you that in the United Nations actual Protocol you see that we are actually worldwide exempting militaries, but moreover ...

Schmit: I would really like to see that because I am actually positive that's not in there.

Goldstein: Well, my partner will offer the Kyoto Protocol.

Schmit: I do want to see that.

Goldstein: But moreover, let's look to the logic of that. If the United Nations really wants the United States to sign, because we are producing so many emissions, then why are they solely going to focus on us and say that we cannot exempt our military?

Schmit: They are solely focusing on us; we are simply saying the U.S. military is not exempt anywhere in the Protocol. The only thing it does talk about with the military is that in UN-sanctioned multilateral actions, which does not include our training, nor our unilateral actions in the war in Iraq, we are not exempted underneath that.

Goldstein: Alright, we disagree because we have evidence otherwise.

Schmit: I would actually like to see that evidence.

Goldstein: Right, as I said, this is a crossfire, we will hand it to you as soon as we can.

Schmit: Okay.

Goldstein: Now I actually have a question for you. You say that climate change can only change one-twentieth of a degree, correct?

Schmit: Yes.

Goldstein: Okay, so as a first step of policy, isn't it absolutely amazing that we are already seeing actual reductions in actual temperature degrees?

Schmit: I actually have a two-part answer to that. First of all, temperatures are still going to increase. According to the Hoover Institute, without the Kyoto Protocol, it is going to increase 1.4 Celsius, with 1.35. The Hoover Institute says that is absolutely no difference, and it's backed up by the National Academy of Science. Second answer: you're acting as if there is going to be a second step, and as we've proved to you in the *National Interest*, it says that both China and India as well as the 134 developing countries are not willing to ratify the Kyoto Protocol post-2012 if restrictions are placed upon them, in which case they will have 85 percent of the future increase, in which case even if it does solve a very tiny bit now, it's just going to take a backward step post-2012.

Goldstein: Okay, understandably, but I'm concerned we both have different transcripts apparently, can we look to the logic ...

Schmit: Can I see your transcript because I'm more than willing to show you ours right now?

Goldstein: Okay, again, this is a crossfire, we'll hand you the evidence as soon as possible.

Schmit: But it's hard to debate over evidence if you're not willing to offer it.

Goldstein: Let's look to logic, then. Logically, would we actually see developing countries pulling out of a protocol when it actually has the ability to create not only better technology under it, but the fact that they can be helped by the clean development mechanism from developed countries?

Schmit: Well, whether or not it's logical, China and India both say they are going to because of the regulations ...

Goldstein: So, is it logical or not?

Schmit: I would say it's logical to pull out of it because of the economic repercussions that are caused by it. And the clean development mechanisms: you told me there are 800 and you told their successes are quoted by the UN. Of course the UN quotes the success.

Goldstein: Okay, now you're questioning our sources? All I'm saying is that the CDMs logically make sense. If you're going to reduce the trade deficit, if you're going to develop technology and spread ideas of technology between countries and reduce your money, then it makes sense. But let's go on to that economics point.

Schmit: Okay.

Goldstein: We've already shown you that through the Conference of Mayors under the exact same standards of the Kyoto …

Schmit: But they're not under the same standards.

Goldstein: Why not?

Schmit: Because they're not under any timetables, they don't hold businesses to any regulations, and they say pretty much if you want to be involved that's great, but they don't force you to be involved. So, of course, businesses like General Electric can do it, but a smaller business cannot—they can't afford it.

VALERIE HOBBS, BISHOP HEELAN (CON SUMMARY SPEECH)

Just so the judges will know, I am going to try my very best to go down her last speech and then return to our own case. Okay, first of all, they claim that it is going to improve international relations, but they can give you absolutely no direct guarantee of this because a large portion of the reason that other countries would be hostile with us is because of our unilateral actions in Iraq and with the war on terror that is not UN sanctioned and not covered under the Protocol, which they have not shown you.

They say it is already being a success, but as we have shown, I have a quote here from one of the mayors: "We will not, however, ask residents and businesses to reach our goal of being environmentally friendly cities in America on their own, and they only ask that you try your best and they don't restrict the small businesses." Of course GE can do that and the examples they're giving you are of very large corporations that can make these, and they can make these cuts, and they can come out better for it. But the small businesses can't. These large corporations are not under any time limits. And it's the time limits and the small businesses that incur the economic repercussions. 2008 to 2012 is just much too short a time period.

They then talk to you about how it doesn't even make sense that China and India. And yet we've given you ... we're completely willing to let our opponents see it ... it says right here that China and India are going to back out post-2012 if they're placed under any commitment period. And they're not even sure they want to do it post-2012 without a commitment. So, it's not going to go on post-2012, so they can't even claim that it's a stepping-stone. One-twentieth of one degree Celsius, not stopping and reversing, but slowing from 1.4 to 1.35, is not significant. Scientists are laughing at it—it won't have any effect on the climate change and that's what the Kyoto Protocol was constructed to do. It was to reverse global warming and it's not.

Then, our national security point, they just say that Congress passed a bill that they won't sign the Kyoto Protocol until our military is exempt. That's what's happening right now—our military is not exempt. No military is exempt, but yet we're the only military right currently involved, or majorly involved, in a unilateral, non-UN sanctioned action. And it doesn't count to our training. Our training is going to reduce our action by six weeks. Six weeks. Imagine what that's going to do during a national crisis—during an environmental crisis. Six weeks—and they've given you no answer to that. We will not allow the UN to have control over the U.S. military; it's just not how it should be.

David Nadle, Stoneman Douglas (Pro Summary Speech)

Let's first look to our case. My opponents have pretty much refused to refute the fact about capitalism. We talk about the point that the United States government ... it's in our best interest to help our businesses to get into this game early and be able to get into the world market—to be able to innovate. However, our opponents simply say that capitalism will lead to that. However, I would like to again point out that the United States government if it were truly in the best interest of its companies would sign the Kyoto Protocol to allow its businesses to get into this game early. Capitalism does work, yet at the same time, the government can initiate moves to help the businesses in the long run. In regards to international relations, they say that our 60 percent foreign investment in renewal technology in the United States is not due to the fact that we haven't signed the Kyoto Protocol, but rather because of the global war on terrorism. However, that simply makes no point. We talk about international relations, and they say well, that's because of the global war on terrorism. That doesn't make any sense. We specifically talked about the fact that foreign investment is down in the renewal technology sector. That's not due to the war on terrorism; my opponents have drawn no link to that.

Next, we need to look to the successes of the Kyoto Protocol in the United States, and they said that there are no timetables. However, I brought up information from the ICLI organization that showed studies that they have reduced their emissions below the Kyoto Protocol already. So, regardless of the fact of whether there are timetables or not, the facts show they have already met it before the timetables would be up. So even if the timetables were initiated form the 2008 to 2012 commitment period, they still would have met them. The timetables in this instance don't make any sense.

Finally in regard to India and China, my partner brought up information about the fact that China is actually implementing cleaner coal technologies inside of their country. And furthermore, so the fact that they bring up that 562 new coal plants are being put in doesn't make any sense because they are actually cleaner coal plants that are actually being used. Furthermore, the fact about the developing countries is another reason to affirm, because if the United States can affirm the resolution, then we can help reduce emissions from developing countries such as India and China. Whereas if you negate the resolution, they continue to pollute and nothing is solved for. If you affirm the resolution, you get developing countries to reduce their emissions and that is what my partner and I would like to go for today.

GRAND CROSSFIRE

Schmit: About foreign investments: you talked about how foreign investments have decreased. But as we told you, in 2003, it's from Thomas Anderson, actually it's 2004, foreign investments have actually increased by 11 percent. Let's even just say that they did decrease, would you not expect that in a capitalistic economy, the profit-driven motive would make companies do better to be more competitive on a global front even without regulations?

Nadle: Well, first of all, your rebuttal was to foreign investment in total, whereas I bring up specific foreign investment in the renewal technology sector, more specifically related to the environment.

Hobbs: And so, how does that change the capitalistic nature of the economy?

Nadle: Well, that's precisely what I want to get to: is it not in the government's best interest to do what it can to help the companies?

Hobbs: I don't ever think it's in the government's best interest to place unnecessary regulations upon small businesses.

Nadle: I didn't say unnecessary regulations.

Schmit: But that's what the Kyoto Protocol would do.

Nadle: Can I ask another question, please?

Hobbs: Sure.

Nadle: You then talk about the fact that it's not in the best interest of the government to help our businesses.

Hobbs: No, that's ...

Nadle: But what I want to show you is that if we affirm the resolution as we've seen in Denmark with their wind technology, we can allow companies the benefit of getting into the game early and be able to invest and, therefore, be more successful. And I believe my partner has a question for you.

Goldstein: We're going to come back to this economy point because it is a major point in the round.

Schmit: Okay.

Goldstein: So we've already shown you from the Council of Mayors themselves that they are holding under the same restrictions that they are specifically focusing on methane, which is more deadly to the environment than CO_2. So again, if we're seeing economic benefits and our emissions reducing, how can you constantly contend that we're going to struggle economically if we implement the Kyoto Protocol?

Schmit: The actual mayor of Chicago as well as the mayor of Seattle, are the two I believe that led the Mayor's Council, say that they are not using the same regulations or standards that the Kyoto Protocol is. Seeing as how businesses and residents do not have to actually follow any regulations, there were very few changes made. And I'd like to point out that Seattle has not produced a report since 2002. If there is a report since 2002, I'd like to see it. The most recent I could find was September of 2002, so they have made no progress in the last four years and probably because they have started to see the economic repercussions.

Nadle: I actually have right here the United States Conference of Mayor's treaty; if you'd like you could look at it.

Schmit: Oh, I have it.

Nadle: It specifically states that they're meeting or exceeding the Kyoto Protocol. Therefore, it shows that they are implementing the Protocol and they are working on the standards.

Schmit: But they haven't done anything since 2002, and why do you think that is?

Goldstein: We're saying ...

Schmit: If it's working so well, and they're making so much money, can you explain why ...?

Goldstein: Do you want us to answer your question?

Schmit: Please.

Goldstein: Okay. All you're saying is that they haven't done any-thing since 2002 according to your standards—that you haven't seen results. But we've had actual, you know, meetings with the U.S. Conference of Mayors that has shown these results. Just because you don't consider them valid from 2002 doesn't mean they aren't valid at all.

Schmit: Do you have any evidence that says that, though? Or do you just assume that they've gone further, because the furthest report I can find is four years ago.

Goldstein: Okay, what does that report say?

Schmit: It simply says that there ... I can read it all to you, but it's kind of long. It's just the point that it comes from 2002 and there hasn't been a report published since. And usually, to me, if there hasn't been a report published since, it's because no progress has been made. And so probably, they began to feel the economic repercussions.

Hobbs: Can we ask you a question?

Nadle: Yes.

Hobbs: You state [timer beeped] ... or not.

MICHELLE SCHMIT, BISHOP HEELAN (FINAL FOCUS, CON)

Judges ready? What this round comes down to is the fact that the Kyoto Protocol doesn't solve for anything. If you don't see an environmental benefit, I'm not very impressed. One-twentieth of one degree Celsius from the Hoover Institute that scientists have deemed laughable. It really makes no difference. And the fact of the matter is that's optimistic. That's only if every single country in the world follows it, and that's clearly not happening. And China and India, which will not follow it post-2012, as we gave you information for, as well as Russia that can actually increase. Anything that gets done, they're just going to undo later because the Kyoto Protocol is simply a flawed treaty. You have to look to the economic repercussions. The reason that those happen is that the timetable is too drastic; you only have four years to make the cuts, and small businesses can't do that. We've quoted a lot of these from the *Journal of Science*, something that actually supports the Kyoto Protocol. It still admits that it will cost $2.2 trillion out of the American people's pockets; I have a real problem with that. National security has also not been answered; six weeks longer to deploy in a crisis. All they can tell you is that Congress thinks that's bad. I think that's bad, too. We cannot accept those kinds of standards that the Kyoto Protocol puts on our military; there are other alternatives. We can do it through market-based incentives. We've been investing in cleaner technologies. Simply, there are other ways to do it. All their economic benefits they discussed were under the Mayors, and the Mayors didn't even follow the Kyoto Protocol very much at all. So, please, I urge a Con ballot.

Jennifer Goldstein, Stoneman Douglas (Final Focus, Pro)

Are the judges ready? The reason you're not going to negate today is for the two reasons they gave you to negate. They talked about developing nations and about how they don't want to participate in 2012 talks. However, they don't substantiate this with evidence nor do they substantiate it with logic, when we've shown that they can benefit through clean development mechanisms. The second reason they gave you to negate is the national security point. And we've already disagreed about Congress's ruling and its importance or not, but we think through it logically that the United Nations will not place sanctions on countries' militaries if they want them to join the Kyoto Protocol. Moreover, we haven't seen any results from these sanctions, so I ask you to question that in this round today. The reason you are going to affirm is because the Kyoto Protocol has hidden benefits and potential benefits. We talked about the economy and how the Conference of Mayors has actually followed the exact Kyoto Protocol standards as outlined in their charter and found that it is successful both economically and environmentally. We have a source from PBS in 2005 which my partner didn't get to say in the Grand Cross. Finally, we ask you to look at the environmental benefits; they say that one-twentieth of one degree is not enough, but we say that it is more than enough. We parallel it to Oxford's train analogy. We show that climate change can't change overnight. You have to do a slow halt, then a stop, then reverse. If a first step of policy is already reversing climate change, it is more than an effective policy. It solves for the two things it must. We talk about businesses and the economy and the environment all benefiting from one Protocol and one signature. That's all you have to do today, judges, is sign one little ballot saying that we're going to benefit economically and environmentally and that our businesses have a foot in the door, which is why you are going to affirm today's resolution.

[Debaters shake hands]

TED TURNER'S COMMENTS

Well, congratulations. This is really terrific. I was once the state champion in Tennessee, but we didn't have enough money to come here. So you've come a lot further than I did, so you're all winners.

PAM McCOMAS (TAB ROOM OFFICIAL)

The judges decided by an 8-3 vote that the Con side won this debate.

ORGANIZATIONS GOVERNING DEBATE COMPETITION

The particular rules governing debate competition vary from tournament to tournament. Every debate league establishes its own rules for everything ranging from the amount of preparation time allowed to the types of arguments that are allowed. Before you begin preparation for debate competition, be sure to check out the rules that apply in your particular debate league. Usually these rules are clearly spelled out at the websites for the debate league.

NATIONAL ORGANIZATIONS GOVERNING DEBATE COMPETITION

National Forensic League (NFL): www.nflonline.org
The NFL in its own words: "The National Forensic League, NFL, is the leading honor society and educational resource for teachers, students, administrators, and parents in the exciting field of speech and debate education. With over 2,800 member schools and 93,000 active student members, we are continuously striving towards our goal of promoting the art of speech and debate. In doing so, we provide educational opportunities, honors, scholarships, and awards

that recognize students at local, regional, and national levels. The NFL is proud of its 80-year tradition of 'Training Youth for Leadership.'"

National Federation of State High School Associations (NFHS): www.nfhs.org NFHS in its own words: "Since 1920, The National Federation of State High School Associations has led the development of education-based interscholastic sports and activities that help students succeed in their lives. We set directions for the future by building awareness and support, improving the participation experience, establishing consistent standards and rules for competition, and helping those who oversee high school sports and activities. The NFHS, from its offices in Indianapolis, Indiana, serves its 50 member state high school athletic/activity associations, plus the District of Columbia. The NFHS publishes playing rules in 16 sports for boys and girls competition and administers fine arts programs in speech, theater, debate, and music. It provides a variety of program initiatives that reach the 18,500 high schools and over 11 million students involved in athletic and activity programs."

National Catholic Forensic Association (NCFL): www.ncfl.org The NCFL in its own words: "The NCFL is an organization of private and public high schools dedicated to promoting and supporting speech and debate activities in the U.S. and Canada. The NCFL sponsors the Grand National Tournament, which is held each year on Memorial Day weekend at a different location each year. At the 2006 Grand National Tournament, held in Chicago on May 27–28, some 2,330 students representing over 500 high schools competed."

National Debate Coaches Association (NDCA): http://ndca. debateteams.net The NDCA in its own words: "The National Debate Coaches Association provides all debate coaches, regardless of type of debate, region, or pedagogical style, with avenues for professional development. The goal of the organization is to strengthen the ability of coaches to provide meaningful learning experiences for their debaters."

National Association of Urban Debate Leagues (NAUDL): www. urbandebate.org The NAUDL in its own words: "The National Association for Urban Debate Leagues (NAUDL) currently has 19 local sites. It works to support their sustainability and qualitative development within the framework of four Organizing Principles: to use debate as a mechanism for urban education improvement, to promote equal access and opportunity to participate in debate, to institutionalize competitive academic debate programs, and to support and professionalize urban high school teachers."

National Christian Forensics and Communications Association (NCFCA): www.ncfca.org   NCFCA in its own words: "The National Christian Forensics and Communications Association (NCFCA) believes that formal speech and debate can provide a means for home-schooled students to learn and exercise analytical and oratorical skills, addressing life issues from a Biblical world view in a manner that glorifies God. To provide these opportunities to home-schooled students, NCFCA shall facilitate qualifying tournaments throughout the country and the annual national tournament."

STATE-BASED ORGANIZATIONS GOVERNING DEBATE COMPETITION

California High School Speech Association (CHSSA): www.cahssa.org

Florida Forensics League (FFL): www.floridaforensics.org

Illinois Speech and Theatre Association (ISTA): www.illinoisspeechandtheatre.com

Indiana High School Forensic Association (IHSFA): www.ihsfa.org

Iowa High School Speech Association (IHSSA): www.ihssa.org

Kentucky High School Speech League (KHSSL): www.wku.edu/khssl

Louisiana High School Speech League (LHSSL): www.lhssl.com

Maine Principal's Association (MPA): http://mpa.cc/id_speech.html

Michigan Interscholastic Forensics Association (MIFA): www.themifa.org

Minnesota Debate Teacher's Association (MDTA): www.mdta.org

Montana High School Association: www.mhsa.org

New York State Forensics League (NYSFL): www.nysfl.org

North Carolina Tarheel Forensic League (TFL): www. ncspeechanddebate.org

South Carolina Forensics Coaches Association: http:// scspeechanddebate.org

Texas Forensic Association (TFA): www.txfa.org

Texas University Interscholastic League (UIL): www.uil.utexas.edu/ academics/speech

Utah Forensics Association: http://utahforensics.org

Wisconsin High School Forensic Association (WHSFA): www. whsfa.org

Wisconsin Debate Coaches Association (WDCA): www.wdca.org

Wyoming High School Forensics Association: www.jcsd1.k12. wy.us/~bhs/WyForensics_ORG/Novice_CX_topics.htm

DEBATE RESOLUTIONS FROM PREVIOUS YEARS

POLICY DEBATE RESOLUTIONS

1939–1940 Resolved: That the federal government should own and operate the railroads.

1940–1941 Resolved: That the power of the federal government should be increased.

1941–1942 Resolved: That every able-bodied male citizen in the United States should be required to have one year of full-time military training before attaining the present draft age.

1942–1943 Resolved: That a federal world government should be established.

1943–1944 Resolved: That the United States should join in reconstituting the League of Nations.

1944–1945 Resolved: That the legal voting age should be reduced to eighteen years.

1945–1946 Resolved: That every able-bodied male citizen of the United States should have one year of full-time military training before attaining age 24.

1946–1947 Resolved: That the federal government should provide a system of complete medical care available to all citizens at public expense.

1947–1948 Resolved: That the federal government should require arbitration of labor disputes in all basic industries.

1948–1949 Resolved: That a federal world government should be established.

1949–1950 Resolved: That the President of the United States should be elected by the direct vote of the people.

1950–1951 Resolved: That the American people should reject the welfare state.

1951–1952 Resolved: That all American citizens should be subject to conscription for essential service in time of war.

1952–1953 Resolved: That the Atlantic pact nations should form a federal union.

1953–1954 Resolved: That the President of the United States should be elected by the direct vote of the people.

1954–1955 Resolved: That the federal government should initiate a policy of free trade among nations friendly to the United States.

1955–1956 Resolved: That the government subsidies should be granted according to need to high school graduates who qualify for additional training.

1956–1957 Resolved: That the federal government should sustain the prices of major agricultural products at not less than 90% of parity.

1957–1958 Resolved: That the United States foreign aid should be substantially increased.

1958–1959 Resolved: That the United States should adopt the essential features of the British system of education.

1959–1960 Resolved: That the federal government should substantially increase its regulation of labor unions.

1960–1961 Resolved: That the United Nations should be significantly strengthened.

1961–1962 Resolved: That the federal government should equalize educational opportunity by means of grants to the states for public elementary and secondary education.

1962–1963 Resolved: That the United States should promote a Common Market for the Western Hemisphere.

1963–1964 Resolved: That Social Security benefits should be extended to include complete medical care.

1964–1965 Resolved: That nuclear weapons should be controlled by an international organization.

1965–1966 Resolved: That the federal government should adopt a program of compulsory arbitration in labor-management disputes in basic industries.

1966–1967 Resolved: That the foreign aid program of the United States should be limited to non-military assistance.

1967–1968 Resolved: That Congress should establish uniform regulations to control criminal investigation procedures.

1968–1969 Resolved: That the United States should establish a system of compulsory service by all citizens.

1969–1970 Resolved: That Congress should prohibit unilateral United States military intervention in foreign countries.

1970–1971 Resolved: That the federal government should establish, finance, and administer programs to control air and/or water pollution in the United States.

1971–1972 Resolved: That the jury system in the United States should be significantly changed.

1972–1973 Resolved: That governmental financial support for all public and secondary education in the United States be provided exclusively by the federal government.

1973–1974 Resolved: That the federal government should guarantee a minimum annual income to each family unit.

1974–1975 Resolved: That the United States should significantly change the method of selection of presidential and vice-presidential candidates.

1975–1976 Resolved: That the development and allocation of scarce world resources should be controlled by an international organization.

1976–1977 Resolved: That a comprehensive program of penal reform should be adopted throughout the United States.

1977–1978 Resolved: That the federal government should establish a comprehensive program to regulate the health care system in the United States.

1978–1979 Resolved: That the federal government should guarantee contracts of medical care for all U. S. citizens.

1979–1980 Resolved: That the United States should significantly change its foreign trade policies.

1980–1981 Resolved: That the federal government should initiate and enforce safety guarantees on consumer goods.

1981–1982 Resolved: That the federal government should establish minimum educational standards for elementary and secondary schools in the United States.

1982–1983 Resolved: That the United States should significantly curtail its arms sales to other countries.

1983–1984 Resolved: That the United States should establish uniform rules governing the procedure of all criminal courts in the nation.

1984–1985 Resolved: That the federal government should provide employment for all employable U.S. Citizens living in poverty.

1985–1986 Resolved: That the federal government should establish a comprehensive national policy to protect the quality of water in the United States.

1986–1987 Resolved: That the federal government should implement a comprehensive long-term agricultural policy in the United States.

1987–1988 Resolved: That the United States government should adopt a policy to increase political stability in Latin America.

1988–1989 Resolved: That the federal government should implement a comprehensive program to guarantee retirement security for United States citizens over age 65.

1989–1990 Resolved: That the federal government should adopt a nationwide policy to decrease overcrowding in prisons and jails in the United States.

1990–1991 Resolved: that the United States Government should significantly increase space exploration beyond Earth's mesosphere.

1991–1992 Resolved: That the federal government should significantly increase social services to homeless individuals in the United States.

1992–1993 Resolved: That the United States government should reduce worldwide pollution through its trade and/or aid policies.

1993–1994 Resolved: That the federal government should guarantee comprehensive national health insurance to all United States citizens.

1994–1995 Resolved: That the United States government should substantially strengthen regulation of immigration to the United States.

1995–1996 Resolved: That the United States government should substantially change its foreign policy toward the People's Republic of China.

1996–1997 Resolved: That the federal government should establish a program to substantially reduce juvenile crime in the United States.

1997–1998 Resolved: That the federal government should establish a policy to substantially increase renewable energy use in the United States.

1998–1999 Resolved: That the United States should substantially change its foreign policy toward Russia.

1999–2000 Resolved: That the federal government should establish an education policy to significantly increase academic achievement in secondary schools in the United States.

2000–2001 Resolved: That the United States federal government should significantly increase protection of privacy in the United States in one or more of the following areas: employment, medical records, consumer information, search and seizure.

2001–2002 Resolved: That the United States federal government should establish a foreign policy significantly limiting the use of weapons of mass destruction.

2002–2003 Resolved: That the United States federal government should substantially increase public health services for mental health care in the United States.

2003–2004 Resolved: That the United States federal government should establish an ocean policy substantially increasing protection of marine natural resources.

2004–2005 Resolved: That the United States federal government should establish a foreign policy substantially increasing its support of United Nations peacekeeping operations.

2005–2006 Resolved: That the United States federal government should substantially decrease its authority either to detain without charge or to search without probable cause.

2006–2007 Resolved: That the United States federal government should establish a policy substantially increasing the number of persons serving in one or more of the following national service programs: AmeriCorps, Citizen Corps, Senior Corps, Peace Corps, Learn and Serve American, Armed Forces.

2007–2008 Resolved: That the United States federal government should substantially increase its public health assistance to sub-Saharan Africa.

Lincoln-Douglas Resolutions

1979–1980

Resolved: The strength of the present methods of funding the Social Security system outweighs the weaknesses.

1980–1981

Resolved: That it is morally unjustifiable to require an individual to join a labor organization as a condition of employment.

Resolved: That military conscription is a superior alternative to a voluntary army.

Resolved: That the protection of human rights should have a higher priority in shaping America's foreign policy.

1981–1982

Resolved: That the rights of the victim should take precedence over the rights of the accused in felony cases.

Resolved: That it is undesirable to expend societal resources on the enforcement of laws against victimless crimes.

Resolved: That the economic health of a nation is more important than social programs for its citizens.

1982–1983

Resolved: That funding for human services programs should take precedence over the development of natural resources.

Resolved: That protection of the environment should take precedence over the development of natural resources.

Resolved: Liberty is more precious than law.

1983–1984

Resolved: Even in a democratic society morality can be legislated.

Resolved: Civil disobedience is justified in a democracy.

Resolved: That uniformity in education leads to mediocrity.

1984–1985

Resolved: Nothing is politically right that is morally wrong.

Resolved: A just social order ought to place the principle of equality above that of liberty.

Resolved: The American media works against the best interest of the American Public.

1985–1986

Resolved: The use of sanctions to achieve U.S. foreign policy goals ought to be immoral.

Resolved: The brotherhood of man transcends the sovereignty of nations.

Resolved: That the restriction of Civil Liberties in the U.S. for the sake of combating terrorism is justified.

Resolved: That allowing innocent people to be harmed is preferable rather than giving into terrorists' demands.

Resolved: Giving Sanctuary to Illegal Refugees in the United States justifiably places moral law above positive law.

1986–1987

Resolved: An unjust government is better than no government at all.

Resolved: That decisions of the U.S. Supreme Court in criminal cases ought to reflect the values of the American people.

Resolved: A Parliamentary system of government would better fulfill the values underlying the American Constitution.

Resolved: When they are in conflict, the right to a free press is a higher priority than the right to a fair trial.

1987–1988

Resolved: That the protection of public safety justifies random, mandatory drug testing throughout society.

Resolved: That the protection of society's health interests through broad based mandatory testing for AIDS ought to be more important than personal privacy rights.

Resolved: That when they are in conflict, the principle of privileged communication ought to be subordinate to the maintenance of Law and Order.

Resolved: That violent revolution is a just response to oppression.

1988–1989

Resolved: That the individual ought to value the sanctity of life above the quality of life.

Resolved: That affirmative action programs to remedy the effects of discrimination are justified.

Resolved: That limitations upon the content of student publications by secondary school administrators are justified.

Resolved: That the public's right to know ought to be valued above U.S. National Security interests.

Resolved: That the American criminal justice system ought to place a higher priority on retribution than on rehabilitation.

1989–1990

Resolved: That all United States citizens ought to perform a period of national service.

Resolved: That communities in the United States ought to have the right to suppress pornography.

Resolved: That development of natural resources ought to be valued above protection of the environment.

Resolved: That individual obedience to law plays a greater role in maintaining ethical public service than does individual obedience to conscience.

1990–1991

Resolved: That competition is superior to cooperation as a means of achieving excellence.

Resolved: That government limits on the individual's right to bear arms in the United States are justified.

Resolved: That showing disrespect for the American Flag is antithetical to fundamental American values.

Resolved: That the pursuit of scientific knowledge ought to be limited by a concern for societal good.

Resolved: That members of the United States Congress ought to value the national interest above constituent's interests when the two are in conflict.

1991–1992

Resolved: A liberal arts curriculum is preferable to an employment-readiness curriculum in U.S. secondary schools.

Resolved: Human genetic engineering is morally justified.

Resolved: A victim's deliberate use of deadly force is justified as a response to physical abuse.

Resolved: The possession of nuclear weapons is immoral.

Resolved: The United States government ought to provide for the medical care of its citizens.

1992–1993

Resolved: That U.S. military interference in the internal affairs of other countries is justified.

Resolved: In the criminal justice system, truth seeking ought to take precedence over privilege communication.

Resolved: When in conflict, the spirit of the law ought to take priority over the letter of the law.

Resolved: The principle of majority rule ought to be valued above the principle of minority rights.

Resolved: The protection of domestic order justifies the curtailment of First Amendment Rights.

1993–1994

Resolved: That secondary education in the United States ought to be a privilege, not a right.

Resolved: The public's right to know is of greater value than the right to privacy of candidates for public office.

Resolved: When called upon by one's government, individuals are morally obligated to risk their lives for their country.

Resolved: Terminally ill patients have the right to die when and how they choose.

Resolved: When in conflict, protection of the innocent is of greater value than prosecution of the guilty.

1994–1995

Resolved: An individual's freedom of expression is of greater value than political correctness.

Resolved: When in conflict, community standards are of greater value than individual liberty.

Resolved: Laws which protect citizens from themselves are justified.

Resolved: On balance, institutional censorship of academic material is harmful to the educational development of students.

Resolved: When in conflict, the safety of others is of greater value than the right to privacy of those with infectious diseases.

1995–1996

Resolved: That individuals with disabilities ought to be afforded the same athletic competition opportunities as able-bodied athletes.

Resolved: The pursuit of feminist ideals is detrimental to the achievement of gender equality.

Resolved: An oppressive government is more desirable than no government.

Resolved: When in conflict, American cultural unity ought to be valued above cultural diversity.

Resolved: That limiting constitutional freedoms is a just response to terrorism in the United States.

1996–1997

Resolved: When in conflict, society's goal of eliminating discrimination ought to transcend an individual's right to participate in exclusive, voluntary associations.

Resolved: When in conflict, a business's responsibility to itself ought to be valued above its responsibility to society.

Resolved: In United States policy, the principle of universal human rights ought to take precedence over conflicting national interest.

Resolved: On balance, individuals ought to have a greater obligation to themselves than to their community.

Resolved: The public's right to know is of greater value than the individual's right to privacy.

1997–1998

Resolved: Global concerns ought to be valued above conflicting national concerns.

Resolved: An adolescent's right to privacy ought to be valued above a parent's conflicting right to know.

Resolved: A just social order ought to place the principle of equality above that of liberty.

Resolved: Civil disobedience is justified in a democracy.

Resolved: In the United States' justice system, due process ought to be valued above the pursuit of truth when they are in conflict.

1998–1999

Resolved: That the individual ought to value the sanctity of life above the quality of life.

Resolved: Capital punishment is justified.

Resolved: In the United States, a journalist's right to shield confidential sources ought to be protected by the First Amendment.

Resolved: Human genetic engineering is morally justified.

Resolved: Capitalism is superior to socialism as a means of achieving economic justice.

1999–2000

Resolved: When they conflict, respect for cultural sensitivity ought to be valued above commercial use of free speech.

Resolved: The use of economic sanctions to achieve U.S. foreign policy goals is moral.

Resolved: Violent juvenile offenders ought to be treated as adults in the criminal justice system.

Resolved: That colleges and universities have a moral obligation to prohibit the public expression of hate speech on their campuses.

Resolved: That establishing a safe educational environment in grades K–12 justifies infringement of students' civil liberties.

Resolved: That the possession of nuclear weapons is immoral.

Resolved: The intervention of one nation in the domestic affairs of another nation is morally justified.

Resolved: Inaction in the face of injustice makes an individual morally culpable.

2000–2001

Resolved: Colleges and universities have a moral obligation to prohibit the public expression of hate speech on their campuses.

Resolved: Establishing a safe educational environment in grades K–12 justifies infringement of students' civil liberties.

Resolved: The possession of nuclear weapons is immoral.

Resolved: The public's right to know ought to be valued above the right to privacy of candidates for public office.

Resolved: On balance, violent revolution is a just response to oppression.

2001–2002

Resolved: Decentralized governmental power ought to be a fundamental goal of democratic society.

Resolved: A lesser developed nation's right to develop ought to take priority over its obligation to protect the environment.

Resolved: Oppressive government is more desirable than no government.

Resolved: Limiting the freedom of expression of adults is justified by society's interest in protecting children.

Resolved: Laws which protect citizens from themselves are justified.

2002–2003

Resolved: When the United States is engaged in military conflict, the demands of national security ought to supercede conflicting claims of individual rights.

Resolved: When in conflict, academic freedom in U.S. high schools ought to be valued above community standards.

Resolved: When in conflict, globalization ought to be valued above national sovereignty.

Resolved: When in conflict, the letter of the law ought to take priority over the spirit of the law.

Resolved: Rehabilitation ought to be valued above punishment in the U.S. criminal justice system.

2003–2004

Resolved: In the U.S. judicial system, truth seeking ought to take precedence over privileged communication.

Resolved: The United States has a moral obligation to mitigate international conflicts.

Resolved: A government's obligation to protect the environment ought to take precedence over its obligation to promote economic development.

Resolved: As a general principle, individuals have an obligation to value the common good above their own interests.

Resolved: Civil disobedience in a democracy is morally justified.

2004–2005

Resolved: Individual claims of privacy ought to be valued above competing claims of societal welfare.

Resolved: The United States has a moral obligation to promote democratic ideals in other nations.

Resolved: Democracy is best served by strict separation of church and state.

Resolved: To better protect civil liberties, community standards ought to take precedence over conflicting national standards.

Resolved: The pursuit of scientific knowledge ought to be constrained by concern for societal good.

2005–2006

Resolved: In matters of U.S. immigration policy, restrictions on the rights of non-citizens are consistent with democratic ideals.

Resolved: Judicial activism is necessary to protect the rights of American citizens.

Resolved: The use of the state's power of eminent domain to promote private enterprise is unjust.

Resolved: Juveniles charged with violent crimes should be tried and punished as adults.

Resolved: In matters of collecting military intelligence, the ends justify the means.

2006–2007

Resolved: A just government should provide health care to its citizens.

Resolved: A victim's deliberate use of deadly force is a just response to repeated domestic violence.

Resolved: The actions of corporations ought to be held to the same moral standards as the actions of individuals.

Resolved: The United Nation's obligation to protect global human rights ought to be valued above its obligation to respect national sovereignty.

Resolved: On balance, violent revolution is a just response to political oppression.

Past Public Forum Resolutions

2002–2003

Resolved: Commercial airline pilots should be armed in the cockpit.

Resolved: That the "Bush" tax cuts should be made permanent.

Resolved: The Federal Government should authorize oil exploration in the Arctic National Wildlife Reserve.

Resolved: The death penalty should be abolished in America.

Resolved: Affirmative action should not be practiced in college and university admission.

Resolved: Awards for pain and suffering in medical malpractice cases should be limited to $250,000.

Resolved: That the United States should assume primary responsibility for the rebuilding of Iraq.

2003–2004

Resolved: Use of a cell phone should be prohibited while operating a motor vehicle.

Resolved: That the United States should comply with United Nations' decisions concerning international peacekeeping operations.

Resolved: That Federal judges should be elected in their district for a limited term rather than appointed by the President for a life term.

Resolved: That Congress should repeal the No Child Left Behind Act.

Resolved: The United States is losing the War on Terror.

Resolved: Americans should be allowed to share copyrighted media over the Internet.

Resolved: The United States should provide universal health insurance to all U.S. citizens.

Resolved: English should be the official national language of the United States.

Resolved: All young adults in every nation should be required to perform at least one full year of national service.

2004–2005

Resolved: That the United States should establish a cabinet-level position to oversee its entire intelligence community.

Resolved: In the United States, public opinion polls positively affect the election process.

Resolved: The United States government should allow Americans to purchase prescription drugs from other countries.

Resolved: Corporate offshoring aids in the economic development of the United States.

Resolved: The United States Constitution should be amended to establish a mandatory retirement age for Supreme Court Justices.

Resolved: In the United States, the current system of federal income taxation should be replaced by a flat rate income tax.

Resolved: Student aptitude should be assessed through standardized testing.

Resolved: The United States should issue guest worker visas to illegal aliens.

Resolved: That, when a choice is required for public high schools in the United States, government funding should prioritize vocational education over college preparatory education.

2005–2006

Resolved: In the United States, colleges and universities should be permitted to pay stipends to their Division I athletes.

Resolved: That the United Nations should be the primary agent to lead and direct the fight against terrorism around the world.

Resolved: That the United States federal government should fund Hurricane Katrina relief and rebuilding by ending President Bush's tax cuts.

Resolved: That the National Basketball Association (NBA) should rescind its dress code.

Resolved: In the United States, public high school science curriculum should include the study of the Theory of Intelligent Design.

Resolved: That the policy decisions of the current Israeli government toward the Palestinian state have improved prospects for peace in the Middle East.

Resolved: That big box retailers benefit the communities in which they are located.

Resolved: That the American media work against the best interest of the American public.

Resolved: That the United States government should ratify the Kyoto Protocol.

2006–2007

Resolved: That the benefits of NASA's space exploration programs justify the costs.

Resolved: Current immigration laws in the United States should be enforced.

Resolved: That participating in multinational diplomatic efforts is beneficial to U.S. interests.

Resolved: Colleges and universities in the United States should end their early admission programs.

Resolved: That lobbyists negatively influence the legislative process in the United States.

Resolved: The costs of legalized casino gambling in the United States outweigh the benefits.

Resolved: That the quantity of credit available to American consumers should be significantly reduced.

Resolved: United States corporations should honor all prior commitments to employee pensions.

Resolved: That the private ownership of handguns should be banned in the United States.

GLOSSARY OF DEBATE TERMS

1AC   The first affirmative constructive speech.

1AR   The first affirmative rebuttal speech.

1NC   The first negative constructive speech.

1NR   The first negative rebuttal speech.

2AC   The second affirmative constructive speech.

2AR   The second affirmative rebuttal speech.

2NC   The second negative constructive speech.

2NR   The second negative rebuttal speech.

a priori   This Latin phrase literally means "before the fact," meaning that something is thought to be true without any need to test or examine experience. A debater might attempt to establish a decision rule by claiming that something is known *a priori*. Philosopher John Rawls argued, for example, that questions of "justice" should be decided from behind a "veil of ignorance." By this he meant that we should decide which standards should define justice before seeking to know the details of a particular situation.

affirmative   The affirmative defends the resolution.

agent of action   This term in policy debate refers to the agency doing the plan or counterplan. For the affirmative, the agent of action is assigned in the resolution—in every resolution since the 1970s, this agent of action has been the "United States federal government." The negative team may propose an agent counterplan in which the agent of action might be the state governments, the United Nations, or the government of another nation.

attitudinal inherency   Inherency is one of the stock issues in policy debate; an *inherency* argument specifies a reason the harm cited by the affirmative will likely continue given the absence of the affirmative plan. Unlike *structural* inherency, an *attitudinal* inherency argument claims that an unwillingness to act on the part of the president or the Congress can constitute an inherent barrier.

ballot   The term given to the piece of paper completed by a debate judge at the end of a round of competition. On the ballot, the judge declares a winner and loser as well as speaker points.

big picture   This is a term debaters use when they want to group an opponent's arguments, rather than to go line-by-line through each argument.

break round   This is a term debaters often give to a preliminary debate round that must be won to advance to elimination rounds. In many tournament competitions, judges announce their decisions at the end of each round. In a six-round tournament, for example, contestants usually must have no more than two losses to qualify for elimination rounds. If a competitor already has two losses, each successive preliminary round is a break round, meaning that just one additional loss would make participation in elimination rounds impossible.

brief   Groups of organized evidence in support of specific arguments are called argument briefs.

brink   A disadvantage in policy debate can be structured either as linear or threshold. A linear disadvantage doesn't have to have a brink, and it doesn't have to be unique. With a linear disadvantage, the negative team argues that something bad is happening now and will become even worse with the adoption of the affirmative plan. With a threshold disadvantage—the most commonly used type of disadvantage—the negative team claims that some action in the affirmative plan will push us over a brink. In other words, the affirmative plan will become the straw that breaks the camel's back. The best brink evidence says that something catastrophic will happen if the present system is nudged just a little bit—a little more deficit spending, any additional terrorist attack in the United States, global warming speeds up (or whatever action is claimed in the disadvantage link).

burden of proof   In policy debate, both affirmative and negative teams have a burden of proof to provide proof for their assertions.

burden of rebuttal   Debaters have the responsibility to respond to the arguments made in the previous speech; if the debater offers no response, the judge has a right to assume that the argument of the opponent is accepted as true.

CEDA debate   Cross Examination Debate Association is one of the formats for debate at the intercollegiate level.

clash   Directly responding to the claims made by an opponent.

comparative advantage case   In policy debate, this is one of the ways to organize an affirmative case; it is an alternative to the traditional need case or the goals/criteria case.

competitiveness   This term refers to a requirement of the negative counterplan in policy debate. Competitiveness imposes a relevancy test on a counterplan; it gives a reason the judge should choose between the plan and the counterplan. Competitiveness answers the question "Why not do both the plan and counterplan?"

con   In public forum debate, the team assigned to oppose the resolution is referred to as the *con* team.

concede   To agree to, or accept as true, a particular argument made by an opponent. A debater might, for example, concede an opponent's argument that fairness should be the criterion for justice.

conditional counterplan   A conditional counterplan—also called a *hypothetical* counterplan—is offered by a negative team in policy debate as a thought experiment. The negative team doesn't really advocate the counterplan, but offers it instead as a test of the resolution. A negative team offering a conditional counterplan typically claims the right to abandon the counterplan at any time during the debate round. Conditional or hypothetical positions are consistent with the hypothesis testing paradigm but conditionality does not fit well within the policymaking or stock issues models.

constructive speeches   Speeches in a debate in which new arguments can be made.

contention   An argument label or heading.

controversy   This was one of the first names given to public forum debate; this form of debate competition is now officially called *public forum debate.*

core value   In Lincoln-Douglas debate, this is the central value advocated by the affirmative or negative case. Some judges believe that every good case must be constructed around a core value, while others see the core value as optional. Examples of core values are justice, safety, and democracy.

counterplan   A negative counter-proposal in policy debate designed to show that the affirmative proposal should be rejected because of the potential to adopt a superior alternative.

critique   Also called *kritik.* In the philosophical context, the *critique,* or *critical theory,* refers to the theorists associated with the Frankfurt School. The members of the Frankfurt School shared an association with the Institute of Social Research in Frankfurt, Germany. Each of these philosophers shared Karl Marx's theory of historical materialism. This theory holds that communism will inevitably replace capitalism as the economic system of choice. Policy and Lincoln-Douglas debaters sometimes use the term *critique* more broadly to describe any questioning of basic assumptions.

cross-apply   Debaters sometimes answer an argument by saying that the judge should cross-apply an answer already given to an earlier argument.

cross-examination   This term is used in policy and Lincoln-Douglas debate to refer to the question/answer periods between constructive speeches.

crossfire   This is the term used in public forum debate to refer to the questioning periods that occur at two points during the constructive speeches. After the first two constructive speeches, the first speakers from each team engage in a free-wheeling interactive period during which there is no preassigned questioner or respondent. The speakers engage one another in a lively exchange, much like on CNN's *Crossfire*—the news program from which this interaction period draws its name. After the second two constructive speeches, the second speakers from each team engage in another free-wheeling interactive period. Only in the "grand crossfire"—an interactive period after the first two rebuttals—are all four contestants allowed to engage in exchanges.

cut evidence   The process of selecting evidence from a book or an article. In the pre-computer era, debaters would physically cut up a photocopy of a section, a book, or an article. Although most evidence is now collected digitally from online or scanned sources, debaters have retained the term *cutting evidence* to refer to the process of selecting particular quotations.

DA   Short-hand reference for a negative disadvantage in policy debate.

debatability   This refers to a standard for deciding the outcome of topicality arguments in policy debate. The debatability standard argues that the judge should select an interpretation of the resolution that best enables good debate on the topic.

decision rule   A decision rule is a standard for determining the outcome of the debate. Either side in the debate can suggest a decision rule. A decision rule might suggest that justice is the first among public virtues and that the judge should always choose the just policy regardless of expediency. Another decision rule might argue that human life is the ultimate value; whatever results in the greater saving of human life should be the preferred policy.

dilemma   When a debater poses a dilemma, he suggests that the opponent must choose between one of two options, both of which are bad.

disadvantage   This is a negative argument in policy debate; a disadvantage claims that if the affirmative plan were to be adopted, bad things would happen. The irreducible minimum for a disadvantage argument is link and impact. Threshold disadvantages also must have uniqueness and brink arguments.

division of labor This term is used in policy debate to refer to the need for the 2NC and the 1NR (back-to-back speeches) to coordinate their arguments so as to avoid needless repetition. Before the beginning of the 2NC, the second negative speaker should discuss with the 1NR which arguments will be left for the rebuttal.

double turn When an affirmative team in policy debate argues a link turn and an impact turn to the same disadvantage, the usual result is a double turn. This type of mistake can often result in the affirmative team losing the round. Consider the example of a deficit disadvantage. First, the affirmative team argues that the plan would not cost more money but would actually save money, thus lowering the federal deficit (this is a link turn). Then the affirmative team later in the answers to the disadvantage argues that a larger deficit is actually good rather than bad in that a larger deficit is needed to stimulate the economy (this is an impact turn). Putting the two arguments together, the affirmative team has argued that adopting the affirmative plan would cause the deficit to be lowered and that lowering the deficit would be a bad thing to do. When the negative team is certain that the affirmative team has committed a double turn, the affirmative team simply grants both halves of the double turn and argues that the affirmative team has provided its own justification for rejecting the plan.

drop Debaters say that their opponents have *dropped* arguments when they did not hear any answer to an argument in an opponent speech. If the judge agrees that the team has not answered the argument, the judge awards that particular argument to the other side; this does not necessarily determine the outcome of the round, however. The round outcome depends on the importance of the argument in relation to the other arguments being won by both sides.

each-word-has-meaning standard for topicality The each word standard in policy debate argues that the framers of the resolution placed each of the words into the resolution for additive meaning; the affirmative plan must, therefore, meet each and every individual word in the resolution. The topicality violation then alleges that there is one word in the resolution that the affirmative plan fails to meet.

effects topicality   In policy debate, some affirmative plans fulfill the terms of the resolution only if certain intervening steps are completed. Most judges and debate theorists would hold that the plan must be topical on its face, meaning that the text of the plan must do directly the things called for in the resolution. We should not have to wait for several months or years to determine whether the change made in the plan will in fact eventuate in the resolutional action. The central theoretical objection to effects topicality is that it collapses the stock issues of topicality and solvency; the topicality of the affirmative plan is provided only if the plan works.

elimination rounds   Debate tournaments are divided into preliminary rounds and elimination rounds. Whereas all attendees participate in preliminary rounds, only the most successful contestants (based on wins and losses in preliminary rounds) participate in elimination rounds. After elimination rounds begin, only the winners of each round advance until the tournament culminates in a final round between the top two competitors.

empirical proof   Proof arising from actual experience.

evaluative term   Some, but not all, propositions of value contain an evaluative term. An evaluative term describes the measure to be used in determining how highly something is to be valued. In the resolution "A just society ought not use the death penalty as a form of punishment," the evaluative term is *just*.

existential inherency   In policy debate, affirmative teams sometimes claim that the problem cited in the case is inherent because it has continued to exist over a prolonged period of time. This approach to demonstrating inherency is referred to as *existential* inherency. Few judges who care about inherency are willing to accept existential inherency—such argumentation circumvents questions of causation and claims that the continued existence of harm is a demonstration of inherency.

extend   When a debater asks the judge to extend an argument, she is really saying that the opponent didn't answer the argument. The debater is simply asking the judge not to forget about this argument.

extratopicality Whereas topicality arguments in policy debate allege that the plan fails to meet the resolution, extratopicality arguments allege that the plan does the resolution and more. The affirmative team is attempting to claim an advantage from a portion of the plan that goes beyond the resolution.

fiat In policy debate, *fiat* refers to the right of the affirmative team to assume that its plan would be adopted in the political structure specified by the plan. Most debate theorists believe that fiat power is created by the *should* term in a policy resolution. We are debating about what should be done, not what will be done. The affirmative team never need worry about whether its plan would be passed by Congress, whether it would be repealed by Congress, or whether the president would sign the bill after it had passed Congress.

field context standard for topicality The field context standard in policy debate argues that the best type of topicality evidence is that which comes from an expert in the professional field related to the resolution. If the resolution deals with economics, a professor of economics would provide the best field contextual evidence.

final focus This is the final speech in public forum debate. The speech is given by the second speaker for the pro and con sides. When public forum debate was first conceived, the final focus speech was limited to the making of a single argument. That requirement has since been relaxed, but the one-minute time limit forces the debater to make only a few arguments.

flow judge A judge who keeps a careful record of the arguments made in the debate. Many lay judges have had very little experience in judging and did not participate as contestants in high school or college debate. When a debater has a flow judge, he knows that line-by-line answers to arguments will likely be necessary. With a non-flow judge, debaters know they probably do not have to answer each and every argument of the opponent; it will probably be sufficient to offer the big picture.

flowsheet Each of the participants in the debate (including the judge) should keep a record of the arguments as they proceed; this record of arguments is called a *flowsheet*.

four-person debate This format for policy debate features two paired teams of two persons each where each team stays on the same side of the resolution. One team debates each round on the affirmative, and the other debates each round on the negative. The total record for the four-person team is the combined win-loss record for the four-person unit.

generic disadvantages This term in policy debate refers to negative disadvantages that apply to broad categories of affirmative plans rather than to specifically address a specific affirmative plan.

goal/criteria case This is one of the organizational schemes for structuring affirmative cases in policy debate. In the goal/criteria case, the affirmative starts by establishing a worthy goal or criteria for solving a problem. The affirmative shows that the present system fails to meet this goal or criteria but that the affirmative plan would best meet the goal or criteria.

grammatical context standard for topicality The grammatical context standard in policy debate argues that the best type of definitions are those that take into account the grammatical structure of the resolutional sentence. The grammatical context standard focuses resolutional interpretation on questions of which word modifies which other word in the resolutional sentence.

grand crossfire In public forum debate, there is an assigned period after the first two rebuttals during which all four contestants engage in a lively exchange. During this period there are no preassigned questioners or respondents.

grouping of arguments When a debater is called upon to answer a large number of similar arguments, the debater often says something like, "group their answers one through four; I will make the following three responses."

harm Harm is one of the stock issues in policy debate that must be demonstrated by the affirmative team in the first affirmative speech.

high-power match A preliminary round paired in such a way that the top competitor meets the second-place competitor, the third meets the fourth, and so on through all the competitors.

high-low power match   This pairing system for preliminary rounds divides all competitors into win-loss brackets, ordered within that bracket by speaker points. The top competitor in a win-loss bracket meets the bottom competitor in that bracket, the second-from-the-top competitor in the bracket meets the second-from-the-bottom competitor in the bracket, and so on in toward the middle. Some debaters make the mistake of thinking that a high-low power match means that the top competitor meets the bottom competitor. This is not the case. Contestants meet other contestants with the same number of wins and losses.

hypothesis testing   This paradigm for judging a policy debate sees debate as analogous to a social scientist who is testing a hypothesis. The hypothesis being tested in the debate is the resolution. Just as a careful scientist would never declare a hypothesis true based on a single test, so the debate judge should not expect the negative team to limit itself to a single test of the resolution; in fact, the responsibility of the negative team is to provide a rigorous test of the hypothesis by attacking it from as many different directions as would be productive. David Zarefsky of Northwestern University and J. W. Patterson of the University of Kentucky are the most widely known advocates of the hypothesis testing model; their debate textbook *Contemporary Debate* is a thorough defense of a hypothesis testing approach.

hypothetical counterplan   See *conditional counterplan.*

impact   The term *impact* could refer to the significance of any argument, but in policy debate usage, it usually is applied to the impact or significance of a disadvantage. Consider a negative deficit disadvantage. If the bottom line of the disadvantage is that the affirmative plan will increase the deficit, the argument is incomplete. The next question is "Why is increasing the deficit bad?" The answer to that question would be the impact of the disadvantage.

impact turnaround   An impact turn argument in policy debate claims that the impact of a negative disadvantage would be good instead of bad. Consider a negative deficit disadvantage that claims that an increased deficit would result from the increased spending in an affirmative plan. A negative impact turn argument would claim that an increase in the deficit would actually be good because deficit spending stimulates the economy and will bring it out of recession.

independent voting issue   An issue that, if won, would be sufficient all by itself to warrant a decision. In policy debate, most judges view topicality as an independent voting issue for the negative. Judges who view the debate from a stock issues perspective see each of the stock issues (significance, inherency, solvency) as independent voting issues for the negative.

inherency   This is one of the stock issues in policy debate; the affirmative team must demonstrate that the harm cited in the case is inherent. One good way to view inherency is that the affirmative team must show that the harm will continue to exist absent the adoption of the plan. Inherency deals with causation—the affirmative team is called on to locate in the present system the cause that will perpetuate the problem.

jurisdiction   This refers to a standard in policy debate for deciding the outcome of topicality debates. One of the reasons topicality is a voting issue is that, within the legal paradigm, the language of the resolution sets the outward limits of the judge's jurisdiction. According to this view, if the plan calls for doing something beyond the resolution, the judge has no power or jurisdiction to enact the plan.

justification   Some negative debaters in policy debate argue that the affirmative team must justify the inclusion of each word in the resolution to show that the resolution is a true statement. If the resolution contains the phrase "federal government," the affirmative team must be able to justify why the federal government as opposed to the state governments should adopt the plan. Working within the hypothesis testing model, a judge might believe that the resolution (or hypothesis) should be rejected unless each part of it is shown to be true. Justification arguments make little sense, however, outside of a hypothesis testing paradigm.

lay judges   Debate judges whose backgrounds do not include debate participation or debate coaching. Some state leagues use local attorneys, businesspeople, or parents as judges for debates.

linear   Some negative disadvantages in policy debate are linear and do not claim to have uniqueness, threshold, or brink. A linear disadvantage alleges that any additional increment of the disadvantage link will produce additional harm. A deficit disadvantage structured as a linear position would admit that the status quo has a huge deficit that is already hurting the economy. The affirmative plan, by increasing spending, will worsen the deficit and produce more of a bad thing.

line-by-line   This refers to a method of rebuttal that methodically answers an opponent's arguments in the same order in which they were presented, responding to each particular argument. This method of argumentation is the opposite of grouping arguments, or offering a big picture. Judges in policy debate typically expect line-by-line answers to an opponent's arguments.

link turnaround   In policy debate, the link turn is an important type of affirmative answer to a disadvantage. The affirmative argument is that the plan not only is innocent of the disadvantage link claim, but also that the plan would actually solve for the problem alleged in the disadvantage.

low point win   This refers to a situation in which the contestant (or team) winning the debate has a lower number of speaker points than the opposing contestant (or team). Judges sometimes assign low point wins because they believe that the winning contestant had the better argument but was inferior in speaking skill to the opponent. Not all debate leagues allow judges to assign low point wins.

Malthus disadvantage   This is a negative disadvantage in policy debate based on the claims of nineteenth-century British economist Thomas Malthus. Malthus argued that population increases geometrically while the food supply (and other resources) increases only arithmetically. The net result, according to Malthus, is that humankind is on a collision course, heading for starvation and environmental devastation. Simply put, the earth cannot sustain huge human populations. Some negative teams have used the Malthus disadvantage to argue that saving lives is actually bad because it contributes to overpopulation. This is the prototypical "bad is good" argument.

mandates   In policy debate, this term refers to the central provisions of an affirmative plan; the mandates list the specific changes offered by the plan.

minor repair   This term in policy debate refers to small changes proposed by the negative designed to fix small defects in the status quo. Advocates of minor repair theory would argue that the affirmative case fails to establish inherency if the negative team can show that small changes in the status quo would alleviate the affirmative harm. Minimum standards for a minor repair argument would be propensity and potential. The negative team would be expected to show that the present system is already moving in the direction of the minor repair (propensity) and that the minor repair, once done, would alleviate the harm (potential).

moving target   Debaters sometimes use this phrase when they want to criticize an argumentative shift by an opponent—the final form of an argument morphed into something totally different from the way it was originally presented.

mutual exclusivity standard for competition   This is a *can not* standard for counterplan competition in policy debate. The mutual exclusivity standard for counterplan answers the question "Why not do both the plan and the counterplan?" by arguing that it is logically impossible to do both the plan and the counterplan. Suppose that the affirmative plan called for national health insurance, while the negative counterplan called for ending all federally sponsored health care, including Medicare and Medicaid. The negative team would argue that it would be logically impossible to combine the plan with the counterplan.

NDT debate   The term *NDT* stands for National Debate Tournament. This is one of the forms of competitive debate at the intercollegiate level.

negative   The negative in policy or Lincoln-Douglas debate opposes the resolution; it defends the status quo or a counterplan of its choice, attacking the plan offered by the affirmative.

negative block   In policy debate, this refers to the back-to-back negative speeches (2NC and 1NR).

net benefits standard for competition   This is a *should not* standard for counterplan competition in policy debate. The net benefits standard for counterplan competition means that the plan plus the counterplan are less desirable than the adoption of the counterplan alone.

new argument   Debaters are not allowed to make new arguments in rebuttal speeches (called the Summary Speech and Final Focus in public forum debate). New evidence can be presented in rebuttal so long as it is used in support of an argument previously made in a constructive speech.

object of evaluation   Every proposition of value contains one or more objects of evaluation. The object of evaluation is the concept or idea being evaluated in the resolution. In the topic "A just society ought not use the death penalty as a form of punishment," the object of evaluation is "the death penalty."

observation   Another name for a contention. Debaters often label their argument as an observation if they believe that it is reasonably obvious—they simply want to establish a grounding for their argument.

overview   An argument made at the top of the flowsheet before beginning the line-by-line responses to an opponent's argument.

paradigm   A paradigm is an interconnected web of assumptions. Debate theorists in policy debate use the term to apply to the assumptions made by the debate judge when approaching a debate. Some judges see a debate from a legal paradigm, where the status quo is innocent until proven guilty. Some judges see a debate from a policymaking paradigm, where the decision asks whether the affirmative policy is shown to be more advantageous than the negative policy. Some judges see a debate from the hypothesis testing paradigm, where the debate round is seen as an experiment in the social sciences designed to test the truth of a hypothesis.

permutation   In policy debate, this is one of the terms used by affirmative teams in answering counterplans. The permutation is suggested by an affirmative team as an example of a way that the essence of the plan could be desirably combined with the essence of counterplan. The permutation is a test of competitiveness.

plan   The affirmative team in policy debate must present a plan; contemporary debate practice requires that this plan be presented in the first affirmative constructive speech. The plan should typically provide answers to the following questions: (1) Who will administer the plan? (2) What will the plan do? (list the plan mandates)

(3) How will the plan be funded? The affirmative team can also choose to specify certain other things such as the date of implementation, the phase-in period, and the means of enforcement.

plan spike   This is a term used in policy debate. A plan spike is provision of an affirmative plan that is designed to preempt an expected disadvantage.

plan-meet-need argument   This is another term for a solvency argument in policy debate. The negative team presents reasons the affirmative plan, even when adopted, will fail to resolve the harms cited by the affirmative team.

policymaker   This paradigm for judging a policy debate sees debate as analogous to the legislative model in which decision-makers choose from competing policy options. The policymaker makes a decision in the debate by answering the simple question "Would the affirmative option be, on balance, more desirable than the option defended by the negative team?" This approach to judging a debate places strong expectations on the negative team to defend something rather than simply to attack the affirmative team. It also requires the negative positions to be internally consistent.

power-matched round   A preliminary round paired in such a way that competitors meet an opponent with a similar record. A competitor who has a 3-0 record (three wins, no losses) will meet a 3-0 opponent. Similarly an 0-3 record (zero wins, three losses) will meet an 0-3 opponent.

preempts   In policy debate, when debaters preempt an argument, they respond to arguments before the other team has made them. Sometimes affirmative teams make a series of preempts at the end of the first affirmative constructive speech.

preliminary rounds   Debate tournaments are divided into preliminary rounds and elimination rounds. The tournament invitation establishes the number of rounds in which every contestant will compete. The number of preliminary rounds ranges from three to eight in interscholastic competition. After the preliminary rounds, the top contestants are determined by the number of wins (ties broken by speaker points). Top contestants then are seeded into elimination rounds where only the winners of each round advance.

prep time   Current debate practice allocates a certain amount of preparation time to each team or contestant for the entire debate. The timer (often the judge) begins timing prep time as soon as the previous speaker has spoken or as soon as cross-examination is over. When the total preparation time for the round has expired, the next speaker must begin speaking immediately to avoid losing time allocated to the speech itself. Five minutes is the typical preparation time for policy debate, four minutes for Lincoln-Douglas debate, and two minutes for public forum debate.

presumption   In policy debate, the negative team traditionally has *presumption*—meaning the negative team will win the round in the event of the judge's perception that the round is tied. The notion of presumption originally comes from Bishop Richard Whately in his 1859 book *The Elements of Rhetoric*. Whately argued that there is presumption in favor of existing institutions.

prima facie case   In policy debate, the term *prima facie* means "first face" or "at face value." This means that the affirmative case must contain all the logical elements of harm, inherency, and solvency in the first affirmative speech. If, for example, the first affirmative speech contained eight minutes of history about the subject matter of the resolution, the first negative debater would have nothing to refute because there is not a complete argument on the floor. The negative team would win even if the affirmative team were granted every position taken. Some debate texts explain a *prima facie* case as one that contains proof "sufficient to convince a reasonable person in the absence of refutation."

pro   In public forum debate, the team assigned to defend the resolution is referred to as the *pro* team.

proposition of policy   A statement that asserts that a course of action should be taken. Policy debate resolutions and many public forum resolutions are propositions of policy.

proposition of value   A statement that asserts that one thing is more important or more valuable than another thing. Lincoln-Douglas debate resolutions are propositions of value.

rebuttal   The closing speeches in a debate. New arguments are not allowed in rebuttal speeches; these speeches are for the purpose of sorting out the arguments made in the constructive speeches.

red herring   This is a type of argumentative fallacy in which a debater proves something that is irrelevant to the question at hand in an attempt to draw attention away from the real issue.

reducing to absurdity   Debaters sometimes seek to reduce the credibility of an opponent's argument by showing that the argument becomes ridiculous when carried out to its logical extreme; this technique is referred to by its Latin name *reductio ad absurdum*.

resolution   The sentence that states the topic to be debated. The debate topic is phrased as a resolution using a single declarative sentence. In policy and Lincoln-Douglas debate, the affirmative says "yes" to the resolution while the negative says "no."

road map   A debater's road map is the brief explanation that precedes a constructive or rebuttal speech. Most judges expect that every debate speech other than the first affirmative constructive will include a road map. Modern flowing practices involve putting each argument on a separate sheet of paper. When the first negative constructive speaker says, "I will present three disadvantages, one topicality argument, and then go to the case," the judge knows that she will need four new sheets of paper before returning to the flow of the affirmative case.

shell   In policy debate, this term refers to a brief version of the negative disadvantage, suitable for brief presentation in the first negative constructive speech. The shell must include all the essential elements of the disadvantage (the irreducible minimum being links and impacts).

shift   An argumentative shift occurs when a debater abandons an original position (in the face of refutation) and adopts a wholly different argument.

solvency   Solvency is one of the stock issues in policy debate; an affirmative case is said to have solvency if it demonstrates that the affirmative plan would, if adopted, resolve the harm cited in the affirmative case. Another term for solvency is *plan-meet-need (PMN)*.

speaker points   In all forms of debate, the judge completes a ballot declaring a winner and a loser for the debate round. In addition, the judge assigns points to each contestant—usually on a 1-to-30 scale—where 30 means perfection. Speaker points are usually assigned only for preliminary rounds of competition; in elimination rounds, judges typically decide only a winner and a loser.

spread debating   This term refers to the tendency of some debaters to make so many answers to an argument that the other team is unable to answer each of them.

squirrel cases   A squirrel case in policy debate refers to an affirmative case that stretches the limits of the topic and is probably nontopical; the affirmative team is attempting to win the debate as a result of surprise.

status quo   Things as they now exist. In policy debate, the negative team generally defends the present system or status quo; the affirmative team proposes to change from the status quo.

stock issues   The traditional approach to the judging of a policy debate is the stock issues perspective. This approach is based on the legal analogy where the criminal law establishes certain independent elements that a prosecutor must prove. In the case of first-degree murder, for example, a prosecutor usually must prove motive, opportunity, forethought, and certain other elements contained in the criminal code of a particular state government. The stock issues in debate are (a) significance of harm; (2) inherency— what will cause the harm to continue absent the adoption of the plan; (3) solvency—how will the affirmative plan resolve the affirmative harm; (4) advantage over disadvantage—will the affirmative advantages outweigh the disadvantages suggested by the negative; (5) topicality—does the affirmative plan meet each of the words of the resolution. Judges who approach a debate from a stock issues perspective will vote negatively if the negative team successfully defeats any one of the five stock issues.

structural inherency   This is the traditional approach to inherency in policy debate; the affirmative team would point to some law or structure in the present system that causes the harm to continue. See also *inherency*.

study counterplan   The study counterplan in policy debate argues that the affirmative plan should be rejected in favor of the establishment of a systematic program to study the affirmative harm area to locate the optimal solution.

summary speech   This is the term used in public forum debate to refer to the first rebuttal; the first speaker for each team gives a summary speech. The second rebuttal speech in public forum debate is called the final focus.

tab room   The place at a tournament where debate schedules are prepared and judges are assigned.

tabula rasa   This paradigm for judging a policy debate establishes the willingness of the judge to be a blank slate or to keep an open mind about the decisionmaking standards for the debate. It is, accordingly, up to each team to present and defend its own standards for determining who wins and who loses. In one debate round, this type of judge might be a stock issues judge and in another round a policymaker.

Ted Turner Debate   This was one of the first names given to public forum debate. Ted Turner, the media entrepreneur who created CNN (Cable News Network), provided early encouragement for the creation of public forum debate competition. The official name is now simply *public forum* debate.

threshold   This is a type of negative disadvantage in policy debate that alleges that there is a definite point beyond which apocalyptic impacts will happen. With a deficit disadvantage, for example, the negative team would argue that our economy has found ways to absorb the multi-trillion-dollar deficit that has been accumulated, but there is a point at which any further increases in the deficit would cause the whole economy to collapse.

topical counterplans   One of the typical requirements for a successful negative counterplan in policy debate is that the plan be nontopical, meaning the counterplan fails to meet at least one of the terms of the resolution. Most debate theorists are adamant in their insistence that a legitimate negative counterplan be nontopical. A significant minority of theorists, however, argues that competition is an adequate test of the relevance of a counterplan and that the nontopicality of a counterplan is a nonissue.

topicality   In policy debate, the affirmative plan must meet each of the terms in the resolutional sentence. Most judges consider that topicality is an independent voting issue, meaning that if the negative team wins topicality, it automatically wins the debate. Most judges will not vote against a case that seems (to the judge) nontopical unless the negative team raises the issue and wins the argument. See also *extratopicality*.

traditional need case affirmative   This is the case structure that dominated policy debate before the middle 1960s (at which point the comparative advantage case structure became ascendant). This case structure is based on a simple problem-solution theme.

turnaround   The most common usage for this term occurs in policy debate when the affirmative team claims that a negative disadvantage is actually an additional advantage for the affirmative. This can happen as a result of either a link turn or an impact turn. In the case of a link turn, the affirmative team argues that the plan actually does the reverse of what the negative team claims (if the negative link argues that the plan would increase the deficit, the link turn argues that the plan would actually increase the deficit). In the case of an impact turn, the affirmative team claims that the impact cited in the disadvantage would actually be advantageous. The term *turnaround* is also used when the negative team claims that the affirmative plan would actually worsen the harm cited in the affirmative case; the negative team would label this a *case turn*. The turnaround is also referred to as a *turn* or a *flip*. See also the following terms: *double turnaround*; *link turnaround*; *impact turnaround*.

underview   An argument made at the bottom of the flowsheet after completing the line-by-line responses to an opponent's argument.

uniqueness   Negative disadvantages in policy debate that are structured as threshold disadvantages must be proven to be unique to the affirmative plan. If the negative disadvantage alleges that any additional increase in the deficit will produce certain disaster, and the affirmative team reads evidence saying that the deficit has just recently increased substantially, the disadvantage is either inevitable or has been proven to be untrue. In either case, the affirmative team has shown the disadvantage to have little or no credibility. See also *disadvantage*.

value criterion   In Lincoln-Douglas debate, the value criterion provides the means for achieving a core value. If the core value is justice, the value criterion might be due process. The debater would be arguing that justice can best be achieved by ensuring due process. Some judges believe that every good case must be constructed around a core value and a value criterion; other judges see this core value/criterion approach as just one among many methods of case construction.

voting issue   In the final rebuttal, a debater typically labels key arguments as voting issues as a way of focusing a judge's attention on those issues.

word economy   This term refers to the skill of explaining an argument using no more words than necessary for clarity and emphasis.

workability arguments   The workability argument in policy debate is a type of solvency argument that could be advanced by the negative team. The argument alleges that the affirmative plan would not work as intended. Potential reasons abound: (1) Sufficient numbers of trained personnel to carry out the affirmative plan do not exist; (2) Raw materials shortages would prohibit the implementation of the plan; (3) The plan assumes technological breakthroughs that will not occur as projected; (4) Affirmative sources of funding would be inadequate; (5) Enforcement mechanisms specified in the plan would not promote compliance; (6) Bureaucratic infighting or ineptitude would preclude solvency; (7) Alternative causes of the problem, unforeseen by the affirmative team, will perpetuate the problem despite the removal of the cause specified by the affirmative. See also *solvency*.

INDEX

E

F

G

O

Y–Z